# ALL THE WORLD'S ANIMALS
# SEA MAMMALS

# ALL THE WORLD'S ANIMALS
# SEA MAMMALS

**TORSTAR BOOKS**
New York · Toronto

# CONTRIBUTORS

PKA   Paul K. Anderson PhD
University of Calgary
Alberta
Canada

SSA   Sheila S. Anderson BSc
British Antarctic Survey
Cambridge
England

KB   Ken Balcomb PhD
Friday Harbor
Washington
USA

RB   Robin Best MSc
Instituto Nacional de
Pesquisas da Amazônia
Manaus
Brazil

WNB   W. Nigel Bonner BSc FIBiol
British Antarctic Survey
Cambridge
England

WDB   W. D. Bowen PhD
Northwest Atlantic Fisheries
Center
St John's, Newfoundland
Canada

PB   Paul Brodie PhD
Bedford Institute of
Oceanography
Dartmouth, Nova Scotia
Canada

IC   Ivar Christensen
Institute of Marine Research
Bergen-Nordnes
Norway

DPD   Daryl Domning PhD
Howard University
Washington
USA

AWE   Albert W. Erickson PhD
University of Seattle
Washington
USA

PGHE   Peter G. H. Evans PhD
University of Oxford
England

FHF   Francis H. Fay BS MS PhD
University of Alaska
Fairbanks, Alaska
USA

RG   Ray Gambell PhD
International Whaling
Commission
Cambridge
England

DEG   David E. Gaskin BSc PhD
University of Guelph
Guelph, Ontario
Canada

TK   Toshio Kasuya PhD
University of Tokyo
Japan

RML   Richard M. Laws PhD FRS
British Antarctic Survey
Cambridge
England

BleB   Burney le Boeuf BA MA PhD
University of California
USA

CL   Christina Lockyer BSc MPhil
British Antarctic Survey
Cambridge
England

IAM   Ian A. McLaren PhD
Dalhousie University
Halifax, Nova Scotia
Canada

DKO   Daniel K. Odell PhD
University of Miami
Miami, Florida
USA

TJO   Thomas J. O'Shea BS MS PhD
US Fish and Wildlife Service
Gainesville, Florida
USA

JMP   Jane M. Packard PhD
University of Florida
Gainesville, Florida
USA

GBR   Galen B. Rathbun BA PhD
US Fish and Wildlife Service
Gainesville, Florida
USA

KR   Keith Ronald
University of Guelph
Guelph, Ontario
Canada

DES   David E. Sergeant PhD
Arctic Biological Station
St. Anne de Bellevue, Quebec
Canada

ABT   Andrew B. Taber BA
University of Oxford
England

POT   Peter O. Thomas
University of California
USA

RSW   Randall S. Wells
Moss Landing Marine
Laboratories
California
USA

BW   Bernd Würsig PhD
Moss Landing Marine
Laboratories
California
USA

## ALL THE WORLD'S ANIMALS
## SEA MAMMALS

**TORSTAR BOOKS INC.**
41 Madison Avenue
Suite 2900
New York, NY 10010

*Project Editor*: Graham Bateman
*Editors*: Peter Forbes, Bill MacKeith, Robert Perberdy
*Art Editor*: Jerry Burman
*Picture Research*: Linda Proud, Alison Renney
*Production*: Bob Christie
*Design*: Chris Munday

*Originally planned and produced by*:
Equinox (Oxford) Ltd
Mayfield House, 256 Banbury Road
Oxford, OX2 7DH, England

*On the cover*: Bearded seal   *page 1*: Humpback whale
*pages 2–3*: South American sea lions and Killer whale
*pages 4–5*: Crabeater seals   *pages 6–7*: Humpback whale
*pages 8–9*: Seal

10 9 8 7 6 5 4 3 2

Printed in Belgium

*Editor*
Dr David Macdonald
Animal Behaviour Research Group
University of Oxford
England

*Advisory Editors*
Dr Peter G. H. Evans
University of Oxford
England

*Artwork Panels*
Priscilla Barrett

Dr Bernd Würsig
Moss Landing Marine
Laboratories
California
USA

**Library of Congress Cataloging in Publication Data**

Main entry under title:

Sea mammals.

(All the world's animals)
Bibliography: p.
Includes index.
1. Marine mammals.   I. Series.
QL713.2.S43   1985   599.5   85–979
ISBN 0–920269–75–3

ISBN 0–920269–72–9 (Series: All the World's Animals)
ISBN 0–920269–75–3 (Sea Mammals)

# CONTENTS

# FOREWORD

*Sea Mammals* is the book that takes you on a journey from comfortable terrestrial surroundings to the disquietingly alien world of ocean and ice floe—a world where distances, empty landscapes and even some of the living creatures are so immense that they seem unreal in their remoteness. From afar, the torpedo-shaped uniformity of marine mammals masks the character and personality of each species. The illusion may be of animals with less individuality than, say, lions or monkeys, but in this book that illusion is banished. Thus the ways of whale and porpoise, of seal and walrus spring intimately to life and, in so doing, emphasize the subtlety and frailty of the natural web, and the dependence of the monumental upon the minute.

The realized aim of the international panel of experts, with whose invaluable help this book has been created, is to gather together the newest information and ideas and to present them lucidly, entertainingly but uncompromisingly. This means that the information will appeal as much to the professional as the schoolchild. Nor are issues of controversy and conservation ignored: thorny subjects from Harp seal culling to the control and regulation of whaling are discussed and evaluated.

A superb collection of photographs and drawings, which capture the essence of marine existence, make the pages of *Sea Mammals* come alive with activity. So vivid are the images that you can almost hear the dolphins "speaking" to each other or imagine yourself swimming alongside the whales, the kings and queens of the oceans.

*How this book is organized*

Animal classification, even for the professional zoologist, can be a thorny problem, and one on which there is scant agreement between experts. This volume has selected the views of many taxonomists but in general follows the classification of Corbet and Hill (see Bibliography) for the arrangement of families and orders.

This volume is structured at a number of levels. First, there is a general essay highlighting common features and main variations of the biology (particularly the body plan), ecology and behavior of the sea mammals and their evolution. Second, essays on each order highlight topics of particular interest, but invariably include a distribution map, summary of species or species groupings, description of skull, dentition and unusual skeletal features of representative species and, in many cases, color artwork that enhances the text by illustrating representative species engaged in characteristic activities.

The bulk of *Sea Mammals* describes families containing either a single species or groups of individual species. The text on these pages covers details of physical features, distribution, evolutionary history, diet and feeding behavior, as well as their social dynamics and spatial organization, classification, conservation and their relationships with man.

Preceding the discussion of each family group is a panel of text that provides basic data about size, life span and the like. A map shows its natural distribution, while a scale drawing compares the size of the species with that of a six-foot man. Where there are silhouettes of two animals, they are the largest and smallest representatives of the group. Where the panel covers a large group of species, the species listed as examples are those referred to in the text. For such large groups, the detailed descriptions of species are provided in a separate Table of Species. Unless otherwise stated, dimensions given are for both males and females. Where there is a difference in size between the sexes, the scale drawings show males.

As you read these pages you will marvel as each story unfolds. But as well as relishing the beauty of these sea mammals, you should also be fearful for them. Again and again, authors return to the need to conserve species threatened with extinction and by mismanagement. Of the 113 species described in these pages, about 84 are listed in the Appendices I through III of the Convention on International Trade in Endangered Species of Wild Flora and Fauna (CITES). The *Red Data Book* of the International Union for the Conservation of Nature and Natural Resources (IUCN) lists 19 species of sea mammals variously at risk. In *Sea Mammals*, the following symbols are used to show the status accorded to species by IUCN at the time of going to press. Ⓔ = Endangered—in danger of extinction unless causal factors are modified (these may include habitat destruction and direct exploitation by man). Ⓥ = Vulnerable—likely to become endangered in the near future. Ⓡ = Rare, but neither endangered nor vulnerable at present. Ⓘ = Indeterminate—insufficient information available, but known to be in one of the above categories. Ⓠ = Suspected, but not definitely known to fall into one of the above categories. The symbol ⊡ indicates entire species, genera or families, in addition to those listed in the *Red Data Book*, that are listed by CITES. Some species and subspecies that have Ⓔх or probably have Ⓔх? become extinct in the past 100 years are also indicated.

# WHALES AND DOLPHINS

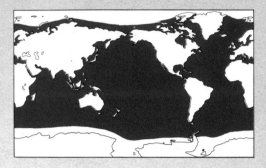

**ORDER: CETACEA** [*]
Nine families: 38 genera: 76 species.

## Toothed whales
Suborder: Odontoceti

### River dolphins
Family: Platanistidae
Five species in 4 genera.
Includes **La Plata dolphin** (*Pontoporia blainvillei*).

### Dolphins
Family: Delphinidae
Thirty-two species in 17 genera.
Includes **Bridled dolphin** (*Stenella attenuata*), **Common dolphin** (*Delphinus delphis*), **Killer whale** (*Orcinus orca*), **Pilot whale** (*Globicephala melaena*), **Risso's dolphin** (*Grampus griseus*), **White beaked dolphin** (*Lagenorhynchus albirostris*).

### Porpoises
Family: Phocoenidae
Six species in 3 genera.
Includes **Common porpoise** (*Phocoena phocoena*).

### White whales
Family: Monodontidae
Two species in 2 genera.
Includes **Narwhal** (*Monodon monoceros*).

### Sperm whales
Family: Physeteridae
Three species in 2 genera.
Includes **Sperm whale** (*Physeter macrocephalus*).

### Beaked whales
Family: Ziphiidae
Eighteen species in 5 genera.
Includes **Northern bottlenose whale** (*Hyperoodon ampullatus*).

To many people, thoughts of whales conjure up a picture of a large mysterious creature living in the gray-green depths of the ocean; fish-like with fins, and scarcely if ever to be seen in one's lifetime. Until 1758, when the great Swedish biologist Linnaeus recognized them as mammals, whales were regarded as fish, and their lifestyles were scarcely known. Only in the last half century has our knowledge of these most specialized of mammals become at all substantial—not a moment too soon as many species are in danger of extinction.

Though superficially resembling some of the large sharks, whales are clearly distinguished by a number of mammalian features—they are warm-blooded, they breathe air with lungs, and they give birth to living young that are suckled on milk secreted by the mammary glands of the mother. Unlike most land mammals, however, they do not have a coat of hair for warmth. External hair or fur would impede their progress through the water, reducing the advantage gained by the streamlining of the body. Of the marine mammal orders Cetacea, Pinnipedia (seals, p86), and Sirenia (sea cows and manatees, p140), it is the whales and dolphins which are most specialized for life in the water; seals must return to land to breed and both seals and sirenians may bask on reefs.

Although in terms of body size, whales dominate the order Cetacea, one half of the order comprises the generally much smaller dolphins and porpoises. Most of the great whales belong to the suborder Mysticeti (see pp62–85), which instead of teeth, have a system of horny "plates" called baleen, used to filter or strain planktonic organisms and larger invertebrates, as well as schools of small fishes, from the sea. However, the vast

## Baleen whales
Suborder: Mysticeti

### Gray whale
Family: Eschrichtidae
One species.
**Gray whale** (*Eschrichtius robustus*).

### Rorquals
Family: Balaenopteridae
Six species in 2 genera.
Includes **Blue whale** (*Balaenoptera musculus*),
**Fin whale** (*Balaenoptera physalus*), **Humpback
whale** (*Megaptera novaeangliae*), **Sei whale**
(*Balaenoptera borealis*).

### Right whales
Family: Balaenidae
Three species in 2 genera.
Includes **Bowhead whale** (*Balaena glacialis*).

[*] All cetaceans are listed by CITES.

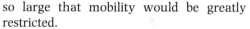

▶ **Tail power.** The tail flukes, powered by huge muscles in the back, are the great whales' sole source of propulsion. The Humpback whale, like other great whales, sometimes produces a loud report by crashing the tail down on the surface (lob-tailing). This may be a signal to other Humpbacks.

◀ **Bursting from the surface,** a Killer whale breaches upside-down. One function of this action may be to communicate with others in the herd; it may also be used to stun or panic fish shoals.

▼ **Leaping dolphin.** Dolphins are perfectly streamlined for rapid swimming. When swimming fast, as in this Pacific white-sided dolphin, they leap to breathe, which is actually more efficient than dragging along at the surface, where resistance is greatest.

majority of cetaceans (66 out of 76 species) belong to the suborder Odontoceti (see pp 24–61). These are the toothed whales, which include the dolphins and porpoises. They feed mainly on fish and squid, which they pursue and capture with their arrays of teeth.

### Body Shape and Locomotion
The largest animal ever to have lived on this planet is the Blue whale, and though its populations have been severely reduced by man's overhunting (see pp72–74), it still survives today. It reaches a length of 80–90ft (24–27m) and weighs 130–150 tonnes, equivalent to the weight of 33 individuals of the largest terrestrial mammal, the elephant. Such an enormous body could only be supported in an aquatic medium, for on land it would require limbs so large that mobility would be greatly restricted.

Despite their size and weight, whales and dolphins are very mobile, having evolved a streamlined torpedo-shaped body for ease of movement through water. The head is elongated compared to other mammals, and passes imperceptibly into the trunk, with no obvious neck or shoulders. All the rorquals, the river dolphins, and the white whales have neck vertebrae which are separate, allowing flexibility of the neck; the remainder of the species have between two and seven fused together. Further streamlining is achieved by reducing protruding parts that would impede the even flow of water over the body. The hindlimbs have been lost, although there are still traces of their bony skeleton within the body. There are no external ears—simply two minute openings on the side of the head which lead directly to the organs of hearing. The male's penis is completely hidden within muscular folds, and the teats of the female are housed within slits on either side of the genital area. The only protuberances are a pair of horizontal fins or flippers, a boneless tail fluke and, in many species, an upright but boneless dorsal fin of tissue which is firm, fibrous and fatty.

In most of the toothed whales the jaws are extended as a beak-like snout behind which the forehead rises in a rounded curve or "melon." Unlike the baleen whales (or any other mammal) they possess a single nostril, the two nasal passages, which are separate at the base of the skull, joining close below the surface to form a single opening—the blowhole; in extreme cases, one blowhole is functionally suppressed, leaving the other as the sole breathing tube. The blowhole is typically a slit in the form of a crescent,

## THE CETACEAN BODY PLAN

▼ **Skeletons** of baleen TOP and toothed whales BOTTOM. The skeleton of whales, although recognizably derived from the basic mammalian plan, is greatly modified. The skeleton does not have to carry the weight of the animal but instead acts as an anchor for the muscles, which may account for 40 percent of the whale's weight. The bones of whales are light and spongy with a thin outer shell. The hindlimbs have been lost completely, except for a vestigial unattached pelvic bone present in baleen whales and some male toothed whales, which acts as an anchor for the penis muscles. The most extreme modification is that of the skull, which is greatly extended in both baleen and toothed whales. The loss of teeth in baleen whales and associated changes have produced a skull with a grotesque form, unlike that of any other animal.

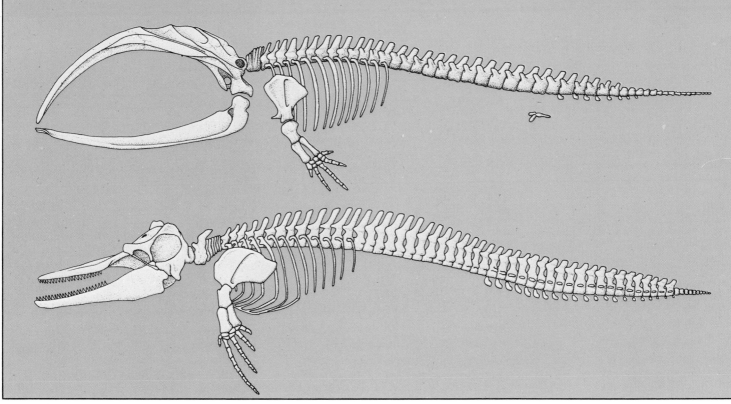

protected by a fatty and fibrous pad or plug which is opened by muscular effort and closed by the pressure of water upon it. The skull bones of the nasal region are usually asymmetrical in their size, shape and position, although porpoises and the La Plata dolphin have symmetrical skulls.

The baleen or whalebone whales differ from toothed whales in a number of ways. Besides being generally much larger, the main difference is in the baleen apparatus which takes the place of teeth in the mouth, and which grows as a series of horny plates from the sides of the upper jaw in the position of the upper teeth in other animals. Baleen whales feed by straining large quantities of water containing plankton and larger organisms through these plates (see pp62 and 63). The paired nostrils remain separate, so that the blowhole is a double hole forming two parallel slits, close together when shut. Other important differences are single-headed ribs and a breast-bone (sternum) composed of a single bone articulating with the first pair of ribs only. Despite variation between species in the size and shape of the skull, all baleen whales have a symmetrical skull.

Like all mammals, cetaceans are warm-blooded, using part of the energy available to them to maintain a stable body-core temperature. How do they maintain a stable muscle-core temperature of 97°–99°F (36°–37°C), without an insulating coat of hair, in the relatively cool environment of the sea, with temperatures usually less than 77°F (25°C)? Insulation is provided by a layer of fat, called blubber—which may be up to 20in (50cm) thick in the Bowhead whale—lying immediately beneath the skin. Larger species have a distinct advantage over smaller forms because of their much more favorable surface-to-volume ratio, and this may be why the smaller dolphins do not occur at very high latitudes. Fat is laid down not only as blubber: the liver is also import-

▶ **Blue whale bones** laid out on King George Island, Antarctica. The skeleton of the largest mammal is much reduced and simplified compared to land mammals. Most of the great bulk is flesh and blubber.

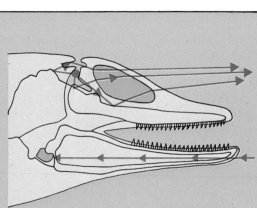

◀ **Baleen apparatus.** Instead of teeth, baleen whales have two rows of fringed plates hanging from the upper roof of the mouth. They evolved from the curved transverse ridges of the palate found in many land mammals. Despite the commercial name applied to them, "whalebone," they are not made of bone, but toughened skin.

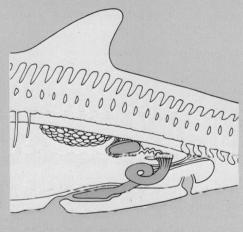

▲ **Acoustic focusing.** Toothed whales have a highly developed capacity for locating objects by means of sound (echolocation). It is thought that the melon, a waxy lens-shaped body in the forehead, focuses sounds produced in the nasal passages. Returning sound waves are channeled through oil-filled sinuses in the lower jaw to the inner ear. It is thought that the extreme sensitivity of this system is assisted by the isolation of the inner ear from the skull by means of a bubbly foam. Sound is thus very precisely channeled without the interference of extraneous resonances.

▲ **The genitals** of whales are internal, only a genital slit being visible. In males, the penis lies coiled on the floor of the abdominal cavity, held there by a retractor muscle. The penis is very mobile and is often used as a sensory organ, particularly during courtship. The penis and testes are shown in blue.

ant for fat deposition and in some species there are significant quantities of fat in the form of oil (as much as 50 percent of the body total) laid down in the skeletal bones of the animal.

Whales drive themselves through the water primarily by the upward stroke of their powerful tail (unlike fishes which propel themselves by a sideways movement of the tail). This movement is powered by a great muscle mass which occupies the upper region of the animal. Most cetaceans have a well-defined dorsal fin which is assumed to stabilize the animal, although it may also help in temperature regulation. The fore-limbs have a skeletal structure similar to that of the human arm, but they have been modified to form paddle-like flippers which are used for steering. Whereas the rigid hull of a ship creates turbulence when it passes through the water, a cetacean minimizes this by its flexible body; its blubber is not tightly fixed to the underlying muscular tissues, and there is a very well-developed system of dermal ridges beneath the skin. From the smooth, outer, cellular layer of the skin epidermis comes a secretion of tiny droplets of a high polymer of ethylene oxide; these droplets assist the shedding of epidermal cells into the water and may help to maintain a laminar flow, reducing turbulence and drag by dissipating the energy of the impeding vortices.

Cetaceans spend nearly all their lives underwater, sometimes at considerable depths. Because they are mammals they breathe air direct, instead of extracting oxygen dissolved in water as fishes do. They must therefore return to the surface at regular intervals to take air, and when they dive they must hold their breath.

When a man dives for longer than he can hold his breath, he takes with him a cylinder of compressed air. This is necessary because the air pressure within his lungs must equal or slightly exceed the pressure of the water around him, otherwise his chest would be crushed. Under compression, the nitrogen of the air dissolves in the fluids and tissues of his body to their full capacity, and when he ascends the dissolved nitrogen comes out of solution in the form of bubbles of the gas. These may appear in any part of the body; in the joints they cause the painful condition called "the bends." In contrast, when a cetacean dives it takes only the amount of air that will fill its relatively small lungs; only a proportion of the air is nitrogen, so that the amount which could dissolve in the body fluids and tissues from one filling of the lungs is rather small. But even this small

amount does not enter the blood and tissues, because as the cetacean dives its lungs compress and drive the air in them into the windpipe and its branches, and into the extensive nasal passages, the thickened membrane linings of which prevent gas exchange to the tissues. In cetaceans the chest is comparatively flexible and the diaphragm set very obliquely, so that the pressure of the abdominal viscera pushing against it on one side makes the lungs on the other side collapse.

As a cetacean returns to the surface, the lungs gradually expand again, its blowhole opens wide and the foul air accumulated during the dive is expelled explosively. This produces a cloud of spray—the spout—and this process, known as "blowing," occurs in all whales, although the spout is less visible in smaller species. It is produced by water from around the blowhole being forced into the air. As soon as the animal has exhaled, it takes in fresh air, the air sacs of the lungs return to their expanded condition for maximum gas exchange, and then it dives again.

Cetaceans remain underwater for quite long periods—perhaps more than an hour in the case of the Sperm whale (see p54). Muscles need to continue functioning and they require oxygen, so how is this achieved on a single breath of air? The muscles of cetaceans contain an unusually large amount of a substance called myoglobin which combines with oxygen to form an oxygen store that allows cetaceans to function without fresh oxygen for longer than land mammals.

There is little light deep underwater, so cetaceans rely mainly on senses other than sight to inform them about their surroundings and to help them locate food. They have a very highly developed sense of hearing, and communicate with each other by making a variety of sounds. The toothed whales, which pursue agile fish and squid, locate their prey by using sonar. They emit intense, short pulses of sound in the ultrasonic range (from 0.25–220kHz). These clicks, and other sounds, bounce off objects in their path producing echoes from which the whale is able to build up a sound picture of its surroundings. The arrangement of bones in the skull may have evolved to function like a parabolic reflector to focus the sounds.

The baleen whales have not yet been shown to use echolocation and may instead rely on sight to locate the dense swarms of plankton on which they feed. Some of them communicate with other individuals by the emission of low-frequency sounds (from 20Hz to 30kHz) which may be audible over tens to hundreds of miles across the deep ocean channels.

## Evolution

The origins of present-day cetaceans are poorly known. Mammals which are recognizable as cetaceans first appear as fossils in rock strata from the early Middle Eocene (about 50 million years ago). These were elongated aquatic animals, up to 70ft (21m) long, with reduced hindlimbs and long snouts, looking rather like a snake or eel. They have been classified within a separate suborder called Archaeoceti (including the

▲ **The Gray whale's spout.** Each whale makes a distinctive pattern as it blows. That of the Gray is vertical and some division of the spout is noticeable, caused by its emission from twin blowholes.

▼ **Evolution of the whale skull,** showing the modification of the bone structure and teeth. (1) *Protocetus*, a land-based creodont with carnivore-like teeth. (2) *Prosqualodon*, an intermediate form. (3) The Bottle-nosed dolphin, a modern toothed whale, showing the uniform teeth. (4) A rorqual, showing the most extreme modification of the bone structure, loss of all the teeth and their replacement by baleen (not shown).

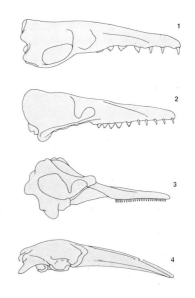

zeuglodonts, so named after the generic name *Zeuglodon* for one of these forms); they flourished during the Eocene epoch but most were extinct before the end of the Oligocene (26 million years ago), and none survived beyond the Miocene (7 million years ago). However, even by the late Middle and early Upper Eocene (40–45 million years ago), these had become so specialized, with sharp incisors and canines for grasping wriggling, slow-moving fish prey, and complex grinding teeth for breaking hard-bodied mollusks and crustaceans, that they could not have been the ancestors of modern cetaceans.

Looking further back in time, members of the terrestrial suborder Mesonychia may have given rise to the zeuglodonts (and thence to all other cetaceans) at the end of the Cretaceous and then colonized the sea during the Paleocene (60 million years ago). These are thought to share with the suborder Arctocyonia (the likely ancestors of present-day ungulates and their relatives) ancestry from the Condylarthra (otherwise known as creodonts). The Mesonychidae resemble the zeuglodonts in a number of skull and dental characters and although the similarities are not all clear-cut, at present they appear to be the most likely ancestors of the Cetacea.

Most of the early zeuglodont remains come from the Mediterranean-Arabian Gulf region, which during the Paleocene formed a narrow semi-enclosed arm of the western part of the ancient Tethys Sea. It is probably here that populations of terrestrial creodonts started to colonize marshes and shallow coastal fringes during the late Paleocene (58 million years ago), exploiting niches vacated at the end of the Cretaceous (65 million years ago) by the vanishing plesiosaurs, ichthyiosaurs and other reptiles. As population pressure on resources intensified during the Eocene, we can speculate that strong selection would have favored adaptations for the capture of fast-moving fish rather than the freshwater and estuarine mollusks and sluggish fish which previously formed their main diet. This was the age of mammals, with massive adaptive radiation into many species; such rapid evolution may help to explain the sparse fossil record for this period, with forms quite quickly developing relatively specialized cetacean characters. During the Eocene, the warm waters of the western Tethys Sea were dominated by the zeuglodonts, but as the climate started to deteriorate and the Tethys Sea enlarged during the Oligocene (38 million years ago), they probably declined in density and abundance, and by the Miocene

(26 million years ago) were being entirely replaced by odontocetes and mysticetes. The progressively more aquatic mode of life resulted in a backward and upward shift of the external nostrils, and the development of ways to seal them against water. The long mobile neck, functional hindlimbs and, eventually, most of the pelvic girdle were all lost, together with any coat remaining from a terrestrial creodont ancestory, and horizontal tail flukes developed as a means of propulsion by an up-and-down stroke action. The body became more torpedo-shaped to provide greater streamlining and a dorsal fin developed, particularly in the smaller species for hydrodynamic control and temperature regulation.

Most modifications of the zeuglodont skull towards an odontocete (toothed whale) form involved telescoping of the front of the skull, which probably paralleled the development of acoustic scanning as a means of locating cues in the dim underwater environment, and aided the capture of agile prey. At the same time, various specialized organs, notably the "melon," spermaceti organ and nasal diverticula developed. Their exact functions are unknown but are probably involved with both the production and reception of sounds, and with diving; later, sexual selection may have favored greater development of some of these in males of species in which inter-male competition for mates is important.

The dentition of zeuglodonts was differentiated into incisors, canines and grinding teeth, which were probably well adapted for

**▲ The Tethys Sea,** the probable center of whale evolution. The dark blue shows the original extent of the Tethys Sea, the pale blue the extent of the expansion. The black line indicates the present-day land mass.

**▼ The evolution of whales.**

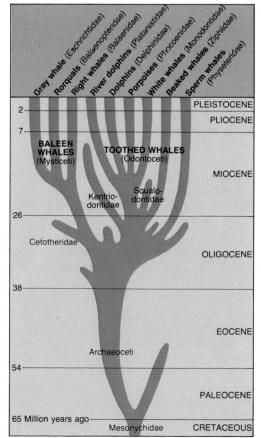

dealing with mollusks and crustaceans, but not for fast-swimming fish. These teeth either became modified during the Eocene, forming the long rows of sharp uniform teeth typical of present-day toothed whales, or later, in the late Oligocene-early Miocene (about 25–30 million years ago), gave rise to the baleen plates: the remarkable feeding structures, present in all mysticetes, which evolved from the curved transverse ridges of the palate in the roof of the mouth. Most present-day forms of baleen whales still have teeth during the early stages of fetal development, a further indication of their common ancestry with the toothed whales, which is also supported by the anatomical and chromosomal evidence.

The earliest true toothed whales were the squalodonts, a group of short-beaked whales (with triangular shark-like teeth) somewhat resembling the modern globicephalids (False killer, Killer and Pilot whales). These were possibly most abundant in the late Oligocene to early Miocene (about 25–30 million years ago), dispersed throughout the Southern Hemisphere, but by the middle Miocene (about 15 million years ago), they were being superseded by representatives of families with living rela-

tives. In particular, the Ziphiidae (beaked whales) can be traced back to a squalodont ancestor, and so can other groups including the Physeteridae (sperm whales) and, in fresh and brackish waters, the Platanistidae (river dolphins), with the Delphinidae (true dolphins) arising a little later in the Pliocene. The relationships of the latter three families are still uncertain, but the sperm whales, which have a much more marked asymmetry of the skull than any other odontocetes, and quite distinct chromosome structure, almost certainly diverged very early in the history of the line.

While the toothed-whale skull was becoming modified to contain acoustic apparatus, the baleen whale skull became modified to a different life-style. The upper margin of the "forehead" of the skull underwent considerable forward extension, probably mainly to combat the stresses on the skull and jaws imposed by the wide opening and closing of the mouth, at irregular intervals, as the animal moves forward to take in gulps of seawater from which its mainly planktonic food is sieved.

## Food and Feeding
Many small toothed whales appear to have

▲ **Krill strainer.** A Minke whale displaying its short, cream-colored baleen plates, with which it filters its crustacean food, krill, from mouthfuls of water.

▼ **Food of giants.** Individual Antarctic krill grow to a maximum of 3in (7.5cm) but exist in staggering numbers, perhaps 500–750 million tonnes. It is the principal food of the large baleen whales, particularly the Blue whale, but also the Fin, Sei and Minke whales.

generalist diets, opportunistically taking a range of shoaling open-sea fishes, but the extent to which diets overlap between species within a region is not known. Amongst the baleen whales, the thickness and number of baleen plates is related to the size and species of prey taken. Thus the Gray whale (see p69), a highly selective sea-bottom feeder, has a shorter stiffer baleen and fewer throat grooves (usually two or three) than the rorquals (with 14–100), and is thereby adapted for "scouring" the sea bottom. In the rorquals (see p71) the baleen is longer and wider. In the largest species, the Blue whale, the plates may reach a width of nearly 2.5ft (0.75m); in the other rorquals they are correspondingly narrower, and this dictates the diet of each. In the Right and Bowhead whales the baleen is extremely long and fine, and these whales feed on the smallest planktonic invertebrates of any of the baleen whales.

Whereas baleen whales and some toothed whales, such as the Sperm whale, Northern bottlenose whale and Harbor porpoise, tend to feed independently of other members of the same species, a number of small toothed whales, for example Dusky and Common dolphins, appear to herd fish shoals co-operatively by a combination of breaching and fast surface-rushing in groups (see pp42–43). Communication between individuals presumably is carried out by vocalization (high-pitched squeaks, squeals or grunts) and perhaps also by particular types of breaching. These latter activities often seem to be quite complex, but until we can follow marked individuals (preferably also below water) we cannot be sure of the extent of co-operation between individuals.

### Ecology and Natural History

The different evolutionary courses which the baleen and toothed whales have taken have strongly influenced their respective ecologies. Generally speaking, the ocean areas with the highest primary productivity (quantities of plankton), and hence fish and squid dependent upon this, are close to the poles, whereas at tropical latitudes productivity is relatively low (though rich upwellings of nutrients do occur patchily). Polar regions show great seasonal variations, and during the summer the rapid increase in temperature, sunlight and daylength and the relatively stable climatic conditions (particularly with respect to wind) allow phytoplankton—and hence zooplankton and higher organisms such as fish and squid—to build up to very high densities.

During the 120-day period of summer

feeding, the great baleen whales probably eat about 3–4 percent of their body weight daily. For an average adult Blue whale this would amount to about 2–2.5 tonnes of food every 24 hours, and correspondingly less for the smaller rorquals. Present-day whale populations in the Southern Ocean (including all species of baleen whales) consume about 40 million tonnes of krill each year. Before these whale populations were exploited by man, this figure may have been as high as 200 million tonnes. Thus during part of the year (about four months in the Southern Ocean but often more than six months in the North Pacific and North Atlantic where productivity is lower), the great whales migrate to high latitudes to feed, and here they may put on as much as 50–70 percent of their body weight as blubber. During the rest of the year, feeding rates may be reduced to about a tenth of the summer value (0.4 percent of body weight daily) and this negative net energy intake results in much of the blubber store being used by the time the whales return to the feeding grounds.

Why should the great baleen whales use up the food they have stored in their blubber to migrate to regions nearer the Equator where there is little food? This is not an easy question to answer. Many smaller cetacean species spend all the year at high latitudes and appear to be perfectly capable of rearing their young in this relatively cool environment, despite being less well insulated, so why should the larger whales travel to these warm waters to breed? It is understandable why they do not breed at high latitudes in winter since the low productivity of food and low water temperatures at this time would almost certainly impose too severe an

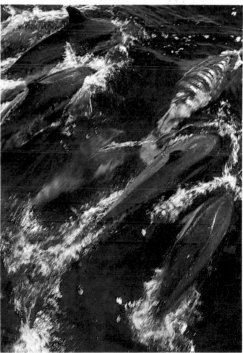

▲ **A short time to live.** TOP Trapped on an ice floe, this Weddell seal will eventually be tipped into the water and eaten by the attacking Killer whales. Killer whales are opportunist feeders.

▲ **Collaborative feeders.** ABOVE Dolphins, like these Common dolphins, cooperate in rounding up shoals of fish, presumably because it is more effective than individual hunting.

energetic strain to rear their young. On the other hand, in summer primary productivity is very high and water temperatures also much more favorable, so it is difficult to see why they do not breed there, alongside their smaller counterparts. Two plausible answers come to mind.

Firstly, it may be that the growth rates required for the young to attain anything like the large size of their parents, together with the energy intake required by the mother to sustain both herself and her calf, would require a longer period of high productivity than is available in a polar summer. It should also be noted that plankton has a short season of abundance whereas fish and squid are available the year round, and the great whales which undergo extensive migrations are all primarily plankton-feeders. Secondly, the answer may be purely historical. The earliest fossil remains of baleen whales, from about 30 million years ago, occur in low latitudes of the North Atlantic. With the juxtaposition of continental land masses by tectonic plate movement and changes in sea temperature, during the Cenozoic era, they radiated and dispersed towards the poles. As with some long-distance migrant bird species, the present-day movements of the great whales may be a vestige of earlier times, in this case when high productivity was in more equatorial regions.

Whereas baleen whales feed primarily upon zooplankton, the toothed whales feed on either fish or squid. All three prey groups have comparable energy values, weight for weight, and although this takes no account of differences in protein, fat or carbohydrate contents, daily feeding rates are comparable across groups. Body size appears to be the factor which determines whether or not they move out of high latitudes in winter; smaller species have relatively higher feeding rates, irrespective of diet (8–10 percent of body weight daily for the smallest species compared with 3–5 percent for the largest), but total daily intake for a smaller individual is obviously proportionately lower. For a 110lb (50kg) porpoise consuming about 9 percent of its body weight per day, this requires the daily capture of 8–10 fish of herring size.

The smaller cetaceans may be found at most latitudes, and though ranging over large areas (for example, the home range of the Bridled dolphin in the North Pacific appears to be 200–300mi (320–480km) in diameter), they do not tend to make strong north-south migrations.

Although the differences in migratory habits cannot be entirely attributed to diet, other features of cetaceans do appear to depend heavily upon their diets. Plankton- and fish-feeding species all have gestation periods of between 10–13 months whatever their size, whereas squid-feeders have longer gestation periods, of the order of 16 months. This may reflect the relative food values (protein, fat and carbohydrate amounts rather than simply energy values) of the different prey, squid perhaps being a poorer quality food, or it may relate to the relative seasonal availabilities of those prey. Amongst large whales, lactation periods are relatively longer in the squid-feeding Sperm whale (about two years) whereas in plankton-feeding baleen whales it is usually around 5–7 months. Amongst smaller cetaceans, the pattern is less clear but

▶ **Tearing itself from the sea,** a Humpback breaches in a cauldron of spray. They do this on the breeding grounds and, as here, in Glacier Bay, Alaska, on the feeding grounds. As with other whales, breaching appears to serve two functions: stunning or panicking fish shoals and communicating information to other herd members.

▼ **The antarctic world of the Humpback.** Barren though it looks, the Southern Ocean in summer swarms with vast quantities of krill, on which the whales feed.

similar: squid-feeding species have lactation periods varying from 12–20 months, whereas in fish-feeding species they are generally around 10–12 months.

The breeding systems of whales can also be grouped according to diet. Thus in the plankton-feeders the males tend to mate with a single female (although some species, such as the Right and Bowhead whales seem to be promiscuous) and the whales appear to spend most of their time either singly or in pairs, although small groups of usually less than 10 individuals may be seen at feeding concentrations or during apparent long-distance movements. There is evidence to suggest that squid-feeders are polygynous, with a male keeping a harem of females and young animals, other groups being made up of bachelor males or all female herds. Lone bachelor males and other individuals which have not been accepted into a herd may travel alone. This system is exemplified by the Sperm whale (see pp52–57) but also seems to occur in other species such as the Risso's dolphin. The killer whale (see pp38–39), which has a mixed diet of squid, fish, marine birds and mammals, also has a polygynous breeding system. Most fish-feeders, on the other hand, have a rather fluid breeding system, with mixed groups or family units (which may simply be mother-calf pairs) that aggregate on the feeding or mating grounds, and also during long-distance movements. Individuals come and go so that the group is not stable although it may have a constant core. In a number of species studied, it appears that there is no stable pair bond and males are promiscuous.

Cetaceans are not randomly distributed over any region but instead appear to be associated with oceanographic features such as upwellings (where food concentrations tend to occur), or undersea topographic features such as continental shelf slopes (which may serve as cues for navigation between areas). Breeding areas for most cetacean species (particularly small toothed whales) are very poorly known, but are better known for some of the large whales.

Gray whales and Right whales seem to require shallow coastal bays in warm waters for calving, whereas balaenopterids such as Blue, Fin and Sei whales possibly breed in deeper waters further offshore. The former group thus has more localized calving areas than the latter

The lengths of the gestation and lactation periods do of course dictate the frequency at which a female may bear young. Cetaceans usually give birth to a single young. In the large plankton-feeding whales an individual female may bear its young every alternate year (in Right whales, perhaps every 3 years); in squid-feeding species this is every 2–5 years; and in the smaller species feeding on fish, a female may reproduce every year. In the Killer whale, with its mixed diet, females reproduce at intervals of 3–8 years. With these relatively low reproductive rates, together with delayed maturation (4–8 years in plankton-feeders; 4–10 years in fish-feeders; and 8–26 years in squid-feeders), it is not surprising that most species are long-lived (14–50 years in the smaller species, but 50–100 years in the large baleen whales, the Sperm whale, and the Killer whale). Natural mortality rates seem to decrease in different whale species as their size increases with (where it has been studied) little apparent difference between juvenile and adult rates. Current estimates are 9–10 percent per annum for Minke whales; 7.5 percent for Sperm whales; and 4 percent for Fin whales. The long maturation in squid-feeders probably results from the need for a long period to learn efficient capture of the relatively difficult and agile squid prey.

During the period of mating, most cetacean species congregate in particular areas. These may be the same warm-water areas as those in which calving occurs during the winter months, as with a number of the larger baleen whales, or they may be on feeding grounds at high latitudes during the summer, as with many small toothed whales. Mating is usually seasonal, but in a number of gregarious dolphin species sexual activity has been observed during most months of the year.

## Whales and Man

Man has interacted with whales for almost as long as we have archaeological evidence of his activities. Whale carvings have been found in Norse settlements dating from 4,000 years ago and Alaskan Eskimo middens, 3,500 years old, contain the remains of whales which clearly have been used for food. It is quite possible, of course, that at this time whales were not being actively hunted but were taken only when stranded upon the coast. However, with the likely seasonal abundance of whales in the polar regions as the oceans warmed after the Pleistocene, it would be surprising if these early hunters had not actively exploited them.

, At about the same time (3,200 years ago) the Ancient Greeks had incorporated dolphins into their culture in a nonconsumptive way, for they appear on frescoes in the Minoan temple of Knossos in Crete, and many Greek myths refer to altruistic behavior by dolphins. Arion, the lyric poet and musician, when returning to Corinth from Italy with riches bestowed upon him at a music competition, was set upon by the crew of the boat in which he traveled. The legend goes that he asked if he might play one last tune and, on being granted this, a school of dolphins was attracted to the music and approached the boat. On sighting them near the boat, Arion leapt overboard, was rescued by the dolphins and carried to safety on the back of one of them. The Greek philosopher Aristotle (384–322BC) was the first to study whales and dolphins in detail, and although some of his information is incorrect and often contradictory, many of his detailed descriptions of their anatomy and physiology are accurate and clearly indicate that he had dissected specimens.

The earliest record of whaling in Europe comes from the Norsemen of Scandinavia between AD800 and 1,000. Slightly later, in the 12th century, the Basques were hunting whales quite extensively in the Bay of Biscay. Early fisheries for whales probably concentrated upon the Right and Bowhead whales (see pp78–85) since they are slow-moving and they float after death (due to their high oil content), so that they could be pursued by men with hand harpoons first from promontories and later from small open boats. It is possible that a Gray whale population existed in the North Atlantic and was hunted to extinction in earlier times.

From the Bay of Biscay, whaling gradually spread northwards up the European coast and across to Greenland, where

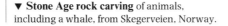

▲ **The grace of dolphins** endeared them to the great Mediterranean and Aegean civilizations. This mural from the Palace of Knossos, Crete, was executed about 1600BC.

▶ **Jonah and the whale,** from a fresco painted by Giotto at the Capella dell 'Arena, Padua, in about 1303–6. At this time, whales were known almost exclusively from ancient literary sources.

▼ **Stone Age rock carving** of animals, including a whale, from Skegerveien, Norway.

▲ **Lancing a Sperm whale.** A painting of a typical scene from the days when large whales were hunted from small boats with hand harpoons.

Sperm whaling flourished until about 1850 but then declined rapidly during the next decade. Whaling for Right whales also started up in the higher latitudes of the Pacific, off New Zealand, Australia and the Kerguelen Islands during the first half of the 19th century, and from 1840 onwards for Bowheads in the Bering, Chukchi and Beaufort seas. However, populations of both species had declined markedly by the end of the century.

In 1868, a Norwegian, Svend Foyn, developed an explosive harpoon gun and, at about the same time, steam-driven vessels replaced the sailing ships. Both these innovations had a significant impact on the remaining great whales, allowing ships to pursue even the fast-moving rorquals.

By the end of the 19th century, whalers concentrated on the waters off Newfoundland, the west coast of Africa and in the Pacific. Then, in 1905, the whalers discovered the rich antarctic feeding grounds of Blue, Fin and Sei whales and the Southern Ocean rapidly became the center of whaling in the world, with South Georgia its major base. All this time, whaling had been land-based, but in 1925 the first modern factory ship started operations in the Antarctic. This had a slipway and winches on the deck which allowed whales to be hauled on board, and hence allowed whaling to operate away from shore stations. A rapid expansion of the whaling industry occurred

▼ **Whales in the early 19th century.** Engravings of baleen whales from Lacépède's *Histoire Naturelle des Cetacés* (1804).

Basque ships were recorded in the 16th century. Whaling was no longer a local subsistence activity and by the next century the Dutch and then the British started whaling in arctic waters, particularly around Jan Mayen Island and Spitsbergen. During the 17th century, whaling was also starting from eastern North America, mainly catching Right whales and Humpbacks as they migrated along the coast. All through this period, the whalers used small sailing ships and struck their prey with hand harpoons from rowing boats. The whales were then towed ashore to land or ice floes, or cut up and processed in the sea alongside the boat. In contrast, whaling in Japan, which developed around 1600, used nets and fleets of small boats.

As vessels improved, whalers started to pursue other species, notably the deep-sea Sperm whale. In the 18th and 19th centuries, the whalers of New England (USA), Britain and Holland moved first southwards in the Atlantic and then round Cape Horn westwards into the Pacific and round the Cape of South Africa eastwards into the Indian Ocean. In the first half of the 19th century, Hawaii became a major whaling base and others started in South Africa and the Seychelles. By this time, the arctic whalers had penetrated far into the icy waters of Greenland, the Davis Strait, and Spitsbergen, where they took Bowhead and Right whales and, later, Humpbacks. Overhunting caused the collapse of whaling in the North Atlantic by the late 1700s and in the North Pacific during the mid-1800s. British arctic whaling ceased in 1912.

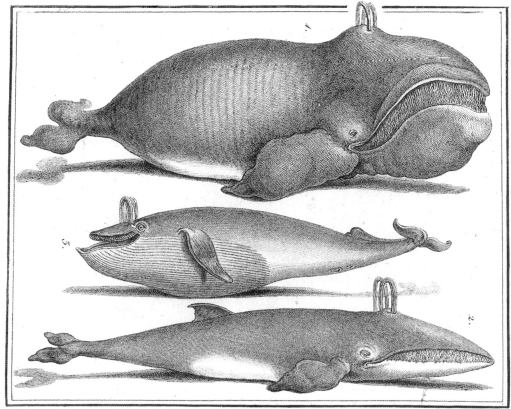

*When the whale comes aboue water ỹ ſhallop rowes towards him and being within reach of him the harpoiner darts his harpingwon at him out of both his hands and being faſt they lance him to death*

*The whale is cut up as hee lyes floting croſſe the ſtearne of a ſhipp the blubber is cut from the fleſh by peeces 3 or 4 foote long and being raſed is rowed on ſhore ſtowards the coppers*

*They place 2 .or 3 .coppers on a roe and ỹ chopping boat on the one ſide and the cooling boate on the other ſide to receiue ỹ oyle of ỹ coppers , the chopt blubber being boyled is taken out of the coppers and put in wiher baſkets or harowes throwgh w the oyle is dreaned and runes into ỹ cooler ʃ iſ ʃ fall ſ water out of w it is convaied by troughs into buts of*

▲ **Whaling in the 17th century,** as depicted in this woodcut of the Spitsbergen whale fishery. According to this account, the whales were cut up in the water.

▶ **Whalebone drying** in the yard at the Pacific Steamship Company, San Francisco, in the 1880s.

in this region, with 46,000 whales taken in the 1937–8 season, until, yet again, populations of successive target species declined to commercial extinction. The largest and hence most valuable of the rorquals, the Blue whale, dominated the catches in the 1930s but had declined to very few by the middle 1950s, and was eventually totally protected in 1965. As these populations declined, attention turned to the next largest rorqual, and so on (see pp74–75).

Following the population collapse of Sperm whales by 1860, whaling continued with a world catch of only about 5,000 annually until 1948. Since then, catches have increased quite rapidly, with about 20,000 a year being taken (mainly in the North Pacific and the Southern Hemisphere) in recent years, although this has now been reduced to a small quota of males only in the North Pacific.

Until the middle of this century, the whaling industry was dominated by Norway and the United Kingdom, with Holland and the United States also taking substantial shares. Since World War II, however, these nations have abandoned deep-sea whaling, and the industry has become dominated by Japan and the Soviet Union, although many nations practice coastal whaling.

Originally, the most important product of modern deep-sea whaling was oil, that of baleen whales used in margarines and other foodstuffs, and that of Sperm whales used in specialized lubricants. Since about 1950, meal for animal foodstuffs, and chemical products became increasingly important, although whale meat (from baleen whales) became highly valued for human consumption by the Japanese. The Soviet Union, the other major whaling nation, on the other hand, uses very little whale meat and instead concentrates upon Sperm whales for oil. Recent figures (late 1970s) indicate that whale catches in the Antarctic yielded 29 percent meat, 20 percent oil and 7 percent meal and solubles.

In the last 15 years, whales have become political animals, as public attention and sympathy have increasingly turned towards their plight. People watching whales in the coastal lagoons of California and dolphins at close quarters as captive animals in dolphinaria throughout the developed world were impressed by their friendliness and ability to learn complicated tricks. But most of the great whales were continuing to decline, as one section of the human population overexploited them. The International Whaling Commission, set up in 1946 to

regulate whaling activities, was generally ineffective because the advice of its scientific committee was often overruled by short-term commercial considerations. In 1972, the US Marine Mammal Act prohibited the taking and importing of marine mammals and their products except under certain conditions, such as by some Indians, Eskimos and Aleuts for subsistence or native handicrafts and clothing. In the same year, the United Nations Conference on the Human Environment called for a 10-year moratorium on whaling. The latter was not accepted by the International Whaling Commission, but continued publicity and pressure, particularly on moral grounds, from environmental bodies (such as World Wildlife Fund, Friends of the Earth, and Greenpeace), and concern expressed by many scientists over the difficulties in estimating population sizes and maximum sustainable yields, finally had an effect. In 1982 a ban on all commercial whaling was agreed upon for the first time in the history of man, to take effect from 1986.

But the story of man's often unhappy relationship with whales does not end here. Even if we terminate commercial whaling forever or acquire sufficient knowledge to manage whale populations in a sustained manner, they continue to face threats from man, and these are likely to increase. Modification of the marine environment is occurring in many parts of the world as human populations increase and become more industrialized, making greater demands upon the sea either by removing organisms for food, or by releasing toxic waste products

into it. Acoustic disturbance comes from sonic testing (for example during oil exploration), military depth charge practice and particularly from motor boat traffic. These probably impose threats to whales in a number of areas of the world, notably the North Sea and English Channel, the Gulfs of California and St. Lawrence, the Caribbean, Hawaii, and tropical Australia. A number of species, such as the Humpback, the Right and Bowhead whales, the Californian Gray whale population, and small toothed whales, such as the Harbor porpoise and the beluga, are particularly vulnerable. Toxic chemical pollution (particularly from heavy metals, oil and persistent chemicals) from urban, industrial and agricultural effluents may also have serious harmful effects in enclosed seas such as the Baltic, Mediterranean and North Seas, and coastal species such as the Harbor porpoise are vulnerable and presently showing declines. Actual removal of suitable habitat by the building of coastal hotel resorts, breakwaters which change local current patterns and encourage silting, and dams which regulate water flow in rivers, all impose threats. Species most vulnerable are usually those that are rare and localized in distribution, such as the Gulf of California porpoise and the Ganges and Indus river dolphins (see pp26–27). Incidental catches in fishing nets of large numbers of dolphins have recently caused heavy mortality (see pp41–46).

Finally, one factor which for whales and dolphins may represent the greatest threat is the increasing need for man to exploit the sea for food. The depletion of the great whales in the early part of this century had repercussions on the populations remaining and on related species (see pp74–75). This was thought to be the result of relaxation of pressures on the food supply through lower competition. It was not only whales that were affected, but also the Crabeater seal (see pp128–129) and various seabird species, all of which showed signs of population increase. The converse now looks as if it might occur as man is beginning to harvest a variety of food organisms (for example krill in the Southern Ocean, capelin, sand eels and sprats in the North Atlantic), which form important links in the marine food chain for cetaceans, seals and seabirds alike. These potential problems are unlikely to evoke the same passions as overexploitation by the whaling nations, but nevertheless will have to be addressed if these magnificent creatures are to continue to grace our oceans.                    PGHE

▼ ▲ **Whaling in the 1980s** – the Faeroes whales hunt. ABOVE Small-scale whaling for Pilot whales is still carried on, with much ritual and folklore, in the Faeroe Islands. BELOW Lining up the catch of Pilot whales at Torshavn in the Faeroe Islands.

# TOOTHED WHALES

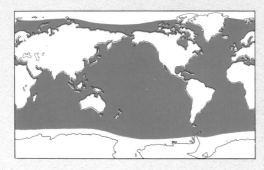

**Suborder: Odontoceti**
Sixty-six species in 33 genera and six families.
Distribution: all oceans.

Habitat: deep sea, coastal shallows and some
river estuaries.

Size: head-to-tail length from 4ft (1.2m) in
Heaviside's dolphin to 68ft (20.7m) in the
Sperm whale; weight from 88lb (40kg) in
Heaviside's dolphin to 70 tonnes in the Sperm
whale.

**River dolphins** (family Platanistidae)
Five species in 4 genera including **Ganges
dolphin** (*Platanista gangetica*), **Indus dolphin**
(*Platanista minor*).

**Dolphins** (family Delphinidae)
Thirty-two species in 17 genera, including
**Common dolphin** (*Delphinus delphis*), **Killer
whale** (*Orcinus orca*), **Melon-headed whale**
(*Peponocephala electra*), **Risso's dolphin**
(*Grampus griseus*).

**Porpoises** (family Phocoenidae)
Six species in 3 genera, including **Finless
porpoise** (*Neophocaena phocaenoides*).

**White whales** (family Monodontidae)
Two species in 2 genera: **Narwhal** (*Monodon
monoceros*), **Beluga** (*Delphinapterus leucas*).

**Sperm whales** (family Physeteridae)
Three species in 2 genera: **Sperm whale**
(*Physeter macrocephalus*), **Pygmy sperm whale**
(*Kogia breviceps*), **Dwarf sperm whale** (*Kogia
simus*).

**Beaked whales** (family Ziphiidae)
Eighteen species in 5 genera, including:
**Northern bottlenose whale** (*Hyperoodon
ampullatus*).

NEARLY 90 percent of the cetacean species belong to the suborder Odontoceti—the toothed whales. Most of these are comparatively small dolphins and porpoises, usually less than 15ft (4.5m) in length, but some, such as the beaked whales, pilot whales and Killer whale, may reach a length of 30ft (9m), and one, the Sperm whale, reaches 60ft (18m) or more. In most of the toothed whales the jaws are prolonged as a beak-like snout behind which the forehead rises in a rounded curve or "melon." As their name suggests, toothed whales always bear teeth, however rudimentary, in the upper or lower jaws, or both, at some stage of their lives. The teeth look alike and always have a single root, so that they are simple or slightly recurved pegs set in single sockets. One set of teeth lasts a lifetime (monophyodont dentition).

The family Platanistidae (river dolphins) is regarded as the most primitive of living cetaceans. The freshwater habit of most members of this family is probably secondary, since platanistid fossils from the Miocene and Pliocene have been found in marine deposits. All the platanistids have a long beak and rather broad short flippers, probably used for obtaining tactile cues from the environment, the eyes are very small and two species (the Indus and Ganges dolphins) are virtually blind. These animals often lie in very turbid water where sight would be of little value, and they have developed instead a relatively sophisticated capacity for echolocation.

Another evolutionary side-arm appears to be the family Ziphiidae (the beaked whales), so named because of the distinct beak which extends from the skull. In all except one species, the teeth are very re-

duced in number and entirely absent from the upper jaw. On each side of the lower jaw of adult males there are only one or two teeth; these are comparatively large, sometimes projecting from the mouth as small tusks. In young males and in females their teeth do not usually emerge from the gums so that these appear as entirely toothless. Another unusual feature is the chromosome number, 42 instead of 44, which is shared by only the almost certainly distantly related sperm whales. Most of the species are extremely elusive, and many are known only from stranded specimens.

The family Physeteridae probably diverged from the main odontocete line as long ago as the Oligocene. They comprise only three living species: the cosmopolitan Sperm whale, the Pygmy sperm whale of the warmer waters of the Atlantic, Indian and Pacific Oceans, and the little-known Dwarf sperm whale of tropical waters. The first of these is the largest of the toothed whales, with the males twice as large as the females. It is characterized by a huge barrel-shaped head containing spermaceti oil, a rounded dorsal hump two-thirds of the way along the back instead of a dorsal fin, and a very narrow underslung lower jaw which lacks functional teeth. The other two species are built similarly but are much smaller, with a less pronounced head and a distinct dorsal fin.

The last three families (Monodontidae, Phocoenidae, Delphinidae) which make up the Odontoceti are all rather closely related and probably diverged sometime in the middle Miocene. The two species of Monodontidae, the narwhal and beluga, are confined to the northern oceans, particularly the Arctic. They are relatively small

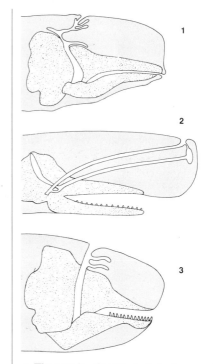

▲ **The nostrils of toothed whales** in general show a migration backwards and towards the top of the skull compared to land mammals. The Narwhal (1) and Pygmy sperm whale (3) are typical. The Sperm whale (2) is unusual, in that its development of the huge spermaceti organ made this pattern unworkable and two new passages were formed, through the spermaceti organ to the front of the nose.

▶ **A Killer bares its teeth.** The Killer whale has fewer teeth than most toothed whales but they are large and strong for seizing large fish, squid and other marine vertebrates. The Killer does not chew its food but swallows it whole or tears off large chunks.

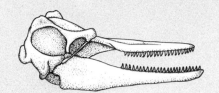

**Bottle-nosed dolphin**  24in

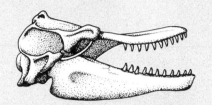

**Killer whale**  47in

## Skulls of Toothed Whales

In the evolution of toothed whales from terrestrial carnivores a telescoping of the skull has taken place, resulting in a long narrow "beak" and a movement of the posterior maxillary bone to the supra-occipital region (top of the skull). These changes were

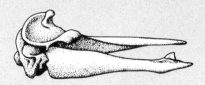

**Gervais's beaked whale**  47in

associated with the development of echolocating abilities and the modification of the teeth for catching fish. The teeth of the toothed whales' ancestors were differentiated into incisors, canines and molars, as in modern carnivores, but the ideal dentition for fish eaters is a long row of even, conical teeth, and this is in fact roughly the pattern in all toothed whales. The Bottle-nosed dolphin is a classic fish-eater, with numerous small sharp teeth. The number of teeth is greatly reduced (10–14 on each side of both jaws) in the Killer whale, which will feed on mammals as well as fish. The beaked whales feed on squid and have become virtually toothless. Those of genus *Mesoplodon*, like Gervais's beaked whale, have a single tooth in the lower jaw.

whales and neither has a dorsal fin. The narwhal is unique in having a tooth modified to form a unicorn's tusk which projects from the snout.

The family Phocoenidae (the porpoises) appears to have radiated and dispersed from the tropics into temperate waters of both hemispheres, probably during the Miocene-Pliocene (about 7 million years ago). One of the six species, the Finless porpoise, may be nearest to the ancestors of this family, with a warm water Indo-Pacific distribution that includes estuaries and rivers. All are small species with a rounded snout, no beak, and a relatively small number of spade-shaped teeth (unlike the conical teeth of most other toothed whales).

The largest odontocete family is the Delphinidae (the dolphins), most of which have functional teeth in both jaws, a melon with a distinct beak, and a dorsal fin, and many have striking black and white countershading pigmentation. The largest of these is the Killer whale, in which the male is twice as large as the female; it also differs from other delphinids in having a large rounded flipper, lacking any beak, and preying upon other marine mammals. Some, for example the genus *Lagenorhynchus*, form species-pairs with an antitropical distribution (ie they are found in both hemispheres away from the tropics); others, for example the genus *Tursiops*, have virtually identical Northern and Southern Hemisphere populations, but with a smaller form in the tropics than at higher latitudes; some, for example the Common dolphin, Killer whale and Risso's dolphin, have a cosmopolitan distribution; still others, such as the Melon-headed whale, have a restricted pantropical distribution.  PGHE

# RIVER DOLPHINS

**Family: Platanistidae**
Five species in four genera.
Distribution: SE Asia, S America.

## Ganges dolphin
*Platanista gangetica*
Ganges dolphin or Ganges susu.
Distribution: India, Nepal, Bangladesh.
Habitat: Ganges-Brahmaputra-Meghna river
system. Length 83–102in (210–260cm);
weight 175–200lb (80–90kg). Skin: light
grayish-brown, paler beneath. Gestation: 10
months. Longevity: over 28 years.

## Indus dolphin E
*Platanista minor*
Indus dolphin or Indus susu.
Distribution: Pakistan. Habitat: Indus river.
Size, coat, diet, gestation and longevity:
as Ganges dolphin (probably).

## Whitefin dolphin I
*Lipotes vexillifer*
Whitefin dolphin or peic'hi.
Distribution: China. Habitat: Yangtze and
lower Fuchanjian Rivers. Length 90–98in
(230–250cm); weight 300–510lb (135–230kg).
Skin: bluish-gray, white underneath.
Gestation: probably 10–12 months.

## Amazon dolphin
*Inia geoffrensis*
Amazon dolphin or boutu.
Distribution: South America. Habitat: Amazon
and Orinoco river systems. Length 82–91in
(208–228cm) (Orinoco), 96–108in (224–247cm)
(Amazon); weight 190–285lb (85–130kg).
Skin: dark bluish-gray above, pink beneath;
darker in Orinoco. Gestation: probably 10–12
months.

## La Plata dolphin
*Pontoporia blainvillei*
La Plata dolphin or franciscana.
Distribution: coast of eastern S America from
Ubatuba to Valdes Peninsula (not in La Plata
river). Length 61–69in (155–175cm); weight
71–115lb (32–52kg). Skin: light, warm brown,
paler beneath. Gestation: 11 months.
Longevity: more than 16 years.

E Endangered.   I Indeterminate.

DOLPHINS with eyes so poor that they are
only capable of distinguishing night
and day, yet are able to detect a copper wire
0.03in (1mm) in diameter—such are the
river dolphins, which rely on their extremely sensitive echolocation apparatus to find
their food. Their vision has been all but lost
in the course of evolution because in the
muddy estuaries that they inhabit visibility
may be only a few centimeters.

The river dolphins are the most primitive
dolphins, retaining certain features of
Miocene cetaceans of about 10 million years
ago. They have a long slender beak bearing
numerous pointed teeth, and the neck is
flexible because the seven neck vertebrae
are not fused. The forehead melon is pronounced, the dorsal fin undeveloped, and the
flippers broad and visibly fingered. The eye
and visual nerve have degenerated in the
descending order: Indus and Ganges dolphins, Amazon dolphin, Whitefin dolphin,
La Plata dolphin. In the Indus and Ganges
dolphins the lens has been lost altogether,
which means that no image can be formed
and only light or dark and the direction of
light can be registered.

The brains of river dolphins are small:
only the Amazon dolphin at 23oz (650g)
and 1.3 percent of body-weight, has a brain
of comparable size to other dolphins. The
small brain size relates to their early weaning and short learning period, and also to
their solitary life, lacking in social behavior
comparable to modern dolphins.

Because of their poor eyesight, river dolphins use echolocation to find their food,
which comprises mostly fish, shrimps and,

▼ **The five species of river dolphins.** Despite
their widely separated habitats, the river
dolphins are very similar in appearance,
differing mainly in skin color, length of beak
and number of teeth. (1) Amazon dolphin (*Inia
geoffrensis*). (2) La Plata dolphin (*Pontoporia
blainvillei*). (3) Ganges dolphin (*Platanista
gangetica*). (4) Indus dolphin (*Platanista minor*).
(5) Whitefin dolphin (*Lipotes vexillifer*).

in the coastal La Plata dolphin, squid and octopus. They emit directed ultrasonic pulses or clicks, at distinctive frequencies for each species, which rebound from any object, allowing the dolphin to judge its distance by the time the pulse takes to return. The nasal air sacs and air sinuses lining the well-developed crest on the upper jawbone direct the pulse to the target. The sensory bristles along the beak also help in locating food on the river bottom. The coastal species, the La Plata dolphin, is thought to find its prey by means of the light they emit (bioluminescence) or by sound.

The teeth are conical and thickened at the base near the back. The Ganges and Indus and the Amazon dolphins have four stomach compartments, including an esophageal compartment for food storage, as in most cetaceans. The La Plata and Whitefin dolphins seem to have lost the esophageal compartment.

Information on growth and reproduction is still fragmentary. The La Plata dolphin matures at 2–3 years and females breed every two years. When growth stops at four years, females are larger than males by about 8in (20cm). This is in contrast to the Indus and Ganges dolphins, in which sexual maturity occurs somewhere around 10 years and growth lasts for more than 20 years. Although females are about 16in (40cm) longer than males, this is entirely accounted for by a greatly extended beak, and the weight difference is small. In both species, calves are weaned before 8–9 months and start their solitary life. The period of growth of the Amazon dolphin is as long as that of the Ganges, but the males are larger and heavier than the females.

Among human factors adversely affecting river dolphins, the most destructive is dam construction. In the Indus River system, the construction of dams for power and irrigation started in the early 1900s, and divided the habitat up into 10 segments, thus inhibiting movement of dolphins and fish. In winter, no water flows to the sea and many upper sections are almost dry. This and hunting for dolphin oil, used in medicine, left a significant number of dolphins only between Guddu and Sukkur barrages, and made the Indus dolphin one of the most vulnerable of all the cetaceans, with a population of about 600.

Although the Ganges dolphin is not vulnerable at present, it too is now threatened by dam construction. In the Yangtze River, the low population of Whitefin dolphins seems to be declining, and here too work is now in progress on dams and drainage systems. Fishing gear often causes accidental death or injury. The South American river dolphins are in a more favorable situation, but here too development is threatening.

Besides these human threats, river dolphins will increasingly come into competition with more adaptive and possibly more intelligent dolphins.                    TK

# DOLPHINS

**Family: Delphinidae**
Thirty-two species in 17 genera.
Distribution: all oceans.

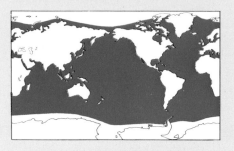

Habitat: generally coastal shallows but some open-sea.

Size: head-to-tail length from 3.5ft (1.2m) in Heaviside's dolphin to 23ft (7m) in the Killer whale; weight from 88lb (40kg) in Heaviside's dolphin to 4.5 tonnes in the Killer whale.

Gestation: 10–12 months (16 months in pilot whales and Risso's dolphin).

Longevity: up to 50–100 years (Killer whale).

Species include: **Bottle-nosed dolphin** (*Tursiops truncatus*), **Bridled dolphin** (*Stenella attenuata*), **Common dolphin** (*Delphinus delphis*), **False killer whale** (*Pseudorca crassidens*), **Guiana dolphin** (*Sotalia guianensis*), **Humpbacked dolphin** (*Sousa teuszii*), **Killer whale** (*Orcinus orca*), **Melon-headed whale** (*Peponocephala electra*), **Risso's dolphin** (*Grampus griseus*), **Spinner dolphin** (*Stenella longirostris*), **Tucuxi** (*Sotalia fluviatilis*).

THE sight of dolphins eagerly performing complicated tricks in oceanaria has probably done more than anything else to put them in a rather special position in the eyes of mankind. It has been argued that their intelligence and developed social organization are equaled only by the primates, perhaps only by man, while their general friendliness and lack of aggression are compared favorably with man.

The family Delphinidae is a relatively modern group, having evolved during the late Miocene (about 10 million years ago). They are the most abundant and varied of all cetaceans.

Most dolphins are small to medium-sized animals with a well-developed beak and a central sickle-shaped dorsal fin curving backwards. They have a single crescent-shaped blowhole, with the concave side facing forwards on top of the head, and they have functional well-separated teeth in both jaws (between 10 and 224 but most between 100 and 200). Most delphinids have a forehead melon although this is indistinct in some species, for example the Guiana dolphin and tucuxi, absent in *Cephalorhynchus* species, pronounced and rounded to form an indistinct beak in Risso's dolphin and the two species of pilot whales, and tapered to form a blunt snout in Killer and False killer whales. Killer whales also have rounded paddle-shaped flippers, whereas the pilot whales and False killer have narrow, elongated flippers. The aforementioned species are not closely related to each other but several genera, particularly *Delphinus*, *Stenella*, *Sousa* and *Sotalia*, contain species which are indistinct from each other.

The extensive variation in color patterns

▲ **Dolphin dapples.** The beautiful patterns on many dolphins may help to conceal them from their prey or their predators. The light patterns near the surface blend with the dolphin's coloration to break up the outline of the dolphin. These are Common dolphins.

▶ **Apparently doing press-ups,** this Indo-Pacific humpbacked dolphin shows why this species rarely strands. It is quite at home in shallow water and can even traverse mudbanks between waters.

◀ **The exuberance of Dusky dolphins** finds expression in graceful leaps. These may not always be functional and at times may simply be for the fun of it.

◀ **Riding the surf,** a Risso's dolphin plows through a wave. This species moves around in herds of stable composition, often one or more males, some females and their young.

between species has been variously categorized. One classification recognizes three types: uniform (plain or evenly marked), patched (with clearly demarcated pigmented areas) and countershaded (black and white). The more conspicuous patched patterns are considered useful for visual recognition by individuals while the others are for concealment from their prey, the uniform ones being related to feeding at depths where light is dim, and the counter-shaded ones to feeding near the surface. The color patterns of some may also be camouflage from predators: the saddle pattern may afford protection from being seen by predators (or prey) through its counter-

lighting effect; the spotted pattern blends directly with a background of sun-dappled water; criss-crossed patterns have both counter-shading and disruptive elements.

The morphological and anatomical differences between dolphins relate partly to differences in diet. Those species with more rounded foreheads, blunt beaks, and often reduced dentition, feed primarily upon squid, or, in the case of the Killer whale, the diet also includes marine mammals and birds. The development of the cranial region may be an adaptation for receiving and focusing acoustic signals to obtain an accurate picture of the location of their agile, fast-moving prey. The other members of the family feed primarily upon fish: all appear to be opportunist feeders, probably catching whatever species of fish they encounter within particular size ranges. Some, for example Bottle-nosed and Humpbacked dolphins, are primarily inshore species, although they may feed upon both bottom-dwelling and open-sea fish. Others, such as members of the genera *Stenella* and *Delphinus*, are more pelagic, ie they feed further out to sea, but take shoaling fish both close to the surface (such as anchovy, herring and capelin) and at great depths (such as lantern fish).

Most dolphins at least occasionally feed upon squid, and even shrimps. This generalist diet makes it very difficult to determine the extent of competition among dolphin species. In the tropical eastern Pacific, however, Bridled dolphins feed largely on open-sea fish near the surface, whereas the related Spinner dolphin feeds at deeper levels; both may also feed at different times of the day.

The more pelagic dolphin species tend to travel in herds of up to 1,000 or more, whose members may cooperate in the capture of shoaling fish (see pp42–43) Inshore species usually form smaller herds of 2–12 individuals. While foraging, dolphin schools often spread out to form a band, varying from about 66ft (20m) to several kilometers wide, and usually comprising small groups of 5–25 but which together may total in the hundreds. They often follow undersea escarpments. At upwellings where plankton fronts develop and shoaling fish concentrate, these groups often coalesce and frenzied feeding activity may follow.

Radio-tracking studies have shown that dolphins may have home ranges varying from about 33sq mi (85sq km) in the Bottle-nosed dolphin to 580sq mi (1,500sq km) in the Dusky dolphin, while individual movements of 190mi (300km) have been recorded in Spinner dolphins and are probably not uncommon for open-sea species.

Although most species have an open social structure, where individuals enter and leave the herd over periods of time, some, such as the Killer whale and Risso's dolphin, appear to have more stable group membership. These latter tend to be polygynous, with an adult male holding a harem of adult females and young, although there are also all-male herds of young animals. The herds of most other dolphins seem to comprise family groups of male, female and calf or mother-calf pairs, which may aggregate to form larger herds, or herds that are segregated by sex and age. Their mating system is not clear but generally appears to be promiscuous. Polygyny may also occur, but whatever the mating system, the male-female and male-calf bonds are relatively weak.

Until recently, virtually all information about dolphins was derived from dead animals that had come ashore on coasts. Most of these have died at sea and have simply been washed ashore, but some strand while alive, and such incidents are most conspicuous when groups of animals strand together, which is most prevalent among Pilot whales (see Box) and False killers. The problem with interpreting

▲ **Characteristic poses** of 13 dolphin species. (1) Bottle-nosed dolphin (*Tursiops truncatus*). (2) Rough-toothed dolphin (*Steno bredanensis*). (3) Atlantic white-sided dolphin (*Lagenorhynchus acutus*). (4) Spotted dolphin (*Stenella plagiodon*). (5) Common dolphin (*Delphinus delphis*). (6) Northern right whale dolphin (*Lissodelphis borealis*). (7) Dusky dolphin (*Lagenorhynchus obscurus*). (8) Atlantic humpbacked dolphin (*Sousa teuszii*). (9) Melon-headed whale (*Peponocephala electra*). (10) Commerson's dolphin (*Cephalorhynchus commersoni*). (11) False killer whale (*Pseudorca crassidens*). (12) Killer whale (*Orcinus orca*). (13) Risso's dolphin (*Grampus griseus*).

fluctuations in the numbers of strandings in a particular region is that the same result may be observed by a change in the population size in that area with constant mortality, or a change in mortality with constant population size.

The Melon-headed whale, for example, was scarcely ever recorded until the 1960s, since when there have been a number of mass strandings. It seems rather unlikely that these species have been overlooked previously and one must conclude that their populations have actually increased. In certain cases, increases in the number of strandings appear to be related to increases in the abundance of particular food fishes which probably attracted dolphins into the area. For example, the recent increase in numbers of Pilot whales stranding in southwest England, mainly in fall-winter (an average of less than one per year between 1913–1947; two per year between 1948–1962; more than five per year between 1963–1978) is mirrored by an increase in sightings of live animals, at the same time as large concentrations of mackerel occur in these waters. However, a number of these are drowning in fishing nets in this region, so mortality may also have increased.

The presence and direction of onshore winds and currents, together with the configuration of the coastline, may all influence where a dolphin that has died may come ashore, and if the species generally spends its time far from the coast, individuals may sink after death and so not be recovered. However, the cause of strandings of live animals is unknown. Theories seeking to explain spectacular mass strandings include: infection of the inner ear by nematode parasites which upset balance or echolocation abilities, the effects of upsetting sounds such as underwater explosions or magnetic disturbances, or disorientation having followed prey into unfamiliar or shallow waters. Obviously, disease and old age are unlikely to lead to an entire herd coming ashore, so the explanation may be that most members are following a leader, which will usually be an older experienced animal. So far as we know, mass-stranding species tend to form fairly stable herds; they are also pelagic, so they are less likely to be familiar with shallow coastal areas, and more likely to become disorientated.

Sexual behavior in dolphins occurs throughout the year although there is usually a peak in calving during the summer months, even in lower latitudes. The single calf remains with the mother for several months, with lactation lasting up to 1.5–2 years. This suggests that many species breed at minimum intervals of 2–3 years. The age of sexual maturity probably ranges between 5 years (Common dolphin) and 16 years (male Killer whale), with most species breeding at about 8–10 years old. Many species undergo seasonal migrations in search of food; these are usually offshore-inshore movements but may be latitudinal. If discrete breeding areas exist, they have rarely been identified, although it is probable that they are in deeper offshore waters where

## The Mystery of Mass Strandings

Strandings of whole herds of Pilot whales are better known than for any other cetacean, probably because of the animals' abundance. Some 95 percent of beach deaths occur in mass strandings, the remainder being of sick and heavily parasitized individuals that drift ashore alone. The mass strandings are of live animals which are not obviously diseased or emaciated, and in this sense resemble strandings of animals driven ashore by fishermen. The composition of a stranded herd is also the same as in a driven herd, indicating that in both types of case all animals of a herd strand together. No one has as yet clearly detected a leader or leading group though it is possible that one or more of the older animals might have this role. If the animals are towed out to sea, all, or many, of them will usually come ashore again at a new site, and die. Mass-strandings occur on all types of coastline and the particular site seems to have no significance. At Newfoundland, stranded herds come from among the massed animals attracted close inshore in late summer by their food supply, immature squid, which themselves make a summer migration up from the continental slope and become exceedingly numerous inshore. The local Pilot whales appear, therefore, to be dependent at this season on a high density of their food resources. This may be the key to their propensity to mass-strand, although the physiological mechanisms involved are not known.                                      DES

there is less turbulence from coastal currents.

Dolphins are gregarious, with some species forming herds of a thousand or more, but these generally occur during long-distance movements or when concentrated at food sources. In most cases, membership of the herd is fluid; that is to say, individuals may enter or leave the group over a period of weeks or months, only a minority remaining within it for a longer time. There is no indication of the stable, well-developed social organization typical of primates.

Dolphins, like other toothed whales, rely greatly upon sound for communication. Their sounds range from trains of clicks of 0.25kHz into the ultrasonic range around 80–220kHz, which appear to be used for echolocation of, and possibly stunning, food, and a pure tone or modulated whistles. Although different whistles have been categorized and associated with particular behaviors, there is no evidence of a language with syntax. The extent to which dolphins cooperate with one another to herd fish is controversial, but even if we accept that

high degree of folding of the cerebral cortex (comparable with primates), considered to be indications of high intelligence, it is likely that these are a consequence of the processing of acoustic information requiring greater "storage space" than visual information. The density of neurones, another feature commonly regarded as suggesting high intelligence, is not particularly high. The often cited lack of aggression amongst dolphins has probably been exaggerated. Several species develop dominance hierarchies in captivity, in which aggression is manifested by directing the head at the threatened animal, displaying with open mouth or clapping of the jaw. Fights have also been observed in the wild when scratches and scrapes have been inflicted by one individual running its teeth over the back of another.

Dolphins may congregate in numbers of up to 2,000 at feeding areas, which often coincide with human fisheries, resulting in a conflict of interests. Gill-nets, laid to catch salmon or capelin, also catch and drown dolphins. Inshore species of porpoises such as Dall's and Harbor porpoises are most at risk, but in the eastern Pacific the purse-seine tuna fishery has caused the death of an estimated 113,000 individuals annually, mainly Spinner and Bridled dolphins, but also Common dolphins, during the late 1960s and early 1970s (see p41). The application of lines of floats at the surface, and similar methods to make the nets more conspicuous to dolphins, reduced the incidental kills to 17,000 by 1980. Similar large incidental catches have occurred in recent years along the Japanese coast, affecting Common and Spinner dolphins, and porpoises such as Dall's porpoise (see p46).

A less obvious threat to dolphins comes from inshore pollution by toxic chemicals, and acoustic disturbance from boats. These may explain apparent recent declines in the Bottle-nosed dolphin in the North Sea and English Channel, although direct evidence of a causal link is generally lacking. The same factors may threaten the Common and Bottle-nosed dolphins in the western Mediterranean and off southern California. The hunting of dolphins is not widespread but in certain areas such as the Black Sea very large numbers (Turkish catches of 176,000 per year reported during the early 1970s) of mainly Common dolphins have been taken. Finally, direct competition for particular fish species may be an important potential threat as man turns increasingly to the marine environment for food.

PGHE

some of the more gregarious species do do this, such behavior is also found among primates, carnivores and birds.

Dolphins can perform quite complex tasks and are fine mimics, capable of memorizing long routines, particularly where learning by ear is involved. In some tests they rank with elephants. Although they are sometimes spontaneously innovative, as are other mammals, there is no proof that they have prior knowledge of the consequences of an action. Although dolphins have the large brain size (relative to body size) and

▲ **Performing dolphins** at San Diego, USA. Such displays of agility, grace and charm have given dolphins a special place in the human imagination, and have probably helped to fuel the outrage felt by many at their continued slaughter at the hands of man.

◄ **Peaceful coexistence.** Two Bottle-nosed dolphins, one primate and a carnivore obviously enjoying each other's company.

◄ **Mass stranding.** Pilot whales appear to strand in large numbers more often than any other whale. TOP Pilot whales at sea. BOTTOM Pilot whales stranded on a beach at Sable Island. Nova Scotia in 1976. Over 130 whales stranded on this occasion. (See Box.)

# THE 32 SPECIES OF DOLPHINS

Abbreviations: HTL = head-to-tail straight-line length. wt = weight

### Killer whale
*Orcinus orca.*
Killer whale or orca

All oceans. Male HTL 22–23ft; wt 8,800–9,920lb. Female HTL 20–21ft; wt 5,500–6,600lb. Skin: black on back and sides, white belly extending as a lobe up the flanks, and a white oval patch above and behind the eye; regional variation in exact position and extent of white patches; indistinct gray saddle over back behind dorsal fin. Rounded paddle-shaped flippers and centrally placed dorsal fin, sickle-shaped in female and immatures, but very tall and erect in male. Broad rounded head and stout torpedo-shaped body.

### False killer whale
*Pseudorca crassidens*

All oceans; mainly tropical and warm temperate. Male HTL 18ft; wt about 4,400lb. Female HTL 16ft; wt about 2,650lb. Skin: all black except for a blaze of gray on belly between the flippers, which have a broad hump on front margin near middle of flipper. Tall, sickle-shaped dorsal fin just behind midpoint of back, sometimes with pointed tip. Slender, tapered head, underslung jaw, and long, slender body.

### Pygmy killer whale
*Feresa attenuata*

Probably all tropical and subtropical seas. Male HTL 7–8ft; wt about 370lb. Female HTL 7ft; wt about 330lb. Skin: dark gray or black on back, often lighter on flanks, extending highest at front of dorsal fin; small but conspicuous zone of white on underside (from anus to tail stock) and around lips, and chin may be entirely white. Flippers slightly rounded at tip. Sickle-shaped, centrally-placed dorsal fin. Rounded head with underslung jaw, and slender body.

◄ **The sinuous ripples** of its wake accentuate the apparent menace of the Killer whale in the foreground. In reality, Killer whales pose little threat to man, unlike the similar (and quite unrelated) sharks. These Killers are in Johnstone Strait, a narrow passage along the north coast of Vancouver Island. Killer whales are found in all oceans.

### Melon-headed whale
*Peponocephala electra*
Melon-headed whale or Many-toothed blackfish.

Probably all tropical seas. HTL 7ft; wt 350lb. Skin: black on back and flanks; slightly lighter on belly; areas around anus, genitals, and the lips pale gray or white. Pointed flippers. Sickle-shaped centrally placed dorsal fin. Rounded head (though slightly more pointed snout than Pygmy killer whale) with slightly underslung jaw, and slender body with slim tail stock.

### Long-finned pilot whale
*Globicephala melaena*
Long-finned pilot whale or Pothead whale.

*G. m. melaena* temperate waters of N Atlantic; *G. m. edwardi* all waters of all seas in S Hemisphere. Male HTL 20ft; wt about 7,700lb. Female HTL 17ft; wt about 3,950lb. Skin: black on back and flanks with anchor-shaped patch of grayish-white on chin and gray area on belly, both variable in extent and intensity (lighter in younger animals). Some have gray dorsal fin. Long sickle-shaped flippers, and fairly low dorsal fin, slightly forward of midpoint, with long base, sickle-shaped (in adult females and immatures) to flag-shaped (in adult males). Square bulbous head, particularly in old males, with slightly protruding upper lip and robust body.

### Short-finned pilot whale
*Globicephala macrorhynchus*

All tropical and subtropical waters but with possible separate form in N Pacific. Male HTL 15–18ft; wt about 5,500lb. Female HTL 12–14ft; wt about 2,900lb. Skin: black on back, flanks and most of belly, with anchor-shaped patch of gray on chin, and gray area of varying extent and intensity on belly (lighter in younger animals). Long sickle-shaped flippers (but shorter than Long-finned pilot whale), and fairly low dorsal fin, slightly forward of midpoint, with long base, sickle-shaped to flag-shaped. Square bulbous head particularly in old males (slightly more robust than in Long-finned pilot whale, with slightly protruding upper lip and robust body).

CONTINUED ►

## Pacific white-sided dolphin
*Lagenorhynchus obliquidens*

Temperate waters of N Pacific. HTL 7ft; wt about 200lb. Male slightly larger than female. Skin: dark gray or black on back, white belly, large pale gray oval area on otherwise black flanks in front of fin above flipper and extending forward to eye which is encircled with dark gray or black; narrow pale gray stripe above eye running along length of body and curving down to anal area where it broadens out; pale gray blaze also sometimes present on posterior part of centrally placed sickle-shaped dorsal fin. Rounded snout with very short black beak and torpedo-shaped body.

## Hour-glass dolphin
*Lagenorhynchus cruciger*

Probably circumpolar in cooler waters of Southern Ocean. HTL 5.2ft; wt 220lb. Skin: black on back, white belly, two large white areas on otherwise black flanks forward of dorsal fin to black beak and backward to tail stock, connected by narrow white band; area of white variable in extent. Centrally placed sickle-shaped dorsal fin, usually strongly concave on leading edge. Rounded snout with very short black beak and torpedo-shaped body.

## Peale's dolphin
*Lagenorhynchus australis*
Peale's or Black chinned dolphin.

Cold waters of Argentina, Chile and Falkland Islands. HTL 6ft; wt 253lb. Skin: dark gray-black on back, white belly; light gray area on flanks from behind eye to anus and, above this, a narrow white band behind the dorsal fin extending backwards, enlarging to tail stock; thin black line running from leading edge of black flipper to eye. Centrally placed sickle-shaped fin. Rounded snout with short black beak and torpedo-shaped body.

## Dusky dolphin
*Lagenorhynchus obscurus*

Circumpolar in temperate waters of S Hemisphere. HTL 6ft; wt 253lb. Skin: dark gray-black on back, white belly; large gray area (varying in intensity) on lower flanks, extending from base of beak or eye backwards and running to anus; light gray or white areas on upper flanks extending backwards from below dorsal fin as two blazes which generally meet above anal region and end at tail stock. Centrally placed sickle-shaped dorsal fin, slightly more erect and less curved than rest of genus, commonly with pale gray on posterior part of fin. Rounded snout with very short black beak and torpedo-shaped body.

## Atlantic white-sided dolphin
*Lagenorhynchus acutus*

Temperate and subpolar waters of N Atlantic. Male HTL 8ft; wt 473lb; Female HTL 7ft; wt 363lb. Skin: black on back, white belly, gray flanks but with long white oval blaze from below dorsal fin to area above anus; directly above but originating slightly behind the front edge of white blaze is an elongated yellow band extending back to tail stock. Centrally placed sickle-shaped dorsal fin, relatively tall, pointed at tip. Rounded snout with short black beak, stout torpedo-shaped body with very thick tail stock narrowing close to tail flukes.

## White-beaked dolphin
*Lagenorhynchus albirostris*

Temperate and subpolar waters of N Atlantic. Male HTL 9ft; wt about 440lb. Female HTL 9ft; wt about 400lb. Skin: dark gray or black over most of back, but pale gray-white area over dorsal surface behind fin (less distinct in young individuals); commonly dark gray-white blaze from near dorsal surface, behind eye, across flanks and downward to anal area; white belly. Centrally placed, tall (particularly in adult males), sickle-shaped dorsal fin. Rounded snout with short beak, often light gray or white. Very stout torpedo-shaped body, with very thick tail stock.

## Fraser's dolphin
*Lagenodelphis hosei*

Warm waters of all oceans. HTL 7ft; wt 200lb. Skin: medium-dark gray on back and flanks, white or pinkish-white belly; two parallel stripes on flanks: upper, cream-white, beginning above and in front of eye, moving back and narrowing to tail stock, lower more distinct, dark gray-black from eye to anus; sometimes also a black band from mouth to flipper; white throat and chin but tip of lower jaw usually black. Small slender slightly sickle-shaped dorsal fin, pointed at tip, centrally placed. Very short rounded snout with short beak. Fairly robust torpedo-shaped body with marked keels above and below tail stock.

## Hector's dolphin
*Cephalorhynchus hectori*

Coastal waters of New Zealand. HTL 4ft; wt 88lb. Skin: pale to dark gray around anus. Rounded black flipper and centrally placed low rounded dorsal fin. Short rounded snout with no melon and a short beak. Small stout torpedo-shaped body, narrowing at tail stock.

## White-bellied dolphin
*Cephalorhynchus eutropia*
White-bellied or Black dolphin.

Coastal waters of Chile. HTL 4ft; wt 99lb. Skin: black on back, flanks and part of belly but with three areas of white, variable in extent, on throat, behind flippers and around anal area; pale gray or white thin margin to lips of both jaws; sometimes pale gray area around blowhole. Low triangular dorsal fin, centrally placed with longer leading edge and blunt apex. Short rounded snout with no melon and very short beak. Small stout torpedo-shaped body with keels above and below tail stock.

## Commerson's dolphin
*Cephalorhynchus commersoni*
Commerson's or Piebald dolphin.

Cool waters of southern S America and Falkland Islands, possibly across Southern Ocean to Kerguelen Island. HTL 4ft; wt 110lb. Skin: dark gray on back but with large white-pale gray cape across front half, extending down across belly, leaving only small black area around anus; white area also on throat and chin so that dark gray frontal region confined to forehead, snout and broad band across neck region to flippers. Rounded black flippers and centrally placed low rounded dorsal fin. Short rounded snout with no melon and very short beak. Small stout torpedo-shaped body.

## Heaviside's dolphin
*Cephalorhynchus heavisidii*

Coastal waters of southern Africa. HTL 4ft; wt 88lb. Skin: black on back and flanks, white belly, extending upwards as three lobes, two on either side of the flipper, and one from anal region up along flanks to tail stock. Small oval-shaped black flippers and centrally placed low triangular dorsal fin. Short rounded snout with no melon and no distinct beak. Small fairly stout torpedo-shaped body.

## Northern right whale dolphin
*Lissodelphis borealis*

Offshore waters of temperate N Pacific. HTL 7ft; wt 154lb. Skin: black on back and flanks, extending down around navel; white belly, in some individuals extending up flanks around flipper so that only the tips are black; otherwise, flippers all black. Juveniles light gray to brown on back and flanks. Dorsal fin absent. Rounded snout with distinct beak and white band across bottom of lower jaw. Small, very slender torpedo-shaped body with marked keel above tail stock.

## Southern right whale dolphin
*Lissodelphis peronii*

Offshore, waters of Southern Ocean, possibly circumpolar. HBL 6ft; wt 132lb. Skin: black on back and flanks, white belly extending upwards to lower flanks behind flippers and forward across forehead in front of eyes so that entire back is white; flippers all white. Dorsal fin absent. Rounded snout with distinct beak. Small, very slender torpedo-shaped body, with underside of tail fluke white.

## Risso's dolphin
*Grampus griseus*
Risso's dolphin or grampus.

All tropical and temperate seas. Male HTL 13ft; wt about 880lb. Female HTL 11ft; wt about 770lb. Skin dark to light gray on back and flanks, palest in older individuals, particularly leading edge of dorsal fin, so that head may be pure white; many scars on flanks of adults; white belly enlarging to oval patch on chest and chin. Long pointed black flippers, tall centrally placed sickle-shaped dorsal fin (taller, more erect in adult males). Blunt snout, rounded with slight melon. No beak. Stout torpedo-shaped body narrowing behind dorsal fin to quite narrow tail stock.

## Bottle-nosed dolphin
*Tursiops truncatus*

Coastal waters of most tropical, subtropical and temperate regions. Three forms recognized: a large race, *T. t. truncatus* in Atlantic, and two smaller races, *T. t. gilli* in temperate N Pacific and *T. t. aduncus* in Indo-Pacific and Red Sea. HTL 11 (small)–13ft (large race); wt about 330–440lb. Usually dark-gray on back, lighter gray on flanks (variable in extent), grading to white or pink on belly. *T. t. gilli* often more brown than gray on back, and has distinct pink area around anus. *T. t. aduncus* sometimes darker than *T. t. truncatus*. Some spotting may be present on belly. Centrally placed, tall, slender, sickle-shaped dorsal fin. Robust head with distinct short beak, often with white patch on tip of lower jaw. Stout torpedo-shaped body with moderately keeled tail stock.

## Rough-toothed dolphin
*Steno bredanensis*

Offshore waters of all tropical, subtropical and warm temperate seas. Male HTL 8ft; wt about 310lb. Female HTL 7ft; wt about 260lb. Skin: coloration variable, often dark gray to dark purplish-gray on back and flanks, and white throat and belly; pinkish-white blotches on flanks round to belly; frequently scarred with numerous white streaks. Centrally placed sickle-shaped dorsal fin. Long, slender beak not clearly demarcated from forehead, with white or pinkish-white along both sides, including one or both lips and tip of snout. Slender torpedo-shaped body, keels above and below tail stock.

## Common dolphin
*Delphinus delphis*
Common or Saddleback dolphin.

Usually offshore waters of all tropical, subtropical and warm temperate seas, including Mediterranean and Black Seas. Possibly separate form *D. d. bairdii*, in N Pacific. Male HTL about 7ft; wt about 190lb. Female HTL about 7ft; wt about 165lb. Skin: coloration variable; black or brownish black on back and upper flanks; chest and belly cream-white to white; on flanks, hourglass pattern of tan or yellowish tan forward becoming paler gray behind dorsal fin where it may reach dorsal surface; black stripe from flipper to middle of lower jaw, and from eye to base of beak; one or two gray lines running longitudinally on lower flanks in *D. d. bairdii*; flippers black to light gray or white (atlantic population). Slender sickle-shaped to erect dorsal fin, centrally placed. Long, slender beak and distinct forehead and slender torpedo-shaped body.

## Striped dolphin
*Stenella coeruleoalba*
Striped, Euphrosyne, or Blue-white dolphin.

All tropical, subtropical and warm temperate seas, including Mediterranean. HTL 8ft; wt 220lb. Skin: dark gray to brown or bluish gray on back, lighter gray flanks, and white belly; two distinct black bands on flanks, one from near eye down side of body to anal area (with short secondary stripe originating with this band, turning downwards towards flippers) and second from eye to flippers; most have additional black or dark gray fingers extending from behind dorsal fin forward and about halfway to eye; black flippers. Slender sickle-shaped centrally placed dorsal fin. Slender, long beak (but shorter than Common dolphin) and distinct forehead. Slender torpedo-shaped body.

## Spinner dolphin
*Stenella longirostris*

Probably in all tropical oceans. Possibly a number of different races. HTL 6ft; wt 165lb. Skin: dark gray, brown or black on back; lighter gray, tan or yellowish tan flanks, and white belly (purplish or yellow in some populations); distinct black to light gray stripe from flipper to eye. Slender erect to sickle-shaped centrally placed dorsal fin, often lighter gray near middle of fin; relatively large black to light gray flippers. Medium to long, slender beak and distinct forehead. Slender to relatively stout torpedo-shaped body which may have marked keels above and below tail stock.

## Bridled dolphin
*Stenella attenuata*
Bridled or Spotted dolphin.

Deep waters of tropical Pacific and Atlantic, probably elsewhere. Some authorities recognize *S. frontalis* as separate species in western N Atlantic, *S. a. graffmani* as separate race (larger, more spotted) in coastal waters of tropical E Pacific. HTL 7ft; wt 220lb. Skin: coloration and markings variable with age and geographically; dark gray to black on back and upper flanks, lighter gray on lower flanks and belly (sometimes pinkish on throat); white spots on upper flanks, dark spots on lower flanks and belly absent at birth but enlarging with age; may give rise to uniform dark gray belly; distinct dark gray-black area (or cape) on head to dorsal fin with black circle around eye, extending to junction of beak and melon, and broad black stripe from origin of flipper to corner of mouth (which tends to fade as spotting increases); these give banded appearance to light gray sides of head. Slender sickle-shaped centrally placed dorsal fin; medium-dark gray flippers. Long slender beak, both upper and lower lips white or pinkish, and distinct forehead. Slender to relatively stout torpedo-shaped body with marked keel below tail stock (sometimes also one above tail stock).

## Spotted dolphin
*Stenella plagiodon*

Tropical Atlantic, possibly other waters. May be a race of Bridled dolphin. HTL 7ft; wt 242lb. Skin: coloration and markings variable with age; dark gray on back and upper flanks, lighter gray on lower flanks and belly, white spots on upper flanks, dark spots on lower flanks and belly absent at birth but enlarging with age; dark gray area (cape) on head to dorsal fin distinctly separated (though less distinct than Bridled dolphin) from light gray flanks; bridling of face and dark line from flipper to mouth both absent; pronounced pale blaze on flanks, slanting up on to back behind dorsal fin; medium gray flippers. Sickle-shaped centrally placed dorsal fin. Long slender beak with upper and lower lips usually pale gray or white, and distinct forehead. Stout torpedo-shaped body.

## Tucuxi
*Sotalia fluviatilis*

Amazon river system. HTL 4ft; wt 79lb. Skin: coloration variable geographically and with age; medium to dark gray on back and upper flanks with brownish tinge, lighter gray sometimes with patches of yellow-ocher on lower flanks and belly; two pale gray areas sometimes extend diagonally upwards on flanks. Small triangular centrally placed dorsal fin. Relatively large spoon-shaped flipper. Pronounced beak (medium to dark gray above, light gray-white below), and rounded forehead. Individuals become lighter with age, sometimes cream-white. Small stout torpedo-shaped body.

## Guiana dolphin
*Sotalia guianensis*

Coastal waters and river systems of S America. HTL about 5ft; wt about 90lb. Skin: generally darker, but otherwise very similar to tucuxi. Blue-gray to dark brown on back and upper flanks, lighter gray on lower flanks, white on belly; sometimes a brownish band extending from anal area diagonally upward to flanks to leading edge of dorsal fin. Small but prominent triangular centrally placed dorsal fin. Relatively large, spatulate flippers. Small, stout torpedo-shaped body.

## Atlantic humpbacked dolphin
*Sousa teuszii*

Coastal waters and river systems of W Africa. Possibly a form of Indo-Pacific humpbacked dolphin which it closely resembles (differs in having fewer teeth and more vertebrae). HTL about 7ft; wt about 220lb. Shape and coloration variable. Skin: dark gray-white on back and upper flanks, lightening on lower flanks to white belly; young uniform pale cream. Small but prominent triangular centrally placed dorsal fin, sickle-shaped in young, becoming more rounded later. Rounded flippers. Long slender beak with slight melon on forehead. Stout torpedo-shaped body, with distinct dorsal hump in middle of back (on which is dorsal fin) and similar marked keels above and below tail stock.

## Indo-Pacific humpbacked dolphin
*Sousa chinensis*

Coastal warm waters of E Africa to Indonesia and S China. Some authorities recognize *S. c. plumbea* (darker), *S. c. lentiginosa* (speckled) and *S. c. chinensis* (white) as separate races. HTL 6ft; wt about 190lb. Shape and coloration variable. Skin: dark gray-white on back and upper flanks, usually lightening on lower flanks to white belly; adults may develop spots or speckles of yellow, pink, gray or brown; young uniform pale cream. Small but prominent triangular centrally placed dorsal fin, sickle-shaped in young, becoming more rounded later. Rounded flippers. Both dorsal fin and flippers may be tipped white. Long slender beak (with white patch on tip in some individuals) with slight melon on forehead. Stout torpedo-shaped body, with distinct dorsal hump in middle of back (on which is dorsal fin) and similar marked keels above and below tail stock.

## Irrawaddy dolphin*
*Orcaella brevirostris*

Coastal waters from Bay of Bengal to northern coast of Australia. HTL about 6ft; wt about 220lb. Skin: blue-gray on back and flanks, lighter gray on belly. Stout torpedo-shaped body and tailstock; robust rounded head with distinct melon but no beak; small sickle-shaped dorsal fin with rounded tip, slightly behind center of back.

*This species is considered by some authorities to be a member of the family Monodontidae.

# Cooperative Killers

*Hunting strategy of the Killer whale*

As they approached the rocky point around which the tide flowed rapidly toward them, the pod of 20 Killer whales was spread in line abreast about 160ft (50m) apart. The whales were swimming slowly near the surface, occasionally rising to breathe and slap the surface with their long, oval flippers and large tail flukes. Underwater, the slaps sounded like muffled gunshots against a background of squeals and ratchet-like clicking sounds. Then came a long, wavy whistling sound, punctuated by a honk like that from a squeeze bulb horn at an Indian bazaar, and the whales converged methodically toward their prey—a school of several thousand Pacific pink salmon they were herding between the rock and the roaring current. For several minutes the whales had the fish loosely but effectively trapped, as one by one they picked out and swallowed several 6.6lb (3kg) salmon from the periphery of the school. Then the whales seemed to lose interest in the hunt and instead rolled lazily in the water and casually "spyhopped" to look around at the boatfuls of salmon anglers floating near the point. With another underwater whistle and a honk, all the whales simultaneously submerged, to reappear five minutes later in a close-knit group beyond the point, upcurrent and far away from the fishermen. They remained in a close group, swimming slowly and silently for two hours toward the next rocky point, where the cooperative hunt was repeated.

Killer whales, or orcas, are the largest and fastest members of the dolphin family. The males, which may approach 33ft (10m) in length, are at once recognizable by the upright triangular fin, up to 6.6ft (2m) tall—the largest of any whale. Females are slightly smaller and the fin is curved back as in a shark. The striking black and white coloration includes a white spot above the eye, a finger-like white patch extending up onto the flank, and a grey "saddle" behind the fin, against the upperside.

The key to the foraging success of these predators is cooperation and exquisite coordination between individuals. All adults and the older juveniles are active participants in the hunt, while younger whales playfully mimic their actions. The coordination is apparently learned and enhanced by the tight social cohesion of Killer whales. Pod members remain together for life, and such ties may persist from one generation to the next, as has been found for some terrestrial predators. The sex and age composition of the group remains fairly stable, with one adult male to three or four adult females and several subadults of both sexes. The pod size

is typically 4–40 whales, larger groups gradually splitting into two or more smaller groups as the population grows. Some pods may inhabit ranges extending for 200–300mi (320–480km). Population control may be accomplished by separating off very small pods of 2–6 whales which are usually doomed to die out within a generation. Partitioning of the food resources may also occur, with the larger productive pods preying upon the most abundant "preferred" prey species, and the smaller pods relegated to foraging on other prey. Both splitting of large pods and partitioning of resources seem to be accomplished without overt aggressive action by these extremely powerful and intelligent creatures.

Sexual maturity is attained at 8–10 years (but may be 16 years in males) and the natural lifespan is estimated to be 50–100 years. An adult female can bear a single calf once every three years, but one calf every eight years is the average. Gestation lasts for 15 months and nursing lasts approximately one year, though a weaned calf may closely accompany its mother for several years. Female calves, at least, remain in the pod of birth.

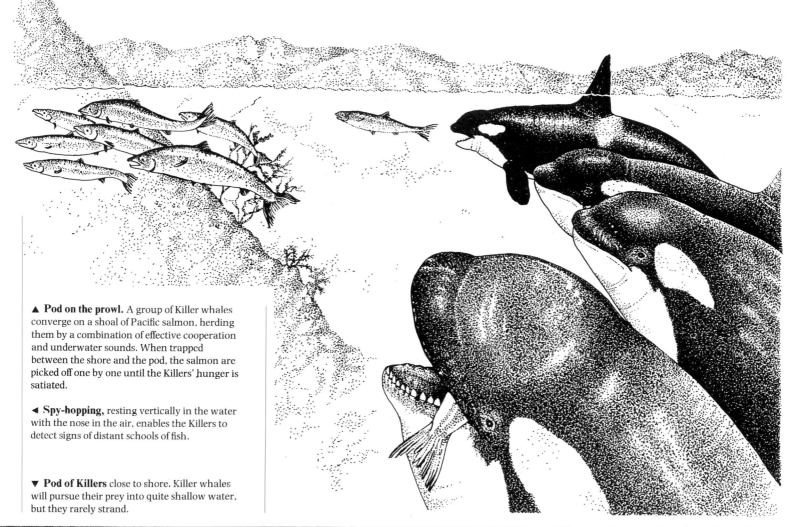

▲ **Pod on the prowl.** A group of Killer whales converge on a shoal of Pacific salmon, herding them by a combination of effective cooperation and underwater sounds. When trapped between the shore and the pod, the salmon are picked off one by one until the Killers' hunger is satiated.

◀ **Spy-hopping,** resting vertically in the water with the nose in the air, enables the Killers to detect signs of distant schools of fish.

▼ **Pod of Killers** close to shore. Killer whales will pursue their prey into quite shallow water, but they rarely strand.

Killer whales are distributed worldwide but are most abundant in food-rich areas at high latitudes. On average, they must eat about 2.5–5 percent of their body weight per day, so they require steady and abundant resources of prey species. They are very flexible predators, eating anything from small fish and invertebrates to the largest whales. Fish and squid form the bulk of their diet, but the Killer whale is the only cetacean that preys on warm-blooded flesh. Dolphins and porpoises are taken with some regularity, and seals, sea lions and seabirds are also eaten. Despite a (undeserved) reputation as a wanton killer, the species actually forbears from attacking another warm-blooded species, man, in the water.

Some Killer whale pods may travel many hundreds of miles to keep up with the movements of prey species, while others maintain relatively restricted ranges where food is abundant all year. Being at the very top of the food chain, Killer whales are not numerous, but the appearance of several large pods of these mobile predators in an area where prey is locally or seasonally abundant can give the false impression that their population is quite large.　KB

# Sleek Spinners

*School life of the Spinner dolphin*

The slender dolphins leap high out of the water, twisting and spinning rapidly around their longitudinal axes. The movement at once identifies these as Spinner dolphins, inhabitants of oceans throughout the tropics and subtropics.

Spinner dolphins of Hawaii spend most of their lives close to shore. During the day, they rest and socialize in tight groups of usually 10–100 animals within protected bays and along shallow coastlines. At night, they move into deep water half a mile or more offshore, and they dive deeply (300ft or more) to feed on fish and squid. At that time, the group spreads out, and 100 animals may cover an area of several square miles.

These groups are ephemeral. During the night, many individual dolphins change their companions so that when they head shoreward at dawn, group membership is reshuffled. However, this daily reshuffling of group composition is not random. Small subgroups of 4–8 animals stay together and change group affiliations together for periods of up to four months and possibly longer. Some dolphins may have close ties which last throughout their lives. It is not known if the members of these more stable subgroups are related or not. Some dolphin mothers and their calves stay together for many years, but the same mothers may also have long-term affiliations with one or more possibly unrelated adult males and females.

In Hawaii, Spinner dolphins shelter in numerous bays, and may range as far as 30mi (50km) along the coast from one day to the next. Each subgroup does however have a preferred "home area" beyond which the dolphins travel with a frequency that declines with distance; they rarely range further than 62mi (100km). There are at least two benefits in seeking out shallow water during the day. The water is usually calmer than in the open ocean, which makes resting and socializing easier, and deepwater sharks which prey on dolphins are not as numerous and are more easily detected in the shallows.

Spinners, like most species of dolphin, are

▲ **Sparring Spinners.** The Spinner dolphin is one of the most acrobatic of all dolphins. These three spinners are playing a sparring game during the evening period of social interaction.

▼ **In mid-turn,** a Spinner dolphin leaps from the water. Spinners are inventive acrobats, but spinning along their axis as they leap is their most characteristic feat.

large-brained social mammals, and they probably recognize many of the individuals with which they associate on a daily basis. They may even recognize individuals which are far from their home area and have therefore only rarely been met. When Spinners meet after a long separation, much social behavior, including vocalizations which may be part of a greeting ceremony, takes place.

Unlike the Hawaiian population, other Spinner dolphins roam throughout the tropical Pacific. These deepwater dolphins do not have the protection of nearby islands. Instead, they associate with a related species, the Bridled dolphin, and the two appear to take turns resting and feeding. While Spinner dolphins feed mostly at night, Bridled dolphins feed mostly during the day. Each species helps the other by guarding against the danger of surprise attack by large, deepwater sharks.

Deepwater Spinners may cover several thousand miles over a few months. It is not known whether the social affinities of deepwater spinners are as transient as those of their Hawaiian relatives. Perhaps the open-ocean school which travels together and may number 5–10 thousand animals has its coastal equivalent in the population of many of the interchanging groups of the Hawaiian coastal region.

Deepwater Spinner dolphins and Bridled dolphins commonly associate with Yellowfin tuna in the tropical Pacific. It is thought that these large fish follow the dolphins because they benefit from the excellent echolocation abilities which dolphins use to help find and identify prey. Since the tuna often swim below the dolphins, movements by the tuna, such as their breaking schooling ranks in the face of an attack by sharks, may be easily detected by the dolphins. In this way, the two dolphin and the tuna fish species each derive mutual benefit from the others.

Because dolphins surface to breathe, they can be seen by the human seafarer more easily than the tuna. Tuna fishermen take advantage of this to set their nets around dolphin–tuna schools. Unfortunately, many dolphins used to become entangled in these nets cast for the tuna and drown. In 1974 about half a million Spinner and Bridled dolphins were killed in tuna nets in the tropical east Pacific.

Tuna fishermen have recently adopted special nets and fishing procedures which greatly reduce this threat to dolphins. A panel of finer mesh—the Medina panel—is employed in that part of the net furthest

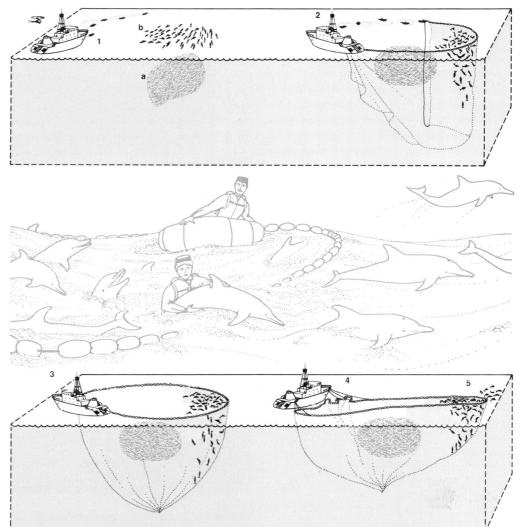

from the fishing vessels where the fleeing dolphins used to get entangled in the large mesh and drown as the net was tightened (pursed). The dolphins can thus escape over the net rim, while the tuna usually dive and are retained in the net. All US tuna fishing boats also have divers stationed in the net to monitor the movement of dolphins and to advise the boat crew when to purse and when to back down.

One further aspect of dolphin behavior has already been recognized, to the benefit of the dolphins' survival. Dolphins caught in tuna nets often lie placidly, as if feigning death (although their rigid state may in fact be due to extreme shock). Such dolphins were previously thought to be drowned and were hauled up onto the deck of the processing vessel, where they did indeed die. Now, the divers who monitor the nets manually help such unmoving animals over the net rim, and make certain that pursing does not proceed until all have been released. The divers may also release any dolphins which do still get entangled in the mesh.

▲ **Saving the Spinners**. To avoid the accidental loss of Spinner dolphins caught in tuna nets, special techniques have been developed. (1) A shoal of tuna (**a**) accompanied by dolphins (**b**), is located by helicopter; the fishing boat approaches and launches inflatables to head off and contain the fish. (2) A purse seine net is pulled around the fish, while the inflatables create disturbances to stop the tuna escaping. (3) The bottom of the net is pulled in beneath the fish. (4) The net is pulled in towards the ship with the fine-mesh Medina panel furthest away from it. Some dolphins may be able to escape over the floats unaided, but they are sometimes assisted by hand from the inflatables or by divers (5).

BW/RSW

# A Dolphin's Day

## Moods of the Dusky dolphin

The sleek, streamlined dolphins were leaping around the Zodiak rubber inflatable at Golfo San José, off the coast of southern Argentina. When the divers entered the cool water, a group of 15 dolphins cavorted under and above them, again and again approaching the humans to within an arm's length, and showing no fear of these strangers to their world.

These were Dusky dolphins, whose playful behavior indicated that they had recently been feeding and socializing, for Dusky dolphins have different "moods," and will not interact with humans when they are hungry or tired.

The behavior of Dusky dolphins varies according to both season and time of day. Off South America, Dusky dolphins feed on Southern anchovy during summer afternoons. Night-time is spent in small schools of 6–15 animals not more than about 0.6mi (1km) off shore. They move slowly, apparently at rest. When danger approaches, in the form of large sharks or Killer whales (see pp38–39), they retreat close inshore, seeking to evade their enemies by hiding in the tubulence of the surf-line.

In the morning, the dolphins begin to move into deeper water 1–6mi (2–10km) from shore, line abreast, each animal 33ft (10m) or more from the next, so that 15 dolphins may cover a swath of sea 500ft (150m) or more wide. They use echolocation to find food, and because they are spread out, they can sweep a large area of sea. When a group locates a school of anchovy, individuals dive down to the school and physically herd it to the surface by swimming around and under the fish in an ever-tightening formation.

The marine birds that gather above the anchovy to feed, and the leaping of the dolphins around the periphery of the fish school, indicate what is going on to human observers as far away as 6mi (10km). Other small groups of dolphins, equally distant, will also see such feeding, and move rapidly toward it.

The newly arrived dolphin groups are immediately incorporated into the activity, and the more dolphins present, the more efficiently they are able to corral and herd prey to the surface. Thus, a group of 5–10 dolphins cannot effectively herd prey, and most such feeding activities die out after an average of five minutes. These small groups will seek to feed further. When dolphin groups aggregate, feeding lasts longer. A group of 50 dolphins has been observed to feed on average for 27 minutes, and 300 dolphins (the total in an area of about 500

◄ **A working leap.** A Dusky dolphin leaping around the edge of a shoal of anchovy. The noise the dolphin makes as it re-enters the water may help to keep the fish contained and the leaps may alert other dolphins to the presence of food. Dolphin sounds travel only about 0.6–1.9mi (1–3km) underwater and while leaping they can spot the tell-tale signs of food, especially circling birds, over considerable distances.

▲ **A playful leap.** After feeding, Dusky dolphins leap acrobatically with spins and somersaults. Such "play" may have a social function.

◄ **The feeding trap.** A dolphin herding anchovy, and using the water's surface as a "wall"—the anchovy thus have one less direction of escape than they would have in deeper water. The dolphins also project loud sounds at the fish, which may cause them to bunch even more tightly and to become disorientated.

sq mi) feed for 2–3 hours. By mid-afternoon, the 300 dolphins which were earlier scattered in 20 to 30 small groups may be feeding in one area. There is much social interaction in such a large group, and considerable sexual activity, particularly toward the end of feeding, with members of both the same and other subgroups.

By this time, the dolphins have rested at night and early morning, have fed—they have taken care of two important biological functions, and can now interact socially and "play." This is perhaps the most important time for these highly social animals. In order for dolphins to function effectively while avoiding predators, hunting for food, and cooperatively herding prey, they must know each other well and must communicate efficiently at all times. Socializing helps to bring this about. Toward the end of feeding, they swim together in small, ever-changing subgroups, with individuals touching or caressing each other with their flippers, swimming belly to belly, and poking their noses at each others sides or bellies. At this time, the dolphins will readily approach a boat, ride on its bow wave if it is moving, and swim with divers in the water.

In the evening, the large school splits into many small groups once again, and the animals settle down near shore to rest, the "mood" changing abruptly to quiescence

once again. Although there is some interchange of individuals between small groups from day to day, many of the same dolphins travel together on subsequent days. Some Dusky dolphins have been observed to stay together for at least two years.

On some days, Dusky dolphins will not find schools of anchovy. They remain in their small foraging parties all day and will not socialize much or associate with boats or divers. Although Dusky dolphins often appear to be carefree and happy in nature, this is probably an impression based on their behavior after successful hunting. Like all wild animals, they have to work for a living, and when food is scarce they are more interested in locating prey than in "play."

In winter, anchovy are not present, so Dusky dolphins feed in small groups mainly at night on squid and bottom-dwelling fish. Such prey does not occur in large shoals, so the feeding dolphins do not form large groups. They rest during the day, and stay quite close to shore at all times, thus avoiding the threat from deepwater sharks. There is little of the "play" or sexual activity of the summer months. Thus, their entire repertoire of group movement patterns and "moods," on both a daily and a seasonal basis, appears governed by food availability, and by the ever-present threat of possible predation.                                    BW

# PORPOISES

**Family: Phocoenidae**
Six species in 3 genera.
Distribution: N temperate zone; W Indo-Pacific; temperate and subantarctic waters of S America; Auckland Islands.

Size: head-to-tail length from 48–59in (120–150cm) in the Gulf of California porpoise to 68–89in (170–225cm) in Dall's porpoise; weight from 66–121lb (30–55kg) in the Gulf of California porpoise to 275–353lb (135–160kg) in Dall's porpoise.

▲ ▼ **Elusive porpoises.** ABOVE Dall's porpoise, seen here apparently plowing a furrow in the sea, is one of the least shy of the porpoises. BELOW Porpoises are retiring at sea but frequently strand, like this Harbor porpoise in Northumberland, England.

HARBOR porpoises often provide people on the coasts of northern Europe and North America with their first sight of live cetaceans—usually a glimpse of small, elusive, rolling dark objects some hundreds of feet from a ferry or a vantage point on shore. Sometimes Harbor porpoises will pass close to a small fishing dinghy, giving a few characteristic snorting "blows" before disappearing. They are also one of the commonest species to strand, which they usually do singly on the sloping shelves of sandy beaches or on mudflats. Yet less is known about these coastal animals than many other cetaceans—a matter of concern especially as numbers of the "Common" porpoise may be declining rapidly, for example off Holland and Denmark, and in Puget Sound on the west coast of North America.

The only species that is readily attracted to moving vessels is Dall's porpoise. They are fast and boisterous swimmers, generating fans of spray visible for hundreds of feet. The Harbor and Finless porpoises are less obtrusive, although the former may make horizontal leaps partly clear of the surface when chasing prey.

In anatomy, true porpoises are a rather uniform group. They lack the "beak" characteristic of most of the dolphins, and all six species are pigmented with various combinations of black, gray or white. They are small, rarely exceeding 6.2ft (190cm) in length at maturity and, with the exception of the Finless porpoise, have small, low triangular fins. The teeth, 60 to 120 in number, are typically laterally compressed and flattened into a spade shape at the tip, in contrast to the pointed teeth of dolphins. The Finless porpoise is the only porpoise to have a bulging "melon" rather like that of the Pilot whale; although lacking the fin, it has a series of small tubercles (found on the leading edge of the fin in other species) along the dorsal ridge. Dall's porpoise is the largest species; as well as having the most striking color patterns it has a prominent dorsal "keel" on the tail stock, and the tip of the lower jaw protrudes slightly beyond that of the upper jaw. The premaxillary bones of porpoise skulls have rather prominent "bosses" just in front of the blowholes, and 3–7 neck vertebrae are fused in adults. In contrast to the 60–70 vertebrae in the other two genera, 95–100 are present in *Phocoenoides*.

Some striking adaptations occur in this family, and some peculiar distributions as well. On the basis of skull characters, limited fusion of neck vertebrae, and general morphology, the Gulf and Burmeister porpoises appear to be the most "typical," even though the rather flattened head and fin spines of the latter are unique. In the Harbor porpoise 6 of the 7 neck vertebrae are fused, and the Spectacled porpoise has somewhat sleeker proportions than the other *Phocoena* species. But despite these and other anatomical modifications both probably derive from a basic *sinus-spinipinnis* stock.

The Finless porpoise appears to be closely related to the *Phocoena* species. Except for the lack of a dorsal fin and the squat foreshortened head with relatively large cranial capacity, *Neophocoena* is a typical member of the family in basic anatomical respects. The differences seem to be adaptations to its turbid river and estuarine habitat where it probably "grubs" for its food on the bottom. It has been suggested that Dall's porpoise should be accorded separate family status. However, the skull and teeth of *Phocoenoides* are those of a porpoise and all the differences appear to be adaptations. The large number of relatively small vertebrae, which probably improves the flexion of the vertical swimming stroke, the complete fusion of all 7 neck vertebrae, the sharply tapered head, and perhaps the tail-stock keel, all appear to be adaptations that contribute to the species' swimming ability. These features have parallels among the deep-sea dolphins. The increased number of ribs, the proportionately large muscle mass and the large thoracic cavity are probably adaptations that enhance the diving capabilities of this oceanic species which, alone among porpoises, exploits prey at some depth (over 330ft/100m).

The porpoises probably emerged as a distinct group in the middle of the Miocene

most tropical Asian coasts and estuaries. *Phocoena*, in the east, first colonized coastal shelves of the Neotropical region, then with further isolation differentiated into parallel Northern Hemisphere (Harbor porpoise) and Southern Hemisphere (Spectacled porpoise) forms. *Phocoenoides* colonized temperate waters of the North Pacific and exploited the food resources along open-ocean current boundaries.

The fossil record more or less supports this picture: porpoise-like fossils have been found in Miocene strata of southern California, but in Europe and the Southern Hemisphere phocoenid fossils occur only in the Pliocene (7–2 million years ago). The isolation of the Black Sea and Sea of Azov population of *P. p. relicta* probably results from warming of the Mediterranean following penetration from the Atlantic through the Mediterranean when the latter was cooler than it is today.

Porpoises feed on relatively small schools of mobile prey items 4–12in (10–30cm) in length. When prey density is low they forage far apart, but they can gather rapidly when large concentrations of prey are located.

Acoustic emissions have been studied extensively only in the Harbor porpoise, although all porpoises probably have a wide repertoire of sounds. Relatively low frequency "click-series" may be used to scan the immediate general environment, high frequencies to echolocate specific objects, including mobile prey. There is little doubt that much hunting is also by sight, and passive listening for fish noise. Fish and squid are swallowed whole or bitten into pieces (not chewed) if large and digested in 3–6 hours.

▲ **Porpoise rescue.** A Harbor porpoise trapped in a herring weir at New Brunswick, Canada, being retrieved by means of a small seine net and manual capture. Once restrained, the animals are usually quite docile if handled slowly, gently and firmly.

period (about 15 million years ago) in the northern part of the Pacific Basin. There is some evidence that shallow water habitats there were more extensive than today. Subsequent changes in that region appear to have isolated three main lines represented by the existing genera. *Neophocoena*, in the west, gradually extended its range along

---

Abbreviations: HTL = head-to-tail length. Wt = weight.
 V Vulnerable.

### Harbor porpoise
*Phocoena phocoena*
Harbor or Common porpoise.

Coastal waters of temperate N Pacific and N Atlantic, Bering Sea, Baltic Sea; Black Sea and Sea of Azov (*P. p. relicta*). HTL 59–75in; wt 119–143lb. Skin: dark gray, paler gray patch on flanks, white beneath. Gray line from flipper to jaw angle. Dorsal fin low, with concave trailing edge. Gestation: 11 months. Longevity: 12–13 years.

### Gulf of California porpoise V
*Phocoena sinus*
Gulf of California porpoise, *cochito* ("little pig").

Gulf of California. HTL 47–59in; wt 66–120lb. Skin: darker than Harbor porpoise, otherwise similar. Dorsal fin with concave trailing edge, but higher than in Harbour porpoise.

### Burmeister's porpoise V
*Phocoena spinipinnis*
Coastal waters of America from Peru to Uruguay; possibly also Falkland Is. HTL about 55–70in; wt 88–154lb. Skin: blackish gray above and on flanks, lighter patches below. Fin low with convex trailing edge, tubercle at base of front of fin characteristically spinose. Gestation and longevity unknown.

### Spectacled porpoise
*Phocoena dioptrica*

Coastal waters of southeastern America, Falkland Is, S Georgia, Auckland Is. HTL 61–80in; wt 132–185lb. Skin: black above, white below, with eyes and lips rimmed with black; gray stripe from jaw angle to flippers, which are often white. Low, straight-edged dorsal fin. Gestation and longevity not known.

### Dall's porpoise
*Phocoenoides dalli*
Dall's or True's porpoise.

Coastal and deep waters of boreal North Pacific and Bering Sea; S Japan to S California. Length 67–88in; wt 298–352lb. Skin: black with variable white patch on belly and flank, and further white areas on fin and flukes. Dorsal fin often largely white, with hooked tip, characteristically higher than in *Phocoena*. Gestation 11.4 months. Longevity: 16–17+ years.

### Finless porpoise
*Neophocoena phocoenoides*
Finless or Black or Black finless porpoise.

Indo-Pacific from Iran to New Guinea and Japan, usually along coasts and in estuaries. HTL 55–65in; wt 66–99lb. Skin: gray, with lips and chin lighter except for dark "chinstrap." No dorsal fin, but dorsal ridge of back bears row of short spinose tubercles. Gestation: 11 months. Longevity: about 23 years.

## Incidental Catches of Porpoises

Because most porpoises prefer to prey on open-sea fish, they are vulnerable to "incidental" capture by certain types of fishing gear set for those fish. In addition to the thousands of porpoises hunted down by gun or harpoon, several thousand Dall's porpoises drown each year after becoming entangled in Japanese gill nets (usually caught by their pectoral flippers). Harbor porpoises are caught in salmon gill nets from New England to Greenland, and in herring weirs in the Maritime Provinces of Canada; Burmeister's porpoises are taken in nets off southern Chile and elsewhere, while the population of the Gulf of California porpoise appears to have been seriously reduced since the late 1940s by gill net fisheries for the commercially important "totoava" and other fish. Some Finless porpoises are trapped in all the areas they frequent off Japan and China.

The porpoises appear to be trapped or entangled while they are pursuing fish—they are simply too intent on their prey to appreciate the danger. They are also caught, especially at night, where they do not anticipate obstruction. Modern synthetic monofilament netting does not reflect porpoises echolocating clicks; there is in any case no reason to assume that porpoise echolocate continuously. Gill net captures are almost invariably fatal, but porpoises caught in Canadian herring weirs or Danish pound nets can be seined out and released alive if the fishermen are so inclined.

At present we do not know if Dall's, Harbor, Burmeister's, and Finless porpoise populations are being reduced by these catches. The herring weir captures in New Brunswick and Nova Scotia do not seem to be serious, but the Gulf of California porpoise may have been reduced to near extinction during the 1970s. Despite current research into the problems of gill net entanglements, no convincing solution is in sight. Acoustic warning devices, which emit continuous pinging sounds, may help, but may not be effective when porpoises are in hot pursuit of prey near the nets, or when they have become habituated to the noise. Considering the number of nets involved, they are also likely to be prohibitively expensive to use, unless the fishermen receive government subsidies.

▲ **The six species of porpoises.** (1) Gulf of California porpoise (*Phocoena sinus*). (2) Burmeister's porpoise (*Phocoena spinipinnis*). (3) Finless porpoise (*Neophocoena phocoenoides*). (4) Dall's porpoise (*Phocoenoides dalli*). (5) Spectacled porpoise (*Phocoena dioptrica*). (6) Harbor porpoise (*Phocoena phocoena*).

All species have a varied diet. Finless porpoises take crustaceans such as prawns as the main prey; Dall's porpoises take oceanic fish such as hake and several species of squid; Harbor porpoises eat mostly clupeid fish (eg herring and sardines), scombroids (eg mackerel) and small gadoids (eg cod and whiting). Gulf of California porpoises eat croakers and grunts, and the diet of the two South American species is not known, but probably comprises pelagic fish such as mullet or anchovies, and squid. An adult Harbor porpoise requires 6.6–11lb (3–5kg) of food per day, Dall's porpoise perhaps 22–26lb (10–12kg). When foraging (often above underwater scarps and mounts, or along boundaries between currents) porpoises execute series of short breathing rolls, separated by dives of 1–4 minutes, in contrast to their traveling behavior, when dives last only 15–30 seconds, between rather regularly spaced surfacings.

North Sea and western North Atlantic Harbor porpoises are sexually mature at 5–6 years and 4–5 years respectively, Dall's porpoises at about 7 years. Little is known about the sex life of porpoises, but Harbor porpoises at least seem not to form lasting pairs. There is evidence for a male sexual cycle in some species, based on seasonal changes in testis size and activity. However, since the pairing season is relatively short (1–2 months), and the animals are relatively small, these changes may be a function of energy conservation. For females, the interval between births is about 2 years in Finless, 3 years in Dall's, and 1–3 years in Harbor porpoises. Lactation probably continues for 6–8 months in Harbor and Finless porpoises but may be as long as two years in the larger, pelagic Dall's porpoise. Mothers with calves are usually segregated from other animals, or form schools of two or more mother-calf pairs. The largest such school seen by the author contained six pairs. The presence of a young animal with a mother-calf combination early in the summer is quite common and may indicate that the weaned calf stays with the mother for some months after it has begun to feed independently; fish remains have been found in the stomachs of Harbor porpoises of 3–4ft (104–111cm) in length, apparently less than one year old. Young Finless porpoises may "ride" their mothers' backs attaching themselves to the ridge of tubercles which are peculiar to adults of this species.

The life spans of porpoises are a matter of some controversy. At least 16–17 years for Dall's porpoise and 23 years for Finless porpoises have been suggested, but most direct estimates for Harbor porpoises indicate an upper limit of 12–13 years.

In contrast to deep-sea dolphins, porpoises are not particularly gregarious. The basic social unit consists of only 2–4 animals in Harbor and Dall's porpoises, and observation suggests that the composition of most groups (with the exception of mother-calf pairs) is rather fluid. One school of Harbor porpoises caught in a herring weir in New Brunswick in late August 1982 consisted of a mother and calf and two immature males. Over 50 percent of Finless porpoises recently observed off Japan were solitary. The small size of the average porpoise school is probably geared to the quantity of prey likely to be encountered while foraging. Larger schools in all three of the most-studied species seem to result from chance meetings or temporary feeding aggregations. During feeding, the small basic groups may split up and individuals dive hundreds of feet apart, but later come together again prior to moving off to a new area. Some sexual segregation occurs: all-male schools of immature Harbor porpoise have been encountered off western Nova Scotia, but since whole schools are trapped only on rare occasions, little is known about sex ratios in small schools.                DEG

# WHITE WHALES

**Family: Monodontidae**
Two species in 2 genera.*
Distribution: North temperate and circumpolar.

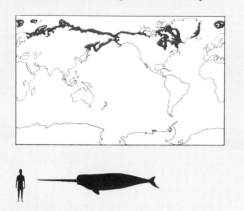

## Beluga
*Delphinapterus leucas*
Beluga, belukha or White whale.
Distribution: N USSR, N America, Greenland.
Habitat: mainly coastal; estuaries and pack ice.
Size: head-to-tail length 10–16ft (300–500cm),
weight 1,100–3,300lb (500–1,500kg).
Skin: adults white; young slate-gray to reddish-brown, changing to medium gray at two years
and white on maturity.
Diet: schooling fish, crustacea, worms,
mollusks.
Gestation: 14–15 months. Longevity: 30–40
years.

## Narwhal
*Monodon monoceros*
Distribution: N USSR, N America, Greenland.
Habitat: coastal and pack ice.
Size: head-to-tail length 13–16.5ft
(400–500cm); male tusk length 5–10ft
(150–300cm); weight 1,760–3,520lb
(800–1,600kg).
Coat: mottled gray-green, cream and black,
whitening with age, beginning with the belly;
young dark gray.
Diet: shrimps, arctic cod, flounder,
cephalopods.
Gestation: 14–15 months.
Longevity: 30–40 years.

*A third species, the Irrawaddy dolphin (*Orcaella
brevirostris*), is considered by some authorities to belong to
the Monodontidae, but is here considered as a member of
the Delphinidae, see p37.

THE white whales—the beluga and the narwhal—are the nonconformists among toothed whales. A large herd of brilliant white beluga makes an impressive enough sight, but a "procession" of narwhal moving along the coast is truly awesome. The body coloration alone is highly unusual: small patches of gray-green, cream and black pigmentation painted on, as it were, by short strokes of a stiff brush. What is more astonishing however is to see the legendary unicorn tusks thrust above the water as the male breaks the surface. Not only does his large spiral tusk—up to 10ft (3m) long and three-fifths of body length—seem out of place on such a relatively small whale but it is oddly offcenter: protruding from the left upper lip and at an awkward angle to the left and pointing downwards. To crown these oddities, the tails of older males appear to be put on backwards! Such is the narwhal, *Monodon monoceros* (one tooth, one horn).

Despite their superficial dissimilarity, the body forms of the beluga and narwhal are similar, although the narwhal is slightly larger. The beluga is notable for its well-defined neck: unusually for whales, it can turn its head sideways to a near right-angle. The beluga has no true back fin, hence its scientific name, *Delphinapterus* = "dolphin-without-a-wing," but there is a ridge along the back, from mid-body to the tail, more darkly pigmented than the body and generally scarred from encounters with ice. In both species, males are about 20in (50cm) longer than females and their flippers increasingly turn upwards at the tips with age. The flippers of beluga are capable of a wide range of movements, and appear to serve an important function in close-quarters maneuvering, including very slow,

reverse swimming. In ageing male narwhals, the shape of the tail changes to one in which the tips migrate forwards, giving a concave leading edge, when viewed from above or below.

The narwhal has only two teeth, and both are non-functional. In the female these are about 8in (20cm) long; in the male, the left tooth continues to grow to form the tusk. About 1–3 percent of males produce twin tusks and a similar proportion of females

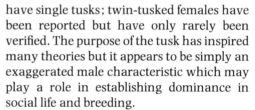

have single tusks; twin-tusked females have been reported but have only rarely been verified. The purpose of the tusk has inspired many theories but it appears to be simply an exaggerated male characteristic which may play a role in establishing dominance in social life and breeding.

Beluga are capable of a wide range of bodily and facial expressions, including an impressive mouth gape displaying 32–40 peg-like teeth which abut one another. There is considerable wear of the surfaces, sometimes to the extent that they appear to be ineffective for grasping prey. This and the fact that they do not fully emerge until well into the second or third year suggest that feeding may not be their prime function: they may serve an equal or greater role in visual threat displays and jawclap noise-making.

▲ **Beluga and calf.** Suckling may last up to two years, during which time the mother and calf are almost inseparable. Newborn beluga are brown and the skin lightens through gray, as in this one-year-old, to white.

▼ **The narwhal,** with its remarkable tusk resulting from spiral growth of the left tooth. The spiral runs counter-clockwise and in old animals the whole tusk may spiral.

The beluga is a highly vocal animal, some of the sounds being easily heard in the air. The sound-spectrum ranges from moos, chirps, whistles and clangs, while the underwater din from a herd is reminiscent of a barnyard and long ago earned them the name "sea canary." In addition to its vocal and echolocation skills the beluga obviously also uses vision for both communication and predation. The versatility of its expressions suggests the likelihood of subtle social communication.

Both beluga and narwhal are diverse feeders: the beluga on a variety of schooling fish, crustacea, worms and sometimes mollusks, and the narwhal on shrimps, Arctic cod, flounder and cephalopods. Beluga are capable of herding schools of fish by working closely together as a group of five or more, forcing the exhausted fish into shallow water or towards a sloping beach. They are equally adept at pursuing single prey on the bottom. The highly flexible neck permits a wide sweep of the bottom and they can produce both suction and a jet of water to dislodge prey. Small stones, bits of seaweed and mud from the stomachs of calves attest to the skills that must be learned by the young. Much of the food gathered during the feeding season is stored as fat or blubber 4–8in (10–20cm) thick, providing insulation as well as an off-season energy supply. The narwhal, with no functional teeth at all, also seems to have a capacity for suction. The tusks appear to play no part in feeding, because the male and the tuskless female have similar diets.

The beluga and the narwhal are similar in their growth and reproduction, although more is known about the beluga. Females become sexually mature after five years, males after eight years. In both sexes the age

of sexual maturity may depend to some degree on the population density. Dominant males appear to mate with many females. Soon after mating, the beluga migrate through the pack ice, often for 185mi (300km) or more to shallow, invariably warmer, often muddy estuaries, arriving in June or July and staying till August or September. Here the young from the previous year's mating are born. Single calves are the norm, with twinning an extremely rare event. Those that are about to calve within the estuary tend to move away from the main herd but may be accompanied by a non-pregnant or immature female. Whether this companion attends to assist the mother or is simply curious, is open to question. It is possible that it may simply be an older calf attempting to maintain maternal ties.

Births have been observed to take place in isolated bays or near shore. Initially, mother and newborn remain separate from the nearby herd and may join up with several other mother–calf pairs. There is a strong bond established and physical contact is maintained even while swimming— swimming so close together that the calf functions almost as an appendage to the mother's side or back. Nursing is accomplished underwater, beginning several hours after birth and at hourly intervals thereafter. Lactation may last two years, at which time the mother is again in early pregnancy. The complete reproductive cycle of gestation and lactation takes three years.

Narwhal move from the offshore pack ice into fjords during mid-summer but, unlike the beluga, do not consistently frequent shallow estuaries during the calving period.

Beluga appear to remain in herds for their entire life, the degree of dispersion depend-

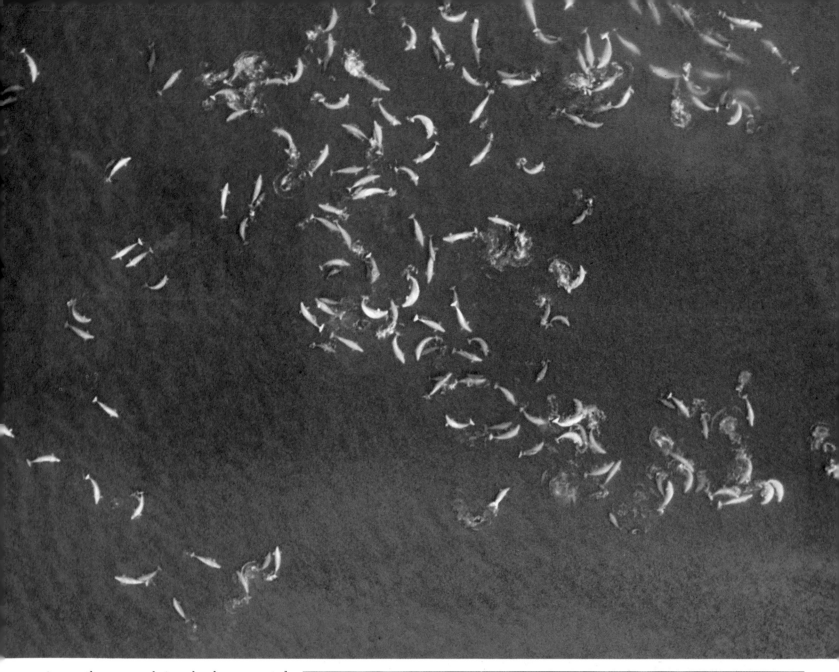

ing on the season: being closely aggregated on the breeding ground or spread out over a larger feeding area. Within the herd there is obvious segregation by age and sex. Groups or pods of adult males can be seen as well as nursery groups of mothers with newborn and older calves. Whether the groups of adult males represent the dominant, breeding animals or are nonbreeders excluded by some dominant bull within the herd has yet to be determined.

Present-day herd sizes may range from hundreds to several thousand, but these numbers may be not so much an indication of the carrying capacity of that region as of the historic and present-day exploitation pressure. While various summering populations may share a common wintering or feeding ground further offshore and away from solid ice, they appear to return to their site of origin for calving. Thus there is no apparent exchange between populations.

Although not as readily observed as beluga, the narwhal herd composition is similar: groups of females with calves;

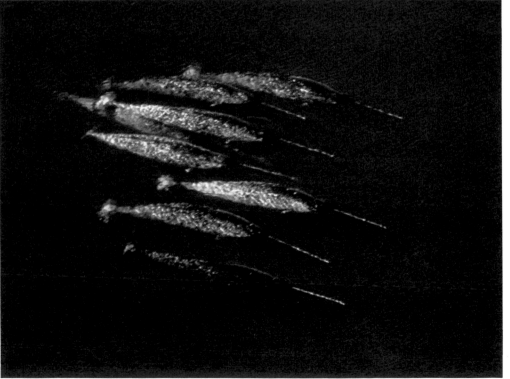

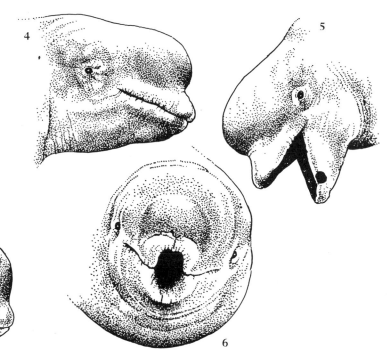

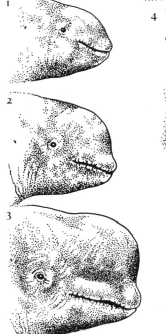

▲ **Smiling beluga**—development of facial features and expressions. Adult beluga have a very pronounced forehead melon, but this is shown to develop: in newborn beluga (1) it is almost absent; in yearlings (2) the melon is quite large but the beak undeveloped; maturity (3) is reached at 5–8 years. The beluga's mouth and neck are highly flexible, and they communicate with each other a great deal by sound and facial expression. In repose (4) the beluga seems to our eyes to be smiling. Beluga are versatile feeders and the pursed mouth (6) is believed to be used in bottom feeding. Besides clicks and bell-like tone, beluga produce loud reports by clapping their jaws together (5).

▶ **Seemingly carved from chalk,** a beluga breaches to breathe, revealing its open blowhole.

◀ **Beluga swarm.** TOP From June to September beluga congregate in hundreds and thousands in traditional estuaries such as the Mackenzie Delta on the Beaufort Sea, Nelson and Churchill rivers in Hudson Bay, and Clearwater Fjord on the coast of Baffin Island, where they give birth.

◀ **Iridescent narwhal** make a dramatic sight, swimming in a dark blue sea between two ice floes.

groups of large males of similar body size, color and tusk length roaming through the herd. Narwhal tend to be more widely dispersed in the fjords, unlike the beluga's tight aggregation in smaller estuaries. Narwhal are not as vocal as beluga, which may, in part, be compensated or displaced by the added feature of tusk display. While the beluga often bite the flukes and flippers of others in rather mild social combat, narwhals perform a "joust" with their tusks and, based upon the body scars observed, some injuries are inflicted. It is not unusual to find both narwhal and beluga in the same fjord and, while they may often be in close proximity, they do not appear to conflict.

The predictable migratory behavior of beluga, dictated by the strict seasonality of higher latitudes and their gregarious nature while summering in estuaries, has made this species particularly vulnerable to exploitation. In the 18th and 19th centuries American and European whalers would force mass strandings of hundreds of beluga in order to "top up" their cargo of whale oil rendered from their primary quarry, the

Bowhead. Aboriginal peoples, being superb animal behaviorists and hunters, were technically capable of taking a large toll of the stocks during the calving season and, no doubt, there were instances of their harvests exceeding immediate needs. By the early 20th century, some stocks, having experienced excessive commercial whaling, continued to be exploited by native hunters both for domestic consumption of oil, meat and edible skin and also for trade in hides and oil.

While some populations have been greatly reduced as a result of past hunting practices they are being monitored by fisheries management scientists, and native hunters are being encouraged to become involved in the process. The beluga's affinity for shallow, coastal areas poses other modern-day problems: those of habitat alteration through the construction of hydroelectric dams and offshore petroleum exploration and extraction via pipelines. It is possible that, as with many wild stocks, beluga will adjust to increased marine activity associated with shipping and petroleum-related activities, provided there is little harassment. In the case of hydroelectric development, there could be significant alteration of habitat either through regulated river flow and/or water temperature.

With the exception of a few complaints of beluga consuming salmon migrating up rivers, their presence has no adverse impact on man and in fact their nearshore migrations make whale watching the basis of small tourist industries in a few areas.

The narwhal's tendency to avoid estuaries and to overwinter further offshore than the beluga reduces several potential threats from industrial development. Environmental studies coincident with the increased pace of mining and petroleum exploration in the Arctic have resulted in a clearer picture of narwhal distribution and population size. While they were originally thought to number some 12,000, the present estimate ranges from 25,000–30,000. The narwhal is not an endangered species but, as in all wild stocks, hunting pressure is not evenly distributed. If there is little exchange with larger populations, isolated populations will be slow to rebuild. This, however, may be more critical with the multi-stock beluga than with the narwhal. The narwhal's tusk is highly valued by collectors and museums, which provides an added incentive for native hunters. Catches are monitored and quotas are imposed, incorporating estimates for those which sink and are lost when killed.    PB

# SPERM WHALES

**Family: Physeteridae**
Three species in 2 genera.
Distribution: worldwide in temperate waters to
latitudes of about 40°; bull Sperm whales to
polar regions.

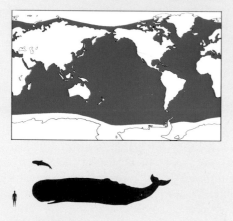

### Sperm whale
*Physeter macrocephalus*
Sperm whale, cachalot, Spermacet whale.
Size: head-to-tail length up to 68ft (20.7m); in
recent years 60ft (18.5m); males considerably
larger than females, up to 39ft (12m); weight:
males 45–70 tons; females 15–20 tons.

Skin: dark gray with white marks and circular
scars (from Giant Squid) especially on head.

Gestation: 14–15 months, possibly 16 in some
areas.

Longevity: up to 70 years.

### Pygmy sperm whale
*Kogia breviceps*
Pygmy, Short-headed, Small or Lesser sperm whale, Lesser
cachalot.
Distribution: populations may be
discontinuous. Size: head-to-tail length up to
11ft (3.4m); weight: about 1,100lb (500kg).

Skin: dark gray, shading to gray-white on
underside; lighter "bracket" marks on side of
head.

Gestation: about 9, possibly 11 months.

Longevity: may be 17 or more years.

### Dwarf sperm whale
*Kogia simus*
Dwarf or Owen's pygmy sperm whale, Rat porpoise.
Size; head-to-tail length up to 9ft (2.7m);
weight: about 770lb (350kg).

Skin: dark gray, shading to gray-white on
underside.

Gestation: probably as *K. breviceps*.

Longevity: unknown.

CELEBRATED as the great white whale
Moby Dick in Herman Melville's novel
of that name, the Sperm whale is the largest
of the toothed whales. At sea it is unmis-
takable for its spout, which issues at a 45°
angle from the tip of a great, blunt head.
When it sounds, lifting its great tail flukes
clear of the water, the Sperm whale may
dive deeper than any other cetacean.

Today a few white Sperm whales exist,
but the giant bulls once reported by whalers
are no longer found. The head occupies
about one-third of the body length in the
Sperm whale. In the smaller species the head
is large but more conical and much shorter
in relation to the whole. The wax organ in
the uppper part of the head probably functions as both an acoustic lens for focusing
sound by refraction through the near-
concentric layers of the wax—used in
echolocation (sonar)—and as a regulator of
buoyancy in deep diving (see boxed feature).

Only in the Sperm whale is the blowhole
placed at the tip of the head but in all species
it is displaced to the lefthand side, and the
nasal bones are markedly asymmetrical.
The lower jaw is small in relation to the
upper jaw, which in the fully grown Sperm
whale can project about 5ft (1.5m) beyond
it. The whales are born without teeth and
teeth often erupt only at sexual maturity
and even then may only appear in the lower
jaw and in the male. In the Sperm whale
there are usually 20–25 similar teeth on
each side of the lower jaw, although not
necessarily paired. In males these teeth may
grow up to 10in (25cm) in length, although
6in (15cm) is a more usual size: both
number and size of teeth are less in females.
In the upper jaw, up to 10, frequently highly
curved teeth up to 4in (10cm) long may
erupt on each side. In the two *Kogia* species
also, the teeth in the upper jaw, if they are
present, do not usually erupt. The number
per side in the lower jaw may be 16 in the
Dwarf and 11 in the Pygmy sperm whale.

In all sperm whales the body is compact
and robust. The flippers are paddle-shaped,
and the body tapers abruptly at the tail
stock. The brain of the Sperm whale is
almost spherical and may be between 25
and 43lb (5.5–9.5kg) in weight, irrespective
of body size or sex. Like some other (mostly
baleen) whales, occasionally a Sperm whale
is found to have vestigial hindlimbs attached
to small pelvic bones. Fossil records indicate
that the family became distinct from other
toothed whales at a relatively early date, in
the Miocene (26 to 7 million years ago), the
genus *Kogia* becoming recognizable at a
later date, in the Pliocene (7 to 2 million

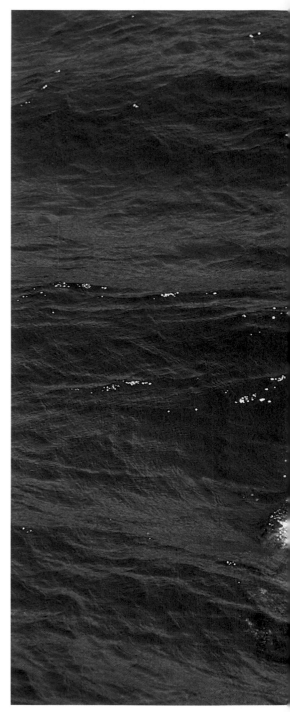

years ago).

Blubber and muscle each form about 33
percent of body weight in the Sperm whale,
and about 22 and 33 percent respectively in
the Pygmy sperm whale. Compared with the
size of the animal, the eye of the Sperm
whale is smaller than in other whales, and it
is not typically mammalian, the anterior
chamber of the eye being almost non-
existent, reduced to a narrow slit between
the pupil and the cornea. The eyeball is fixed
in its socket and as it cannot swivel there is a
"blind" area both forward and aft.

Sperm whales have "taste" receptors
(chemoreceptors) in the mouth which can

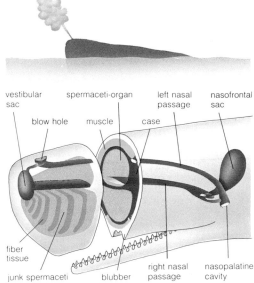

vestibular sac    spermaceti-organ    left nasal passage    nasofrontal sac

blow hole    muscle    case

fiber tissue

junk spermaceti    blubber    right nasal passage    nasopalatine cavity

▲ **The corrugated skin** of a Sperm whale calf catches the sun's glint as it breaks the surface. These corrugations give mature whales a shriveled appearance, but in this calf the effect is curiously slug-like. The lop-sided blowhole is clearly visible on the left.

▶ **Head of the Sperm whale.** TOP The unique oblique blow, to the left of the animal's direction and at a forward angle of 45°. BELOW A cross section shows the huge volume of spermaceti wax which the whale can cool or warm to alter its buoyancy by the passage of water through the nasal passages.

probably detect minute changes in the salinity and chemical components of the water.

Sperm whales show an interesting differential distribution: females and juveniles are usually restricted to equatorial and subtropical waters while males range from the Equator to polar regions. It is possible that the males' use of more distant food resources thus relieves pressure on the food resources of the females and young, who need female protection and have insufficient blubber to meet the polar waters.

There are probably at least two stocks (east and west) of Sperm whale in the North Pacific and possibly a third in western

coastal areas. The wide range of the North Atlantic stock was demonstrated when a hand-harpooned individual broke loose and escaped off the Azores in August 1980, and was caught again off Iceland a year later, a distance of 1,600mi (2,560km). Another individual marked off Nova Scotia in 1966 was captured seven years later off Spain. In the Southern Hemisphere there may be 7–9 different stocks. It is thought that Northern and Southern Hemisphere stocks do not mingle, even though there may be some movements across the Equator. There may be some migration towards higher latitudes in the summer months; regular seasonal migration by males to the polar waters is less certain.

Pygmy and Dwarf sperm whales are generally restricted to warmer latitudes. They strand fairly frequently off the USA, South Africa, Australia, New Zealand, India and Japan. The Pygmy sperm whale appears to prefer more oceanic waters, whilst the Dwarf sperm whale inhabits waters of the continental shelf. Little is known of migratory habits, and even this appears contradictory for different areas. Off Japan there is a seasonal occurrence, whereas off South Africa animals have been observed all year round.

Sperm whales almost certainly use echolocation (sonar) to find their prey as they dive into total darkness to at least 3,950ft (1,200m) for up to an hour (see boxed feature). Indeed, totally blind Sperm whales have been captured in perfect health and with food in their stomach. Sperm whales are often found along current lines and in areas of oceanic upwelling, where prey are usually abundant. Squid form about 80 percent of the Sperm whale diet,

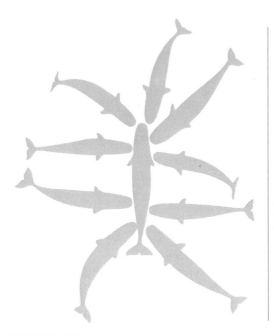

▶ **The three species of sperm whales.** (**1**) The Sperm whale (*Physeter macrocephalus*) diving for squid, which it sometimes catches at extraordinary depths. (**2**) The Pygmy sperm whale (*Kogia breviceps*). (**3**) The Dwarf sperm whale (*Kogia simus*).

◀ **The marguerite formation** in which members of a pod will encircle an injured Sperm whale while it remains alive. Such supportive behavior used to be disastrous for the whales, allowing them to be picked off one-by-one by the whalers.

## Champion Divers

Sperm whales may be considered to be the champion divers among all aquatic mammals. They have been accurately recorded by sonar as diving to 3,936ft (1,200m) and carcasses of Sperm whales have been recovered entangled in cables from 3,740ft (1,140m), where they had probably been feeding on the bottom-dwelling squid that form the bulk of their diet. One of two bulls observed diving for one to nearly two hours each dive, was found on capture to have in its stomach two specimens of *Scymodon*, a small bottom-living shark. The depth of water in the area was about 10,500ft (3,200m), suggesting an amazing diving ability. The fact that Sperm whales dive right to the seabed for food is borne out by the discovery of all manner of strange objects in their stomachs, from stones to tin cans, suggesting that they literally shovel up the bottom mud.

Bulls are the deepest and longest divers, and females may dive to 3,280ft (1,000m), for more than one hour. Juveniles and calves dive for only half this time to about 2,300ft (700m). Females often accompany young whales and this may be what limits their diving range rather than an inability to dive deeper. However, the gregariousness and caring behavior within the nursery school means that young calves may temporarily be adopted by other females, thus enabling the mother to dive deeper for food than she might otherwise be able to do.

If diving as a group, Sperm whales appear to remain close and do almost everything together throughout a dive. They are able to recover quickly from a long deep dive and dive again after only 2–5 minutes. After several long dives, they reach their physiological limit and need to recover by lolling on the surface for many minutes.

The descent and ascent rates are astonishing. The fastest recorded averaged 550ft (170m) per min in descent and 450ft (140m) per min in ascent. The adaptations that enable the Sperm whale to perform these prodigious feats are largely similar to those of other cetaceans (see p13) but more efficient. For example, the muscle in Sperm whale can absorb up to 50 percent of the total oxygen store—at least double the proportion in land mammals, and significantly more than in baleen whales and seals.

A unique feature of the Sperm whale is the vast spermaceti organ, which fills most of the upper part of the head, and is thought to be an aid to buoyancy control. The theory is that the nasal passages and sinuses which permeate the organ can control the cooling and warming rate of the wax, which has a consistent melting point of 84.2°F (29°C). As the whale dives from warm surface waters to the colder depths, the flow of water into the head passages is controlled to quickly cool the head wax from the whale's normal body temperature of 92.3°F (33.5°C). As a result, the wax solidifies, shrinking as it does so, increasing the density of the head, and thus assisting the descent. On ascending, the blood flow to the capillaries in the head can be increased, so warming the wax slightly and increasing buoyancy, to provide lift to the exhausted whale. This is the Sperm whale's trump card for survival, ensuring that it will always rise with the minimum of effort after a dive.

the remainder being octopus, fish and crustaceans, mostly shrimp and crabs. The smaller species have a similar diet, but the type of prey suggests that the Pygmy sperm whale feeds in oceanic waters to at least 330ft (100m), while the Dwarf sperm whale frequents waters of the continental shelf at depths less than 100m. How the Sperm whale captures its prey is not known. One suggestion is that its white teeth attract the squid on which it feeds. Another is that the whale transmits a beam of very high-frequency sound which creates a short-term field of high pressure capable of temporarily stunning the prey.

Most food items recovered from the Sperm whale's stomach are complete—even Giant squid of 39ft (12m) or longer; worn, broken teeth do not affect feeding ability, nor do broken or badly deformed lower jaws. However, the Sperm whale clearly does not always capture its meal easily—the heads of many whales are covered in disk-shaped scars and wounds made by the suckers of squid which have fiercely resisted capture. Sperm whales may consume up to 440lb (200kg) at a time (a Giant squid found in one individual weighed this much), although the first stomach (there are three) is large enough to hold more. Probably the Sperm whale fills its stomach up to four times a day.

Sperm whales appear to have a high gut parasite load which is presumably transmitted via the food. They frequently have vast quantities of roundworms (nematodes) in the stomach with no detrimental effect, and tapeworms are found both in the worm stage in the intestine and in the larval cyst form in the blubber.

The peak breeding and calving season in the two hemispheres are some six months out of phase; southern stocks conceive in December and they give birth in

February–March, some 14–15 months later. These activities all occur in warm temperate waters, at times when the bulls seek the nursery schools, as decribed below.

Suckling calves remain in nursery schools, and continue to suckle, for at least two years. They may even suckle after weaning for several more years, suggesting a social rather than a feeding function. At weaning the calf is 22ft (6.7m) long and weighs about 6,175lb (2,800kg). The female matures sexually at 7–12 years (determined as in all Sperm whales from dentinal growth layers in the teeth) when she is about 28ft (8.5m) long. Unlike the female, the male matures in uneven stages with a growth spurt towards sexual maturity. Puberty in males is prolonged—from 9–11 up to maturity at 18–19 years, when they are some 39ft (12m) in length. The males may then move to polar waters, and be successful in obtaining harem bull status, serving several females, but they are not socially mature until about 26 years old and some 45ft (13.7m) long.

Newly mature females are only about half as fertile as the older ones—perhaps because they are still growing. The demands of pregnancy and lactation may require the female to consume 30 percent more food, even 60 percent in the newly mature female. The mother must supply her calf daily with about 44lb (20kg) of milk, containing about one-third fat.

Unlike Sperm whales, female Pygmy and Dwarf sperm whales frequently conceive while they are still nursing. At sexual maturity female Pygmy sperm whales are some 9ft (2.7m) long, males 9–10ft (2.7–3.0m). Both sexes of the Dwarf sperm whale are 7ft (2.1–2.2m) in length at maturity.

The Sperm whale forms several different types of school according to season, age, sex and place. In polar waters only large adult males (bulls) are found and they are usually solitary. In warmer waters, five types of school have been observed: bull school, bachelor school (young adult males), juv-

enile school, nursery school (adult females, calves and juveniles of both sexes), and harem school (a nursery school temporarily joined by one bull for the breeding season). The size of schools varies from one to over 100, averaging 20 in coastal and 3–7 in oceanic waters. Some schools, notably of the nursery type, tend to keep their integrity. In one instance, a female marked with a tag was found to be still in the same company of other tagged females 10 years later.

A harem school served by one bull may contain 10–40 females, but usually numbers about 14 females. The bull may have to fight established males to gain control of a harem; in such competition the male uses his more prominent teeth, as well as butting with the head. Females may help to drive out old bulls.

The Dwarf sperm whale probably occurs in groups of less than 10 animals. Adult females and their calves probably form groups, as may juveniles, and sexually adult males and females may occur together.

▲ **The power of the Sperm whale** is dramatically apparent as this pod forges ahead in formation. The dorsal hump, slightly suggestive of a submarine, is prominent here, and the individual on the right is demonstrating its oblique blow.

◀ ▼ **Sperm whaling.** LEFT In the 19th century, the Sperm whale was a prime target for whalers, and it was hunted so ruthlessly in the 1850s that the population collapsed in 1860. BELOW Modern Sperm whaling at Nova Scotia. This whale being flensed, ie stripped of its skin and blubber, demonstrates the narrow bottom jaw and conical teeth.

behavior, common to many cetaceans, is mass stranding (see p32), when an entire school of dozens of Sperm whales may beach.

In the 18th and, particularly, the 19th centuries, the main target of New England whalers was the Sperm whale, taken for sperm oil. Today a small commercial whaling operation in the Azores uses the methods the islanders were taught by New Englanders before the advent of steam—the whales are harpooned by hand from canoes driven by oars and sail.

Whaling is still active for Sperm whales (the two *Kogia* species are taken only incidentally) in the Antarctic, North Pacific and Atlantic coasts. Most of this is based on factory vessels served by whaling ships. Modern whaling began with the use of faster steam-driven whaling ships and continued with the invention about 1868 of the explosive harpoon gun by Svend Foyn.

Any whale species taken in fishing operations must be considered to be under threat. In the Southern Hemisphere alone, the estimated original stock of 170,000 males and 160,000 females is now reduced to about 71,000 and 125,000 respectively. However, extinction now seems extremely unlikely for all three species. Certain Sperm whale stocks are already afforded protection and all Sperm whaling is scheduled to cease before the end of 1985 (a decision made by the International Whaling Commission in July 1982) although this ruling may not prevent individual nations from continuing to whale in coastal territorial waters.

There is considerable concern over depletion of the male population. Because of the "harem" social structure, most males have been considered by some people to be "surplus." This view is now being challenged because of the falling pregnancy rate in some areas.

In addition to exploitation in the modern whaling industry of the flesh (for human consumption) and blubber (for oil), the Sperm whale yields two products which are unique and have long been valued. The spermaceti oil obtained from the head, and the body oils provide a high-grade lubricating oil that is used in many industries, including, today, space research. The other well-known Sperm whale derivative is the "ambergris" used as a fixative in the perfume and cosmetic industries. Ambergris is found in the intestine and is thought to be a form of excrement. A huge lump of this material from a 49ft (15m) male taken in the Antarctic was found to weigh 926lb (421kg)!

The Sperm whale is often said to be protective, and not only the female towards her calf. In one instance, after the shooting of the largest in a school of 20–30 whales, the others formed a tight circle around the injured whale with heads towards the centre and tails outstretched—the so-called "marguerite flower" formation.

Interaction between whales ranges from play, such as tossing timber baulks, leaping and lob-tailing, to fighting, in which wounds and injuries such as broken jaws may result.

Sperm whales produce "clicks" under water in the 5–32kHz range, each click comprising up to nine short pulses. These clicks are heard when groups meet. Individual whales have unique clicking patterns called "codas," which they repeat 2–60 times at intervals of seconds or minutes. Other sounds produced by the Sperm whale resemble low roars and "rusty-hinge" creaks.

One mystifying aspect of the family's

CL

# BEAKED WHALES

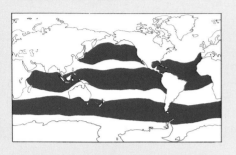

▶ **Barrelheads.** The massive forehead of the
Northern bottlenose whale led Norwegian
whalers to call them "barrelheads" or "gray
heads." Bottlenose whaling ceased in 1972 and
the Northern bottlenose whale was declared a
provisional protected species in 1977.

THE 18 species of beaked whales tend to be elusive creatures, and indeed one species, Longman's beaked whale, has never been seen in the flesh—two skulls, one found in 1822 and the other in 1955, are the sole evidence for its existence. Similarly, Shepherd's beaked ·whale is known from only 10 specimens and may never have been seen alive. Not all, though, are quite as shy as this: about 50,000 Northern bottlenose whales were caught by whalers between 1882 and 1920 and the Baird's beaked whale has been taken off Japan.

The beaked whales are amongst the most primitive of whales, along with the river dolphins. The beak (strictly, elongated upper and lower jaws) that gives them their name varies from long and pointed in Shepherd's beaked whale to short and stubby in the whales of genus *Mesoplodon*. The scientific name Ziphiidae derives from the Greek *xiphos* = sword; hence Ziphiidae: "the sword-nosed whales." They have become specialized feeders, generally on squid, and in some genera—*Hyperoodon*, *Ziphius* and *Mesoplodon*—only one pair of teeth develops fully, in the lower jaw. In the genus *Berardius* there are two pairs of teeth in the lower jaw and in Shepherd's beaked whale there are many teeth in both jaws.

In all the beaked whales except Shepherd's beaked whale and those of genus *Berardius* the teeth of females never erupt from the gums. It is possible to determine the species, sex and maturity of a beaked whale skull from the teeth: their number and place in the jaw determine the species; teeth with filled or virtually filled pulp cavities provide a criterion of maturity; teeth exhibiting natural wear as a sign of having erupted in life signify male; teeth exhibiting no such wear but with pulp cavities completely or virtually filled out signify adult female.

The beaked whales are medium-sized whales, some of them smaller than 20ft (6m) long (*Mesoplodon*), others up to and exceeding 40ft (12m) (*Berardius*). Under the throat, there are two characteristic grooves which make a V shape, but they do not meet. There is no notch in the tail fluke. Sexual dimorphism becomes very marked by adolescence: sometimes the male is bigger, as in the Northern bottlenose whale, and sometimes the female, as in Baird's beaked whale. The forehead of old males often has a pronounced bulge, which in some species, such as the Northern bottlenose whale, becomes white. At sea, it is difficult to distinguish between immature specimens and females of almost all beaked whales because the foreheads are similar in shape. All beaked whales except the Northern bottlenose whale are liable to have a pattern of scars on their backs, inflicted by the teeth of other members of the same species. These scars are usually more pronounced in older males—the result of fights. Most species of beaked whales live in the

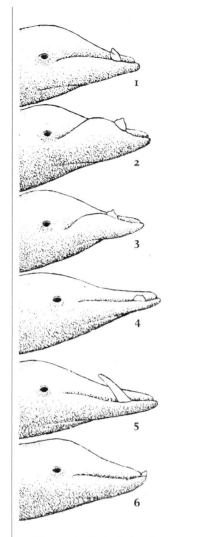

▲ **The one-toothed whales** of genus *Mesoplodon*. Beaked whales feed on squid, which do not require many sharp teeth either to catch or to eat them. Nevertheless the 12 species of *Mesoplodon* have a single tooth, whose position in the jaw is characteristic for each species. (1) Arch beaked whale (*M. carlhubbsi*). (2) Blainville's beaked whale (*M. densirostris*). (3) Ginkgo-toothed beaked whale (*M. ginkgodens*). (4) Gray's beaked whale (*M. grayi*). (5) Strap-toothed whale (*M. layardii*). (6) True's beaked whale (*M. mirus*).

deep-sea areas outside the continental shelf. They all appear to eat squid and sometimes deep-sea fishes.

Most beaked whales are hard to identify at sea. They are usually encountered singly or in groups of two or three, but some of them may be seen in schools of 25–40 animals. They are deep divers and some of them possibly dive deeper than any other cetaceans. A diving time of up to 2 hours is recorded for the Northern bottlenose whale.

Records of the distribution of beaked whales are often based upon reports of stranded animals. Such records also involve dead animals which have been washed ashore, although the death of the animal may have occurred far from the stranding area. This is demonstrated by the Northern bottlenose whale, which is recorded in the Baltic and the White Sea, even though its main area of distribution is outside the continental slope. The reason that presumably healthy animals become stranded is not fully understood (see p32). Mass strandings seldom or never occur in beaked whales. It is still not known how deep-sea species of whales navigate across thousands of miles in the open sea, but it is possible that they orientate themselves by water currents and the contours of the sea bottom.

The ancestors of the "modern" beaked whales are found in fossils from the Miocene (about 20 million years ago). They were once classified with the sperm whales in a superfamily because of the many similarities between the two families. Later research has shown that the chromosomes of beaked and sperm whales are quite different, which indicates that these two groups of animals diverged early and independently.

The Northern bottlenose whale is one of the few species for which there is any knowledge of its migratory and social behavior. This species is widely distributed in the North Atlantic, occurring as far north as the edge of the ice in the summer. In the winter it occurs as far south as the Cape Verde Islands, off West Africa, in the east, and off New York in the west. Local concentrations of bottlenose whales off Spitsbergen, the coast of Norway, around Iceland and Jan Mayen Island and off Labrador may represent separate stocks. Herds of bottlenose whales are seen as early as March in the waters off the Faeroes. A great number occurs between Jan Mayen Island and Iceland at the end of April, in May and early June. At the same time they are found off Spitsbergen and Bear Island. The southern migration starts at the beginning of July.

Bottlenose whales recorded on the coast of Europe are animals which have stranded mainly in the late summer and fall. Many of these whales seem to have been caught by the shallow water in the North Sea on their southern migrations. Only one bottlenose whale has been reported caught at sea in the period 1938–1972 in the shallow waters of the North Sea. In spite of intensive whaling for small whales in the Barents Sea, not a single bottlenose whale has ever been reported caught in this shelf area. These findings conflict with several reports that this species is distributed as far east in the Barents Sea as Novaya Zemlya. Reports of bottlenose whales caught by Norwegian whalers show that the greatest number has been caught at depths of more than 3,300ft (1,000m). Geographical segregation of males and females may occur; fully grown males are generally found closer to the ice than females and younger males.

In the North Atlantic, bottlenose whales usually occur in herds of 2–4 animals, but groups of up to 20 animals have been seen. Groups including two or three whales are usually animals of the same sex and age. Groups of four animals are often dominated by older males. Mother and calf usually appear alone, but sometimes two females with their calves form a group. A group of animals will usually stay with an injured companion until it is dead. If a calf approaches a ship, the mother will swim between the ship and the calf.

Male Northern bottlenose whales become sexually mature at a body length of 23–25ft (7.3–7.6m) at the age of 7–9 years; females attain sexual maturity at 22–23ft 6.7–7.0m), at an age between 8 and 14 years, with an average of about 9 years. Mating and birth occur mainly in April. The calf is about 120in (300cm) long at birth, and weaning takes place when the calf is about one year old. They give birth every second year.

Growth curves of Northern bottlenose whales based upon age determined from growth layers in the teeth (the teeth erupt when the animal is 15–17 years old) show that males continue their growth till they are about 20 years old; Females stop growing at about 15 years of age.

Obscurity has largely saved the beaked whales from exploitation, but although there has been little pressure from whaling, their future is uncertain. Like other primitive, highly specialized species such as the river dolphins, they would seem to be incapable of exploiting changes in the ecosystem and hence may well succumb to competition from more adaptable species.

1

2

# THE 18 SPECIES OF BEAKED WHALES

Abbreviations: HTL = head-to-tail straight-line length. wt = weight (estimated from a weight-length key for the Northern bottlenose whale).
[v] Vulnerable.

## Genus *Tasmacetus*

Beak long and slender; two large conical teeth at tip of lower jaw, with 26–27 conical teeth on lower jaw and 19–21 similar teeth on upper jaw.

### Shepherd's beaked whale

*Tasmacetus shepherdi*
Shepherd's beaked whale or Tasman whale.

Circumpolar (known only from 10 specimens recorded in S Hemisphere, including New Zealand, Argentina, Chile and Tierra del Fuego). Female HTL 22ft; wt about 5.6 tons. Skin: dark gray-brown above, flanks lighter, belly almost white.

## Genus *Ziphius*

Head slightly concave; beak less developed than in bottlenose whales, distinctly goose-like.

### Cuvier's beaked whale

*Ziphius cavirostris*
Cuvier's beaked whale or Goosebeaked whale.

All oceans except high latitudes. Strandings from Atlantic Ocean north to Cape Cod in west, North Sea in east; Mediterranean and south to Cape of Good Hope; Pacific Ocean north to Bering Sea and Alaska, south to Tierra del Fuego. Male HTL 22ft; wt about 5.6 tons; female HTL 23ft; HTL at birth 7ft. Male sexual maturity at 18ft, female at 20ft. Skin: very variable; mustard to dark umber in Pacific, gray or smoke blue in Atlantic; white patches on belly caused by parasites.

## Genus *Hyperoodon*

Forehead bulbous, becoming more pronounced with age, particularly in males. Older males with a single pair of pear-shaped teeth that erupt at the top of the lower jaw.

### Northern bottlenose whale [v]

*Hyperoodon ampullatus*
Widely distributed in N Atlantic, to edge of the ice in summer; in winter, south to Cape Verde Islands in the east and off New York in the west. Male HTL 29ft; wt about 10 tons; female HTL 23–28ft; HTL at birth about 10ft. Male sexual maturity at 24–25ft. Skin: very variable; greenish-sienna above, smoke gray beneath, lightening to cream all over with age; calves uniform umber brown. Gestation: 12 months. Longevity 37 years.

### Southern bottlenose whale

*Hyperoodon planifrons*
Southern or Flower's or Flat-headed or Antarctic bottlenose whale; Pacific beaked whale.

Temperate waters in the Southern Hemisphere. Strandings in Argentina, off Falkland Islands, Brazil, Chile, Australia, New Zealand, South Africa. Male HTL 23ft; wt about 6.2 tons; female HTL 25ft; wt about 7.9 tons. Skin: deep metallic gray, lightening to bluish on the flanks and paler beneath (these are colors of dead animals; in life they may be more brown than blue).

## Genus *Berardius*

The largest of the beaked whales. Unlike other Ziphiidae, 2 pairs of strongly compressed functional teeth near tip of lower jaw, 3in in front and 2in behind, erupt in both sexes. Weals and other wounds on the body of males, particularly older ones.

### Arnoux's beaked whale

*Berardius arnuxi*
Arnoux's or New Zealand beaked whale.

Throughout Southern Ocean south of 30°S. Strandings reported from S Australia, New Zealand, S Africa, Argentina, Falkland Islands, S Georgia, S Shetlands, Antarctic Peninsula. HTL about 29–32ft; wt about 9.8–10.6 tons; HTL at birth 11ft. Skin: blue-gray with sometimes a brownish tint; flippers, flukes and back darker; old males dirty white from head to dorsal fin. Gestation: probably 10 months.

### Baird's beaked whale

*Berardius bairdii*
Baird's beaked or Northern giant bottlenose or Northern fourtooth whale.

Widely distributed in N Pacific from about 30°N to S Bering Sea (from Pribilof Islands and Alaska to S California in NE Pacific, and from Kamchatka and Sea of Okhotsk to Sea of Japan in W Pacific. Offshore waters deeper than 3,300ft. Male HTL 39ft; wt about 13.5 tons; female HTL 42ft, wt about 15 tons; HTL at birth 14ft. Male sexual maturity at 31ft, female at 33ft. Skin: bluish dark gray, often with brown tinge; underside lighter with white blotches on throat, between flippers, around navel and anus; female lighter. Gestation: 17 months.

## Genus *Mesoplodon*

A single pair of teeth in the lower jaw (the name *Mesoplodon* means "armed with a tooth in the middle of the jaw" and is derived from the position of the teeth in *M. bidens*, the first species of the genus to be described). Position, shape and size of the teeth, which erupt only in older males, are used to separate the species. Skin: dark gray to black. Deep divers.

### Strap-toothed whale

*Mesoplodon layardii*
Circumpolar in relatively cool water in the Southern Hemisphere south of 30°S. Strandings in New Zealand, S Australia, Falkland Islands, Uruguay, Tierra del Fuego. HTL about 16ft; wt about 3.4 tons; HTL at birth about 7ft.

### Gray's beaked whale

*Mesoplodon grayi*
Gray's beaked or Scamperdown whale.

Circumpolar in all cool temperate waters of Southern Hemisphere. Strandings in S Africa, S Australia, New Zealand, Patagonia, Argentina south of 30°S. HTL 20ft; wt 4.8 tons.

### Hector's beaked whale

*Mesoplodon hectori*
Circumpolar in all temperate waters of the Southern Hemisphere. Strandings in Tasmania, New Zealand, Tierra del Fuego, Falkland Islands, S Africa. HTL 12ft; wt about 2 tons. Known mainly from skulls.

◄ **Representative species of beaked whales.** (**1**) Northern bottlenosed whale (*Hyperoodon ampullatus*). (**2**) Shepherd's beaked whale (*Tasmacetus shepherdi*). (**3**) Baird's beaked whale (*Beradius bairdii*). (**4**) Cuvier's beaked whale (*Ziphius cavirostris*). (**5**) Sowerby's beaked whale (*Mesoplodon bidens*).

## Andrew's beaked whale

*Mesoplodon bowdoini*

Cool temperate waters of the central Indo-pacific areas. Strandings in New Zealand, Tasmania and W Australia. HTL 14ft; wt 2.6 tons.

## Longman's beaked whale

*Mesoplodon pacificus*

Probably SW tropical Pacific and Indian Ocean. Known only from two skulls, the first from a specimen stranded at Mackay, Queensland, found in 1822, the second found in 1955 in Somalia, on the east coast of Africa.

## Blainville's beaked whale

*Mesoplodon densirostris*

Tropical and warm temperate waters on both sides of the equator: in Atlantic from Madeira to the east coast of Canada and Florida; in N Pacific strandings from Hawaii and Formosa, and in Indian Ocean from Seychelles. HTL 17ft; wt 3.6 tons. A marked protuberance located near the corner of the mouth gives the head a distinctive character in adult males.

## True's beaked whale

*Mesoplodon mirus*

Temperate waters in N and S Atlantic, with *M. densirostris* in the middle. Strandings on French coast, Outer Hebrides and Orkney Islands, coast of Ireland. More abundant on American side of North Atlantic; strandings here from Florida, N Carolina, New England, Canada; also strandings on the east coast of S Africa. HTL 16ft; wt about 3.2 tons.

## Gervais' beaked whale

*Mesoplodon europaeus*
Gervais' or Antillean or Gulfstream beaked whale.

Deep water in temperate and warmer areas of N Atlantic. Strandings in N America from New York to Florida, in the Gulf of Mexico and Caribbean Sea; one record from English Channel; overlaps partly with *M. mirus*. HTL 22ft; wt about 5.6 tons. Slender in form, somewhat laterally compressed. Teeth about one-third of the way from the tip of the snout to the corner of the mouth.

## Sowerby's beaked whale

*Mesoplodon bidens*
Sowerby's or North Sea beaked whale.

N Atlantic. Strandings in Canada, France, the Netherlands, UK, Ireland, Norway, Sweden. Earlier literature suggested a distribution in the North Sea because of many strandings in the area, but the only observations in open sea are outside the continental shelf at 3,300–9,900ft depth. HTL about 16ft; wt about 3.4 tons. HTL at birth about 6ft.

## Stejnegeri's beaked whale

*Mesoplodon stejnegeri*
Stejnegeri's or Bering Sea beaked whale.

N Pacific, between 40°N and 60°N, but mainly between 50°N and 60°N.

Strandings from Bering Sea to Japan in western Pacific and to Oregon in eastern Pacific. HTL 20ft; wt about 4.8 tons. Sometimes caught by whalers from Japanese coastal stations.

## Arch beaked whale

*Mesoplodon carlhubbsi*

Distribution in temperate waters of N Pacific from 50°N to 30°N, south of the range of Stejneger's beaked whale. Strandings in Japan, Washington and California. HTL about 16ft; wt about 3.4 tons.

## Ginkgo-toothed beaked whale

*Mesoplodon ginkgodens*
Ginkgo-toothed or Japanese beaked whale.

Warm waters of the Indo-pacific from Sri Lanka, Japan to California. HTL 17ft; wt 3.6 tons.

# BALEEN WHALES

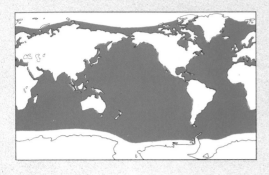

**Suborder: Mysticeti**
Ten species in 5 genera and 3 families.
Distribution: all major oceans.
Habitat: deep sea.

Size: head-to-tail length from 6ft (2m) in the
Pygmy right whale to 90ft (27m) in the Blue
whale; weight from 3 tons in the Pygmy
right whale to 150 tons in the Blue whale.

**Gray whale** (family Eschrichlidae)
One species in 1 genus: *Eschrichtius robustus*.

**Rorquals** (family Balaenopteridae)
Six species in 2 genera, including **Blue whale**
(*Balaenoptera musculus*), **Humpback whale**
(*Megaptera novaeangliae*).

**Right whales** (family Balaenidae)
Three species in 2 genera: **Right whale**
(*Balaena glacialis*), **Bowhead whale** (*Balaena
mysticetus*), **Pygmy right whale** (*Caperea
marginata*).

THE suborder Mysticeti, or baleen whales, contains rather few living species, although they make up for this by their size, the Blue whale being the largest animal ever to have lived on earth. In baleen whales teeth are present only as vestigial buds in the embryo. Instead, they have evolved a new structure, the baleen plates, which are totally unconnected to teeth. These act to strain small zooplanktonic organisms, krill, which the whales ingest in large quantities. The baleen plates are fringed with bristles and the organisms are dislodged from the baleen by the tongue.

The baleen whales are thought to have evolved in the western South Pacific, where rich zooplankton deposits in Oligocene strata, together with the occurrence of fossils of the earliest mysticete forms (early cetothere ancestors), suggest that these may have favored the evolution of baleen and a filter-feeding mode of life. From here they may have dispersed into the Pacific and Indo-Pacific regions along lines of high productivity during the late Cenozoic, although the rorquals appear to have been originally distributed in the warm temperate North Atlantic. The Gray whale is the sole member of the family Eschrichtidae, and is confined to the North Pacific (although a North Atlantic population became extinct in comparatively recent historical times). It has a rather narrow gently arched rostrum, two (rarely four) short throat grooves and no dorsal fin.

The slim, torpedo-shaped rorquals, members of the family Balaenopteridae (which also include the Humpback), have a series of throat pleats which expand as they ingest water filled with plankton, and then contract to force the water over the baleen plates. This leaves the plankton stranded on the fibrous mat that forms the frayed inner edges of the plates. The Humpback differs from other rorquals in being rather stoutly built, with fewer and much coarser throat grooves, and a pair of very long robust flippers. The head, lower jaw and flipper edge are covered with irregular knobs, and the trailing edge is indented and serrated. The rorquals, with the exception of the tropical Bryde's whale, are found throughout the world's oceans, the Bowhead has a restricted arctic distribution, the Right whale occurs only in the North Atlantic, and the Pygmy right whale is confined to the Southern Ocean.

Two of the three species of the family Balaenidae, the Right and Bowhead whales, have much larger heads, up to one-third of the total length of the body, the rostrum is long and narrow, and arched upwards, though the bones of the lower jaw are not. This leaves a space which is filled by the huge lower lips that rise from the lower jaw and enclose the long narrow baleen plates hanging from the edges of the rostrum. Neither of these species has a dorsal fin, unlike the relatively primitive Pygmy right whale, though all three species have the seven neck vertebrae fused into a single mass.

PGHE

▶ **Skimming the water** for food organisms, this Southern Right whale demonstrates its regular array of baleen plates.

▼ **Baleen types.** Although the principle of baleen functioning is similar in all such whales, there are variations. The two extremes are typified by the Right whale (**1**) and the rorquals such as the Sei whale (**2**). The Right whale has a narrow rostrum and long baleen plates. It feeds by skimming the surface, collecting food organisms which it then dislodges with the tongue. The Sei whale has a wide rostrum with short baleen plates. It gulps huge mouthfuls and raises the tongue to force the water through the baleen plates, leaving the food behind. Baleen plates from the ten species of Mysticeti (all to scale) are as follows: (**a**) Minke, (**b**) Bryde's, (**c**) Sei, (**d**) Pygmy Right, (**e**) Gray, (**f**) Humpback, (**g**) Fin, (**h**) Blue, (**i**) Right, (**j**) Bowhead.

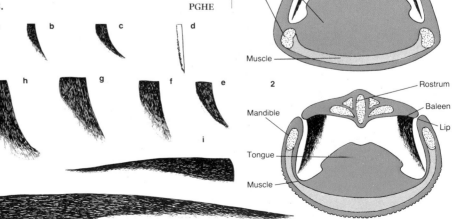

## Skulls of Baleen Whales

Baleen whales show a more extreme modification of the skull than do toothed whales, so much so that it is at first hard to believe that such bones could support the head and enclose the brain of these creatures.

The principal modifications are the extension of the jaws, the upper one (rostrum) supporting the baleen plates, forward movement of the supraoccipital region (back of the skull) over the frontal, and consequent merging of the rostral and cranial bones. In the Bowhead whale the rostrum has a pronounced curve to accommodate the long baleen plates. In rorquals, like the Humpback whale, the rostrum is broader and only gently curved. The Gray whale is a bottom feeder, "plowing" the sea bed, and its jaws are shorter and thicker than the other species, the upper supporting short, stiff baleen. For the baleen characteristics of all the baleen whales, see below left.

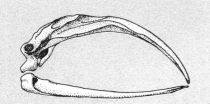

**Bowhead whale**   197in

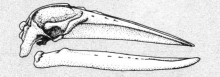

**Humpback whale**   138in

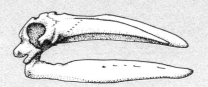

**Gray whale**   94in

# GRAY WHALE

***Eschrichtius robustus***
Gray whale, California gray whale or devilfish.
Family: Eschrichtidae.
Sole member of genus.
Distribution: two stocks, one from Baja
California along Pacific coast to Bering and
Chukchi seas; Korean stock from S Korea to
Okhotsk Sea. Usually in coastal waters less than
330ft (100m) deep.

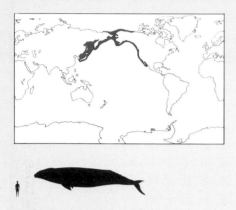

Size: head-to-tail length (male) 39–47ft
(11.9–14.3m); weight 16 tons; head-to-tail
length (female) 42–50ft (12.8–15.2m); weight
(pregnant) 31–34 tons.

Skin: mottled gray, usually covered with
patches of barnacles and whale lice. no dorsal
fin, but low ridge on rear half of back. Two
throat grooves. White baleen. Spout paired,
short and bushy.

Diet: bottom-dwelling amphipods, polychaete
worms and other invertebrates.

Gestation: 13 months.

Longevity: sexually mature at 8, physically
mature at 40 years; maximum recorded 77
years.

Gray whales are the most coastal of the baleen whales and are often found within half a mile of shore. This preference for coastal waters, and the accessibility of the breeding lagoons in Mexico make them one of the best-known cetaceans. Gray whales migrate each fall and spring along the western coast of North America on their yearly passage between summer feeding grounds in the Arctic and winter calving areas in the protected lagoons of Baja California. Thousands of people watch the "grays" swimming past the shores of California each year. Their migration is the longest known of any mammal; some individual Gray whales may swim as far as 12,500mi (20,400km) yearly from the Arctic ice-pack to the subtropics and back.

The Gray whale averages about 40ft (12m) in length but can reach 50ft (15m). The skin is a mottled dark to light gray and is one of the most heavily parasitized among cetaceans. Both barnacles and whale lice (cyamids) live on it in great abundance, barnacles particularly on top of the relatively short, bowed head, around the blowhole and on the anterior part of the back, adding greatly to the mottled appearance; one barnacle and three whale lice species have been found only on the Gray whale. Several albino individuals have been sighted. Gray whales lack a dorsal fin but do have a dorsal ridge of 8–9 humps along the last third of the back. The baleen is yellowish-white and is much heavier and shorter than in other baleen whales, never exceeding 15in (38cm) in length. Under the throat are two longitudinal grooves about 16in (40cm) apart and 6.6ft (2m) long. These grooves may stretch open and allow the mouth to expand during feeding, thus taking in more food.

While migrating Gray whales swim at about 4.5 knots (8km/h), they can attain speeds of 11 knots (20km/h) under stress. Migrating Grays swim steadily, surfacing every 3–4 minutes to blow 3–5 times. The spout is short and puffy and is forked as it issues from both blowholes. The tail flukes often come out of the water on the last blow in the series as the whale dives.

The Gray whale's sound repertoire includes grunts, pulses, clicks, moans and knocks. In the lagoons of Baja California calves emit a low resonant pulse which attracts their mothers. But in Gray whales sounds do not appear to have the complexity or social significance of those produced by other cetaceans.

At present there are only two stocks of Gray whales, the Californian and the separate Korean or western Pacific stock. Gray whales once inhabited the North Atlantic but disappeared in the early 1700s, probably due to whaling.

The Californian Gray whale calves during the winter in lagoons, such as Laguna Ojo de Liebre and Laguna San Ignacio, on the desert peninsula of Baja California, Mexico. They summer in the northern Bering Sea near Saint Lawrence Island and north through the Bering Straits into the Chukchi Sea, almost to the edge of the Arctic pack ice. The Korean Gray whale summers in the Okhotsk Sea off the coast of Siberia and migrates south each fall to calve among the

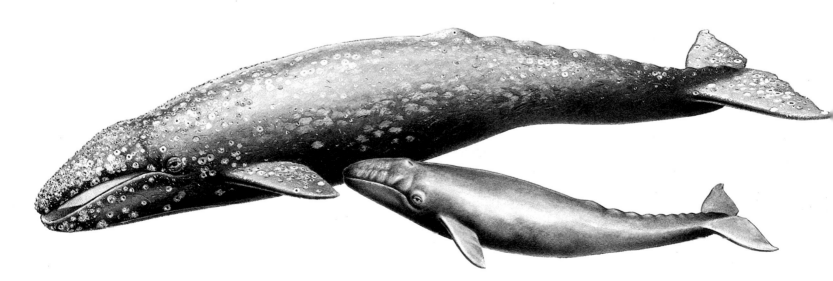

▲ **Gray whale blowing.** Gray whales
swimming just below the surface appear very
pale, almost white. The vertical spout,
emerging from twin blowholes, may or may not
appear divided.

▶ **Barnacle clusters** create a world of tiny
bejewelled grottoes on the Gray whale's skin.
Most of the great whales have barnacles, but
the Gray is particularly well decorated.
INSET Around the barnacles live whale lice, pale
spidery creatures about 1 in (2.5cm) long.

◀ **Gray whale mother and calf.** Young gray
whales are smooth and sleek compared to their
encrusted elders.

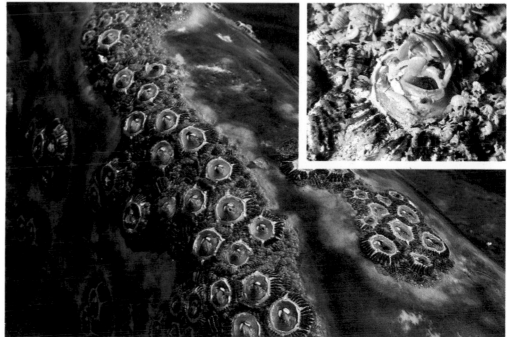

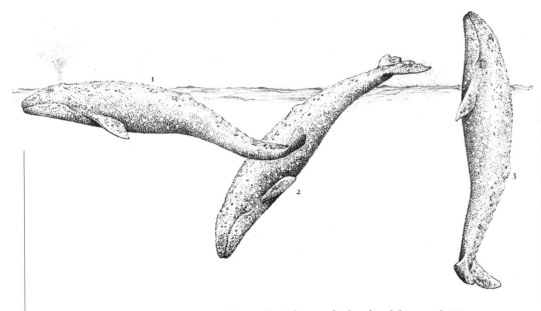

▲ **Characteristic attitudes** of the Gray whale. (**1**) Blowing. (**2**) Diving. (**3**) Spy-hopping.

▼ **Two years in the life of the Gray.** The gestation period of Gray whales is just over a year, 13 months in fact, which leads to a 2-year breeding cycle. Not all whales migrate the full distance but the extremes of the range represent a 12,675mi (20,400km) round trip.

inlets and islands of the south Korean coast. Much research has been done on the California Grays and most of the facts presented here refer to that stock.

Gray whales reach puberty at about 8 years of age (range 5–11 years), when the mean length is 36ft (11.1m) for males and 38ft (11.7m) for females, and they attain full physical maturity at about 40. Like the other baleen whales, females of the species are larger than males, probably to satisfy the greater physical demands of bearing and nursing young. Females give birth on alternate years, after a gestation period of 13 months, to a single calf about 16ft (4.9m) long.

Gray whales are adapted to migration, and many aspects of their life history and ecology reflect this yearly movement from the Arctic to the Tropics. The Californian Gray spends from June to October in arctic waters feeding heavily on bottom-dwelling invertebrates.

At the start of the arctic winter their feeding grounds begin to freeze over. The whales then migrate to the protected lagoons, where the females calve. The calves are born within a period of 5–6 weeks, with a peak occurring about 10 January. At birth the calves have coats of blubber too thin for them to withstand cold arctic water, but they thrive in the warm lagoons. For the first few hours after birth the breathing and swimming of the calf are uncoordinated and labored, and the mother sometimes has to help the calf to breathe by holding it to the surface with her back or tail flukes. The calves are nursed for about seven months, beginning in the confined shallow lagoons, where they gain motor coordination and perhaps establish the mother-young bond necessary to keep together on the migration north into the summering grounds where they are weaned. By the time the calves have arrived in the Arctic, they have built up thick insulating blubber coats from the milk of the nursing females. In the lagoons

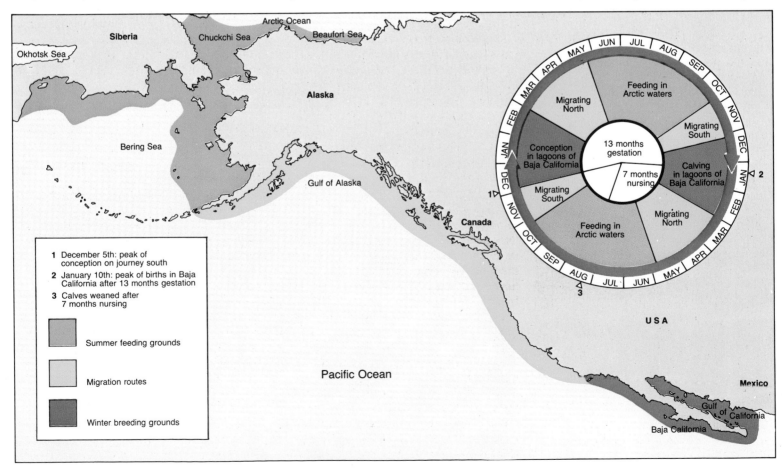

1 December 5th: peak of conception on journey south

2 January 10th: peak of births in Baja California after 13 months gestation

3 Calves weaned after 7 months nursing

Summer feeding grounds

Migration routes

Winter breeding grounds

▲ **Gray whales mating** in a warm lagoon of Baja California, Mexico. Occasionally, triads have been reported, in which an additional animal supports the mating pair.

▼ **A young Gray,** in San Ignacio Lagoon, Baja California, showing its large blowhole, and already considerable collection of barnacles.

▷ **Like a giant tusk** OVERLEAF, the head of a Gray whale protrudes from the water as it surveys its surroundings. This maneuver, spy-hopping, although seen in many whales, is very prominent in the Gray whale.

and off southern California, the calves stay close to and almost touching their mothers; but when they reach the Bering Sea in late May and June the calves are good swimmers and may be seen breaching energetically away from their mothers.

Since the migration route follows the coast closely, the whales may navigate simply by staying in shallow water and keeping the land on their right or left side, depending on whether they are migrating north or south. At points of land along the migration route Gray whales are often seen "spy-hopping." To spy-hop a whale thrusts its head straight up out of the water and then slowly sinks back down along its horizontal axis. This contrasts with the breach, where a whale leaps half way or more out of the water and then falls back on its side, creating a large splash. It is possible that Gray whales spy-hop to view the adjacent shore and thus orient their migration.

Mating and other sexual behavior have been observed at all times of year throughout the range, but most conceptions occur within a three-week period during the southward migration, with a peak about

5th December. Sexual behavior may involve as many as five or more individuals rolling and milling together. Unfortunately, little is known about the sexual behavior of Gray whales, although some authors have speculated that the extra animals are necessary to hold the mating pair together. If so this would be an extreme example of cooperation.

The migration off California occurs in a sequence according to reproductive status, sex and age-group. Heading south, the migration is led by females in the late stages of pregnancy. Next come the recently impregnated females who have weaned their calves the previous summer. Then come immature females and adult males and finally the immature males. The migration north is led by the newly pregnant females, perhaps hurrying to spend the maximum length of time feeding in the Arctic to nurture the developing fetus inside them. The adult males and non-breeding females follow, then immature whales of both sexes, and finally, meandering slowly north, come the females with their newborn calves.

Observers have noticed changes in the sizes of groups as the migration progresses past a certain point. In the early part of the southward migration single whales predominate, presumably mostly females carrying near-term fetuses, and almost no whales are in groups of more than six. These leading whales swim steadily, seldom deviating from the migratory path, which suggests that they are hurrying south to give birth to the calves. During the remainder of the migration, groups of two predominate, but there are as many as 11 in one group in the middle of the procession. These later whales seem to have a tendency to loiter more *en route*, particularly toward the end of the migration.

In the calving grounds the males and subadults are concentrated in the areas around the lagoon mouths where much rolling, milling and sexual play can be seen, while the mothers and calves seem to use the shallower portions deep inside the lagoons. In the Arctic 100 or more Gray whales may gather to feed in roughly the same area.

Some individuals do not make the entire migration north. Gray whales can be found in most of the migration areas during summer months. Off British Columbia some individuals stay in the same area for three months or more, apparently to feed. These residents seem to include both sexes and all age groups, including females with calves. Many of the same individuals return for

several summers to the same area. This is perhaps an alternative feeding strategy to making the full migration, but it is one that only a few whales can afford, since feeding areas south of the northern Bering Sea are probably rare and can only support a fraction of the population.

The only known non-human predator on the Gray whale is the Killer whale. Several attacks have been observed, most often on cows with calves and presumably in an attempt to get the relatively defenseless calf. Killer whales seem to attack particularly the lips, tongue and flukes of the grays, the areas that may most readily be grasped. Adult Grays accompanying calves will place themselves protectively between the attackers and the calves. When under attack, Grays swim toward shallow water and kelp beds near shore, areas which Killer whales seem hesitant to enter. Gray whales respond to underwater playback of recordings of Killer whale sounds by swimming rapidly away or by taking refuge in thick kelp beds.

The Korean Gray whale is currently endangered and may be on the edge of extinction. Heavy whaling pressures in the first third of this century and sporadic whaling since are undoubtedly responsible for this decline. Eskimo, Aleut and Indian whaling tribes took Gray whales from the California stock for thousands of years in the northern part of its range. In the 1850s Yankee whalers began killing Gray whales both in the calving lagoons and along the migration route. The whaling pressures were intense and by 1874 one whaling captain, Charles Scammon, was predicting that the Californian Gray would soon be extinct. Whaling virtually ceased by 1900, with the California stock reduced to a mere remnant of its population before commercial whaling, estimated at about 30,000. In 1913 whaling resumed, and it continued sporadically until 1946, when the International Whaling Commission was formed, which prohibited a commercial take of Gray whales. The Soviet Union, however, was permitted an aboriginal take of Gray whales for the Eskimo people living on the Chukotsky peninsula. At present the Soviet Union has an annual quota of 179 Gray whales. With the decline in whaling, the California stock began to show signs of recovery. The present population is estimated at 15,000–17,000 and is still growing.                                    ABT

## Deep Harvest

Gray whales are adapted to exploiting the tremendous seasonal abundance of food that results as the arctic pack ice retreats in spring, exposing the sea to the polar summer's 24-hour daylight and thus triggering an enormous bloom of microorganisms in the water from the surface down to the sea floor. While present in the Arctic from June to October, Gray whales store enough fat to sustain them virtually without feeding through the rest of the year, as they migrate to calve in warm waters while their summer feeding grounds are covered with ice. By the time they return to their feeding grounds they may have lost up to one-third of their body weight.

The whales feed in shallow waters 15–330ft (5–100m) deep on amphipods and isopods (both orders of crustaceans), polychaete worms and mollusks that live on the ocean floor or a few inches into the bottom sediment. The gammarid amphipod *Ampelisca macrocephala* is probably the most commonly taken species. To feed, Gray whales dive to the sea floor, turn on their side (usually the right), and swim forward along the bottom forcing their heads through the top layer of sediment, sucking or scooping up invertebrate prey, mud and gravel and trailing a large mud plume behind. The whales then surface, straining sediments through the baleen to leave food items inside the mouth which are then swallowed; they take a few breaths, and

dive again. As Gray whales feed they leave a shallow scrape. Some scientists have speculated that they may thus effectively plow the sea floor, possibly increasing its productivity in subsequent years.

Although Gray whales feed primarily during the months spent in arctic waters, they will feed, if the opportunity arises, in other parts of their range. Grays have been found surface feeding on both small fish and shrimp-like kelp mysids (*Acanthomysis sculpta*) off the coast of California while migrating.

Several species of seabird associate with feeding Gray whales, such as Horned puffins, Glaucous gulls and Arctic terns. These birds apparently feed on crustaceans which escape through the baleen during the straining process while the whales are surfacing. The discovery of this association answered the perplexing question of how large numbers of bottom-dwelling invertebrates, from beyond the birds' diving depth, got into their digestive tracts.

Abbreviations: HTL = head to tail length. wt = weight.
[E] Endangered. [V] Vulnerable.

### Blue whale [E]
*Balaenoptera musculus*

Polar to tropical seas.
HTL 88ft; wt 150 tons.
Skin: mottled bluish-grey; flippers
pale beneath. Baleen plates:
270–395, blue-black. Throat
grooves: 55–88. Longevity: 80 years.
Subspecies: 2. **Blue whale**
(*B. m. musculus*). **Pygmy blue whale**
(*B. m. brevicauda*). S India Ocean,
S Pacific. HTL 79ft; wt 70 tons.
Skin: silvery-gray; baleen plates:
280–350, black; throat grooves:
76–94; longevity: 65 years.

### Fin whale [V]
*Balaenoptera physalus*

Polar to tropical seas.
HTL 82ft; wt 80 tons.
Skin: gray above, white below,
asymmetrical on jaw; flipper and
flukes white below. Baleen plates:
260–470, blue-gray with whitish
fringes, but left front white. Throat
grooves: 56–100.

### Sei whale
*Balaenoptera borealis*

Polar to tropical seas. HTL 59ft; wt 30
tons. Skin: dark steely-gray, white
grooves on belly. Baleen plates:
320–400, gray-black with pale
fringes. Throat grooves: 32–62.

### Bryde's whale
*Balaenoptera edeni*

Tropical and subtropical seas. HTL
43ft; wt 26 tons. Skin: dark gray.
Baleen plates: 250–370, gray with
dark fringes. Throat grooves: 47–70.

### Minke whale
*Balaenoptera acutorostrata*

Polar to tropical seas. HTL 36ft; wt 10
tons. Skin: dark gray above, belly
and flippers white below; white or
pale band on flippers, especially in
N hemisphere; pale streaks behind
head. Baleen plates: 230–350,
yellowish-white, some black. Throat
grooves: 50–70. Longevity: 45 years.

### Humpback whale [E]
*Megaptera novaeangliae*

Polar to tropical seas. HTL 52ft; wt 65
tons. Skin: black above, grooves
white; flukes with variable white
pattern below. Baleen plates:
270–400, dark gray. Throat grooves:
14–24. Longevity: 95 years.

4

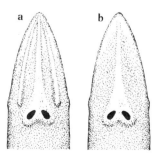

▲ **Species of rorquals.** (1) Humpback whale (*Megaptera novaeangliae*). (2) Minke whale (*Balaenoptera acutorostrata*). (3) Bryde's whale (*Balaenoptera edeni*). (4) Fin whale (*Balaenoptera physalus*). (5) Blue whale (*Balaenoptera musculus*). The Sei whale, not shown here, is similar to Bryde's whale, but they can be distinguished by the top of the head, which has three ridges in Bryde's whale (**a**), only one in the Sei (**b**).

area at a particular time may show an imbalance. The breeding group in these animals tends to be a male and female pair, although the duration of the pair-bond is not known.

It is characteristic of whales, as of many other animals, that they reach sexual maturity at a given body size, which is most conveniently measured in terms of length. Because it appears that there has been an increase in the growth rates of at least the Blue, Fin, Sei, and Minke whales in the Southern Hemisphere since the major reduction in the population numbers of the Blue and Fin whales, all these species are now reaching the critical sizes at which they become sexually mature earlier than before.

For Fin whales born before 1930 the mean age at maturity was a little over 10 years. From the mid-1930s onwards this mean age declined and is now about 6 years. Sei whales up to 1935 had a mean age at maturity of just over 11 years. This age fell to a little under 10 years by 1945 and now has decreased to 7 years in some areas. Even greater reductions are indicated in southern Minke whales, in which the age at sexual maturity has decreased from around 14 years in 1944 to 6 years now.

The future of the rorquals depends on the success of the protection they have received in recent years and, in the Southern Hemisphere, on the conservation of their food-base, krill. There is evidence of increasing numbers in some species, but because of their very slow birth-rate, it will be many decades before there is full recovery, if ever.

RG

# In the Wake of the Giant

*The ecological consequences of overexploitation of the Blue whale*

The sheer size of the Blue whale made it peculiarly vulnerable to exploitation. The oil from its body was used in edible foodstuffs, and it very soon became the prime target for whalers, once they had developed adequate technology to chase, kill and hold on to such a massive carcass, which sinks when dead. This development came in the 1860s, and Norwegian and other European whalers soon caught so many Blue and other large whales in the North Atlantic and adjacent waters that they were forced to find new areas in which to operate.

Rorquals are equally at home in northern and southern polar waters but it was not until 1906 that the whales of the Southern Ocean were discovered. European whalers were quick to exploit these vast whale resources of the Antarctic. The coastal Humpbacks were quickly reduced by shore-based whaling from subantarctic islands and tropical coasts before the oceanic Blue whales became the prime targets. This fishery accelerated in the mid-1920s, with the development of free-ranging floating factory ships on which the whales, killed by a fleet of fast catcher boats, could be processed. The island of South Georgia became the center of the whaling industry.

Over 29,000 Blue whales were killed in the single summer season of 1930/31, and the stocks could not sustain so great a slaughter. The record of the Blue whale fishery in the Antarctic is a tragic illustration of the depletion of a major resource by gross over-catching. The whaling nations continued to reduce the Blue whale stocks despite the warnings of scientists, until they were reduced to about one-thirtieth of their original abundance. The

▲ **The churning power** of the Blue whale at sea, a sight that, earlier this century, almost disappeared from the earth forever.

◄ **Last of the giants.** A Blue whale waiting to be cut up at a whaling station on South Georgia in 1926, during the peak period of Blue whale exploitation.

▼ **Diminishing catch.** Fin whales at Grytviken, South Georgia, in 1961. As the catch of Blue whales dwindled, attention turned to the smaller rorquals, until they too were depleted.

Antarctic industry was maintained by diverting its attention to the smaller Fin whales, and Blue whales were not given total protection from hunting in the Southern Hemisphere until 1965. By this time the original population of some 200,000 Blue whales had been reduced to about 6,000, with about the same number of Pygmy blue whales, a form which has been described as a separate subspecies, paler in color, rather shorter in the tail region and with relatively shorter baleen plates than the ordinary Blue whale. The Pygmy blue whale was first recognized in the southern part of the Indian Ocean, but has also been identified in the waters off Chile.

In the Antarctic, all rorquals tend to have the same food, krill, as the mainstay of their diet. It is not surprising, therefore, that the reduced abundance of the large Blue, Fin and Humpback whales in particular has had some effects on the smaller Sei and Minke whales, and also on the reproductive potential of the larger whales themselves. Now, some 50–55 per cent of mature non-lactating female Blue whales are pregnant. This is an approximate doubling of the rate before the 1930s and reflects a halving of the average interval between successive births. The same change has occurred in Fin and Sei whales, while in Minke whales up to 90 percent of the females sampled in the Antarctic fishery are pregnant (this very high figure may be the result of sampling bias if the catching operations happen to fall on this component of the segregated populations). Proper management of the natural renewable resources represented by the great whales should be based on a harvesting policy which ensures that only the surplus after making good natural deaths is cropped. Because many of the rorquals have been so heavily depleted in the past, the International Whaling Commission has protected them from capture in recent years. This should allow the most rapid rebuilding of the stocks. Those stocks which are still numerous, such as the Minke (more than 425,000) and Bryde's whales (90,000), can at present only be captured in numbers which will not reduce their abundance and there is the prospect that all commercial whaling will end in 1986.

If Blue whales are reproducing more frequently and from an earlier age than in former years, it might be expected that their numbers will start to increase. Unfortunately, the research devoted to monitoring their abundance is insufficient to provide very firm evidence. However, there are some signs from sightings by survey vessels in parts of the Southern Hemisphere that the Blue whales there are slowly increasing, as well as in the North Atlantic, while the stocks in the North Pacific appear to be at least stable rather than declining.

It seems unlikely that total protection will lead simply to a recovery of rorqual populations to their pre-1906 levels. The release of vast quantities of krill that was once consumed by the whales has led to large increases in the populations of other krill-eating species, especially the Crabeater seal (see pp267–268), the Antarctic fur seal (see pp108–109), penguins and other seabirds. The effects of protection of the whales on this complex food-chain, based on krill, will be watched with great interest.    RG

# Water Voices

*The songs of the Humpback whale*

Snores, groans, whos, yups, chirps, ees and oos ... These are some of the "words" man has inadequately used to describe the unique songs of the Humpback whale. Although complex, these songs are repeated according to identifiable patterns, and some can be detected by hydrophones at a range of more than 100 nautical miles (185km).

Like so many discoveries, the songs of Humpbacked whales became known to science almost by chance: attention was first drawn to the songs because they interfered with naval acoustic surveys. The songs' existence has probably been common knowledge to sailors for centuries, since the sounds are transmitted through the hulls of ships. However, the fact that the noises stem from whales has only recently been confirmed by means of directional arrays of underwater hydrophones and simultaneous surface observation. Live skin sampling of the singing subject, and subsequent sexing of the skin chromatin, has so far indicated that it is solitary males in their coastal winter breeding and calving grounds of the warm subtropics who sing, perhaps seeking mates for the first time.

The sounds usually range in frequency between 40Hz and 5kHz, and the song itself is a true song, consisting of an ordered sequence of themes comprising motifs and phrases, like that of birds. It can last from 6 to 35 minutes, and forms part of a "song session" which can continue throughout the day and night with only brief pauses of a minute or so, for breathing, between successive songs. In a session, each song is well defined, following a set sequence, with a beginning and ending, which is usually indicated by the so-called "surface ratchet" noise, followed by blowing. If there is a temporary interruption in singing, the whale recommences where it broke off, and the sequence remains intact.

The song consists of six basic themes which are composed, in descending order of complexity, of so-called phrases, motifs, and approximately 20 syllables, which are often described onomatopeically. Throughout all the themes are interspersed individual "chirps," "cries" and other sundry notes and syllables. The motifs and phrases may be repeated any number of times (a phenomenon known as redundancy) and while the basic song is continually repeated in sessions, the individual phrases can vary in length considerably, which explains the great variability in overall song duration.

While songs of individual animals have their own characteristics, within one season all whales in one region sing what is recognizably the same song. There are at least three regionally distinct dialects in (a) the North Pacific (Hawaii and Pacific Mexico), (b) the North Atlantic (West Indies and Cape Verde Islands) and (c) Tonga in the Southern Hemisphere. The song slowly changes over several seasons: the content of phrases within themes changes slightly throughout each season, new motifs are included or old ones dropped; exceptionally, an entire theme may disappear from an individual's repertoire from one season to the next.

Individual whales appear to have voice characteristics that confer a personal signature on their songs, and the differences between individuals remain recognizable even when within-song variations occur. This may enable females to identify particular mates at any time and any place.

The versatility and acoustic range of vocalizations within the song may increase the efficiency of transmission of information in a noisy environment, and also avoid monotony. The song's repetition of phrases probably reinforces communication and can be detected at least 17 nautical miles (31km) away. The low frequency notes of snores and moans are of high amplitude (60 db.u bar$^{-1}$) and the detection range of such sounds is over 100 nautical miles (185km).

▶ **Humpback themes.** The basic unit of the songs is the syllable, rendered onomatopeically as "yups," "cries," "chirps," etc. These are the equivalent of the notes in our music and are shown here as their sonogram patterns. Motifs, recurring groupings of these syllables, are combined into phrases, which make up the themes. There are six basic themes.

▼ ▶ **The underwater world of the Humpback** is eerily beautiful, both in the songs they sing and their movement. The extremely long flippers have a white leading edge which gleams against the dark blue of the water.

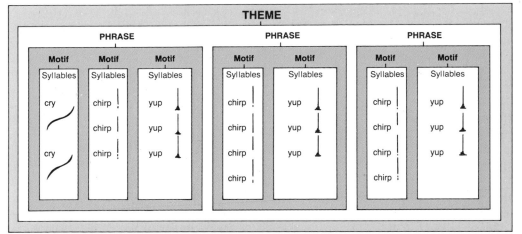

THEME

| PHRASE | | | PHRASE | | PHRASE | |
|---|---|---|---|---|---|---|
| Motif | Motif | Motif | Motif | Motif | Motif | Motif |
| Syllables | Syllables | Syllables | Syllables | Syllables | Syllables | Syllables |
| cry | chirp | yup | chirp | yup | chirp | yup |
| | chirp | yup | chirp | yup | chirp | yup |
| cry | chirp | yup | chirp | yup | chirp | yup |
| | | | chirp | | chirp | |

While most singing is in relatively shallow coastal water, calls (if made) in the range 20–100Hz in colder, deeper water could be detectable at even greater distances. The changing frequencies could also be used to determine range and bearing, so that whales could home in on each other.

It is clear from its continuous nature and ordered sequence that the song potentially contains much information, but its precise function is not known. Most evidence at present indicates that the prime function of the song is sexual.

Humpback whales migrate to the warm 75–82°F (24–28°C) subtropical (latitude 10–22°S) waters for the winter breeding season. On the breeding grounds, the strongest bond is that between cows and their calves. The female, whether with a calf or not, forms the nucleus of any group formation that develops while on these grounds. All the whales appear to return to the same sites from year to year. The males arrive on the grounds and commence singing. They favor shallow coastal areas of depth 65–130ft (20–40m) with smooth bottom contours which probably help sound propagation. Females appear to attract the attentions of the males to a different extent throughout the season, perhaps reflecting whether or not they are receptive or already pregnant. Some believe that the female may experience several receptive cycles while on the grounds if conception fails initially, so optimizing her chances of conceiving.

The female initially attracts a single male escort who for that day or for a few hours acts as her "principal" escort. Soon, other male "hangers-on" jostle for position close to the female. The males all struggle to oust each other by tail-thrashing, lunging and creating bubble-streams. The group size around the female may range from one to six or so males. The principal escort may change daily or even more frequently throughout the season, so that fidelity to one mate does not seem likely, at least in the pre-mating stage.

When the whales join an animal at the center of the group (the "nuclear" animal) they are frequently singing. They then stop until they leave, when they usually resume singing. The nuclear animal never sings, and this, together with the facts that this animal often has a calf, and that the singing escorts are solitary before joining strongly suggest that the nuclear whale is female and that the newcomers are males. One role of the singing is thus likely to be sexual, and probably advertises availability.

# RIGHT WHALES

**Family: Balaenidae**
Three species in 2 genera.
Distribution: arctic and temperate waters. One species in the north only, one in the south only, one in both hemispheres.

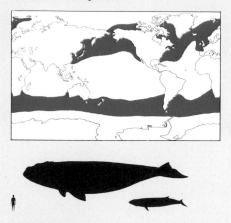

## Right whale E

*Balaena glacialis*
Distribution: temperate waters of both hemispheres; recorded as far south as Florida and as far north as Southern Brazil respectively.
Size: length 16–60ft (5–18m), average adult about 45ft (15m); weight about 50–56 tons.
Skin: black, with white patches on the chin and belly, sometimes extensive. Head and jaws characteristically bearing several large irregular skin callosities infested with parasites. Baleen gray or grayish-yellow, up to 8ft (2.5m) in length.
Gestation: about 10–11 months.
Longevity: not known but probably greater than 30 years.

Subspecies: 3. *B. g. glacialis*; N Atlantic.
*B. g. japonica*; N Pacific. *B. g. australis*; Southern Ocean.

## Bowhead whale E

*Balaena mysticetus*
Distribution: Arctic Basin, with winter migration into Bering and Labrador Seas.
Size: length 11–66ft (3.5–20m), average adult about 51ft (17m); average adult weight probably 60–80 tons.
Skin: body black, except for white or ochreous chin patch; no callosities. Baleen narrow, dark gray to blackish, up to 13ft (4m) in length.
Gestation: 10–11 months.
Longevity: not known, but probably greater than 30 years.

## Pygmy right whale

*Caperea marginata*
Distribution: circumpolar in southern temperate and subantarctic waters. Not a true Antarctic species.
Size: length 6–21ft (2–6.5m), average adult about 15ft (5m); weight about 3–3.5 tons.
Skin: body gray, darker above and lighter below, with some variable pale streaks on the back and shoulders, and dark streaks from eye to flipper. Baleen plates relatively long for its size, whitish with dark outer borders.
Gestation: probably 10–11 months.
Longevity: not known.

E Endangered.

THE Right whale might well wish it had been christened differently. It was so called because it was the "right" whale to hunt—it swam slowly, floated when killed and had a high yield of baleen and oil. In consequence, it is unlikely that any other whale—the Blue whale included—was hunted to such precariously low levels as were the Right whale and its close relative, the Bowhead. Even today, after decades of protection from industrial whaling, the entire Bowhead population still numbers only about 3,000, and the scattered breeding herds of Right whales perhaps barely 4,000 animals.

Despite the definitive-sounding name, there is in fact not one right whale but three—Right whale, Bowhead whale and Pygmy right whale which share certain characters that distinguish them from the rorquals. These include an arched rostrum, giving a deeply curved jawline in profile, in contrast to the nearly straight line of the rorqual mouth; long slender baleen plates instead of relatively short ones as in the rorquals; and only two throat grooves in the Pygmy right whale and none in the large species, compared to many in all rorquals. There are also a number of marked differences in cranial features, not visible in the living or stranded specimen: in particular, the upper jawbone is narrow in right whales and broad in rorquals. In all three species the head is large in proportion to the rest of the body; the two large species are exceptionally bulky in comparison to the rorquals.

A unique feature of the Right whale is the group of protrusions or callosities on the head in front of the blowhole. These outgrowths are infested with colonies of barnacles, parasitic worms and whale lice. The largest patch, on the snout, was called the "bonnet" by old-time whalers, and is a feature by which the species is easily recognized at sea. The function of the callosities is unknown but they are useful in enabling cetologists to identify individuals. In the Bowhead whale the curved jawbone is at its most pronounced and the head may be up to 40 percent of the total body length. The Pygmy right whale is a small, slim species, more like a rorqual in build than either of its large relatives; unlike the other two species, it has a small triangular dorsal fin.

Nothing is known of vocalizations in the Pygmy right whale, and little of those of the Bowhead, but the Right whale has an extensive repertoire. One of these, best described as a loud lowing or bellowing, is

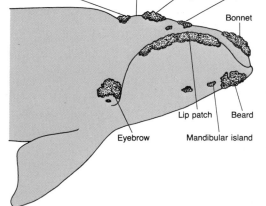

▲ **Basking Right whales** off Península Valdés, South America. The callosities give them a strangely crocodile-like apearance.

◄ ▼ **The Right whale's bonnet** LEFT and other callosities BELOW. Unlike the Gray and Humpback whales, which have parasites scattered randomly over their bodies, the Right whale has concentrated outgrowths, one of which, the bonnet, is always present on the top of the head. The pattern of callosities is individually unique and so facilitates recognition of individuals by scientists.

Post blowhole island  Nostrils  Coaming  Rostral island

Bonnet

Lip patch  Beard

Eyebrow  Mandibular island

made when the animal's head (or at least the nostrils) is above the water. On a quiet day it can be heard for several hundred yards. Low-frequency sounds have been recorded underwater during travel, courtship and play. Vocal activity is said to be greatest at night. Right whales do not seem to produce repeated sequences like the "songs" of Humpback whales (see pp76–77), but make many single and grouped sounds in the 50–500Hz range, some lasting as much as one minute, variously described as "belches" or "moans." The latter may be the sound sometimes heard above the surface. There is also a pulsed sound with a wide frequency spread (30–2,100Hz). Functions are not yet assigned to any of these calls, but it is known that a variable 2–4kHz noise taped during surface feeding is made by water rattling across partially exposed baleen plates.

All the three species feed primarily on copepods, but the North Atlantic Right whale also takes the larvae of krill, and the Southern Ocean population appears to eat adult krill regularly as well. Bowhead feeding is usually associated with restricted belts of high productivity in arctic areas, such as the edge of the plume from the Mackenzie River, where nutrient enrichment and water clarity are both optimal for active photosynthesis by phytoplankton, resulting in turn in relatively high zooplankton production. Both Bowhead and Right whales generally feed by skimming with their mouths open through surface concen-

trations of zooplankton; this is in contrast to the feeding methods of most rorquals (other than Sei whales) which tend to gulp patches of highly concentrated shrimp or fish. In the Bay of Fundy, eastern Canada, Right whales feed as often below the surface as above, diving for 8–12 minutes at a time. Some of the feeding areas there are thickly scattered with fragments of floating rockweed, torn from the beaches by surf action and carried back and forth by the large tides of Fundy; surface feeding runs tend to be short and the whales stop frequently to clean debris from the baleen; they seem to be able to use the tongue to roll the weed into a bolus, and flick it from the mouth, rather like a spent wad of chewing tobacco. When prey concentrations are dense, Right whales feed side by side; under other circumstances because of their considerable food requirement, it is presumably advantageous for animals of such large size to separate to feed. Based on work on rorquals, Bowhead and Right whales probably need 2,200–5,500lb (1,000–2,500kg) of food per day. The Pygmy right whale might require 110–220lb (50–100kg); little is known of its feeding habits, except that two animals taken by the Russians had stomachs full of copepods.

The migratory habits of the Right whale are not fully known, and it is difficult to generalize from the only two areas where rather intensive studies have been made—the Bay of Fundy to Cape Cod region in the North Atlantic, and the Patagonian shelf in

the South Atlantic—since the former is a summer ground and the latter a winter ground. Combined data suggest that calves are born in the late spring–early summer and that mating leading to conception occurs during mid and late summer in the respective hemispheres. The implication, therefore, is that the mating activity observed during the southern winter is more related to social bonding than actual reproduction. The migrations are rather diffuse in comparison to those of the Bowhead, reflecting the less rigorous habitat provided by the temperate zones of the world. Southern populations generally winter off the coasts of southern America, South Africa, Australia and New Zealand, and spend the summer feeding in the Southern Ocean. The North Atlantic population is probably centered somewhere along the Cape Cod to Carolinas region in winter, and spends the summer from Cape Cod to southern Newfoundland, scattered along the edge of the productive North Atlantic Drift.

The Right whale social unit is small, 2–9 animals, and fluid in its composition. Recognizable individuals may be seen alone at some times of day, and within one or other groups later on that day, or on other days. In the Bay of Fundy, they separate, sometimes by as much as several miles, when they begin to feed. Breaching behavior (leaping from the surface) and lobtailing (slapping the water with the flukes) occur frequently in this species; sometimes during courtship, but they are also believed to be a method of indicating position, especially when disturbance increases sea surface noise and limits the range at which vocalizations might otherwise be heard. It is parti-

cularly common in calves, which are especially playful (see pp84–85).

Mating appears to be promiscuous. The reproductive cycle is at least two, and probably three years long, so less than half the adult females in a given area may be receptive to males each year. A female may be surrounded by 2–6 competing males. "Triads" are very common, in which one male supports the female from below while the other copulates. The female circles and dives, with the males accompanying her, in what looks like a courtship "dance" or ritual. She may refuse their advances, either by swimming away or by lying on her back with both flippers in the air, so that her

genital region is inaccessible. Males will then attempt to roll her over in the water, sometimes successfully, other times not. Many of the scars and gouges on the skin of these animals result from pushing and head-butting activity; the callosities are rough enough to inflict abrasions.

The mating activity of Right whales in the Bay of Fundy takes place not only in the summer when most activity might be expected to be directed towards feeding, but also over deep water (more than 660ft; 200m); in contrast, on the coasts of the southern continents, mating is invariably in shallow waters (16–66ft; 5–20m). Probably shallow-water southern winter mating is non-reproductive in nature. No significant shallow-water mating has been noted in the North Atlantic in modern times. Is the Bay of Fundy–Gulf of Maine population a remnant that has adapted to the loss of former shallow-water habitat now that the eastern seaboard of North America is densely settled? Or did this population escape the depredations of coastal whaling because of this offshore-mating and calf-rearing habit? These questions remain unanswered.

The annual migratory cycle of the Bowhead is best seen in the Bering Sea–Beaufort Sea population, which is by far the largest surviving stock of this species, and the best-known in the Arctic. Distributions are closely connected with seasonal changes in the position and extent of ice-free areas. The route and timing of migration in any given year are dictated by the patterns of development of open channels (leads) between the ice floes from the northern Bering Sea eastward to the Amundsen Gulf during the spring and summer months.

Bowheads winter in the Bering Sea, particularly in the vicinity of St. Lawrence and St. Matthew Islands, and it is here that the calves are born. Mating occurs during the first stage of the northeastward migration in the spring. Aerial and satellite photographs reveal that the ice in the northern Bering and southern Chukchi Seas develops series of fractures in April which first open to Cape Lisburne and then Point Barrow. The leads are relatively close to shore, so that most of the population passes Barrow on their way

▲ **The three species of right whales.** (1) Right whale (*Balaena glacialis*), showing its huge baleen and tongue, deeply arched lower jaw and callosities. (2) Bowhead whale (*Balaena mysticetus*), with an even more pronounced curve to the lower jaw than the Right whale, but no callosities. (3) Pygmy right whale (*Caperea marginata*), which has a dorsal fin and only moderate bowing of the lower jaw.

◄ **The mating chase.** ABOVE Northern Right whales mating in the Bay of Fundy, Canada. BELOW A female Southern Right whale pursued by three males in shallow water at José Gulf, off Patagonia.

into the Beaufort Sea. Beyond Barrow, however, the winds and current circulation open large offshore leads and the eastward migration shifts further from land. Whales reach Cape Bathurst and the Amundsen Gulf as early as May. The slow breakup of coastal ice east of Alaska normally prevents Bowheads utilizing the Mackenzie Delta and Yukon shore in any numbers until the second half of July.

Eskimo hunters state that there is segregation by age and sex during this migration (as in Australian Humpback whales). The migration certainly takes place in "pulses," with animals during May and June straggling in a column along the whole length of the route from Barrow to southwestern Banks Island. The return migration to the Bering Sea in late summer-early fall tends not only to be rather rapid (according to old whaling records) but also further offshore along the route, and hence less easy to observe.

Until recently the Pygmy right whale was one of the least known cetaceans, ranking with the rarer beaked whales. It is easy to confuse at sea with the Minke whale. In the 1960s, however, some South African biologists noted unusual whales in False Bay, which proved to be Pygmy right whales. Prior to this, most information had come from specimens stranded in southern Australia, Tasmania and southern New Zealand. In 1967 the species was sighted again in South Africa, in Plettenberg Bay, and this time some underwater cine film was obtained.

The species resembles the Right whale in its preference for relatively shallow water at some times of year, and there is speculation that mating occurs during this inshore phase. Nevertheless, Pygmy rights have been seen during most months of the year in all the regions from which it has been reported, so it may be a species which has localized populations and limited migrations. There, however, the resemblance to its large distant cousins ends; no deep diving for long periods has been noted despite an earlier suggestion that the peculiar flattening of the underside of the ribcage might indicate that it spent long periods on the bottom. There is none of the exuberant tail-fluking or lob-tailing and breaching characteristic of the large species. It swims relatively slowly, often without the dorsal fin breaking the surface, and the whole snout usually breaks clear of the water at surfacing, behavior similar to that of Minke whales. The respiratory rhythm of undisturbed animals is regular, somewhat

less than one blow per minute, in sequence of about five ventilations, with dives of 3–4 minutes between them. Its general behavior has been characterized as "unspectacular"—another feature, coupled with its small size, that has certainly contributed to the lack of records of the species. It appears to be present in subantarctic and southern temperate zones right around the globe; areas of low human population density and relatively little land mass.

All remaining concentrations of Bowhead and Right whales are but remnants of much larger populations. The earliest Right whale hunting, by the Basques, began shortly after the Norman invasion of Britain, and the last Right and Bowhead whaling by Europeans and Americans was in the 1930s; they were finally given almost total protection, except for the arctic Eskimo hunt, in 1936. Much Right whale hunting was carried out in Southern Hemisphere bays; some of the richest hauls were made on the coasts of New Zealand, sometimes at considerable risk of attack from the war-like Maori tribes of the notorious Cloudy Bay and elsewhere. Traditionally, the whalers would attempt to take a calf first to draw the mother close inshore for an easy kill and retrieval. This tactic hardly favored replenishment of the exploited populations. The carcasses were hauled ashore, or into the shallows, and the baleen cut out. If the oil was taken, the blubber was stripped and cut into pieces to be "rendered down" in large cast iron "try pots." Some of these pots, several feet in diameter, have been preserved; one is on

▲ **The importance of the Bowhead** to Alaskan Eskimos is symbolized by this print, *One Chance*, by Bernard Katexac; 1974.

▶ **Cutting up a Bowhead.** Alaskan Eskimos are still heavily dependent on the Bowhead (see Box).

▼ **Going down.** The tail of a Southern Right whale about to disappear beneath the waves. Right whales are noted for their exuberant lob-tailing, bringing the tail crashing down onto the sea's surface.

## The Alaska Bowhead Hunt

The Eskimo peoples of Alaska hunted Bowhead whales with ivory or stone-tipped harpoons and sealskin floats for thousands of years; when the whale population in the Bering Sea region still numbered 10,000 or more, the effect of this village hunt was negligible. In the 19th century, American and European whalers reduced both western and eastern Bowhead populations to a few hundreds or less in a matter of decades. This type of whaling ceased in the 1930s but the Eskimo hunt persists and may now be having a significant impact on the recovery of at least the western (Bering Sea) Bowhead population. Other factors, such as predation by Killer whales and death by crushing or suffocation under ice they cannot break, may also be implicated in the failure of the eastern population to recover to its pre-mass-exploitation levels.

The traditional hunting methods of the Eskimos have been replaced by modern rifles and grenade-tipped darting guns. This has increased the catch, but the number of animals wounded but not landed has not decreased as might have been expected—in fact, this may actually have increased. While some wounded animals obviously survive, it is probable that many more do not, so that the landed catch of Bowheads represents only part of the annual mortality caused by hunting. The Bowheads follow the inshore lead in the pack ice eastward in the spring, making them vulnerable to the Alaskan

hunters even when they are present in very low numbers.

Many world conservation groups, and the scientific committee of the International Whaling Commission, have recommended that the hunt cease. The Alaskan Eskimo vehemently insist that it is materially and culturally necessary for their own welfare, and must continue. Biologists have recently concluded that present population size and the annual production rate of western Bowhead whales can permit only the most limited catch, to prevent the population from decreasing again, if indeed it has not already done so. What little evidence there is suggests that Bowheads are slow to mature and that females do not give birth more often than once every two or three years. Preferably, there should be no catch at all, so that the population can increase at the maximum rate. It is clear that the United States government will have to make a politically unpleasant choice in the relatively near future between the "cultural survival" of the whale-hunting communities, and the physical survival of the Bowhead. They rejected the thesis that Bowhead whale products were necessary for the *material* survival of the Eskimo communities in the 1980s. The question of *cultural* necessity defies definition, but these authors suggest that substitution of a small catch of the much more numerous Californian Gray whale by the Eskimo could satisfy both nutritional and cultural needs.

display at Kaikoura on the east coast of the South Island of New Zealand.

Although, technically, Right whales have worldwide protection, the Bowhead is still hunted by some Eskimo on the coast of Alaska, and there are some acute threats locally to their shallow, coastal habitats. The relatively large southwest Atlantic population shelters in the Golfo Nuevo and Golfo San José region of Patagonia, perilously close to oil rigs and other industrial activity sanctioned by Argentina.

What then is the general prospect for Right whales? Some evidence has been presented that the Southern Ocean and western North Atlantic populations of the Right whale might be increasing, but in each case the figures are inconclusive. The North Pacific population appears to have stabilized at a few hundred. The Bowhead population of the western North American Arctic is in a perilous situation, yet would seem to have more prospect of survival than the remnants of the eastern Arctic and European Arctic stocks. The inshore habit of both the large species will continue to render them vulnerable to the expansion of human regions, and the consequent impact of interference and pollution. Unless the right whales are given active protection in some critical areas, it is possible that only the Pygmy right whale will survive long into the 21st century.                DEG

# Life in the Nursery

*The playful Right whale calf*

In Right whales the period of nursing is prolonged and the antics of the young calves notably boisterous and playful. Southern Right whale females bear a single calf every three years. The 18ft (5.5m) long infant is born in mid-winter after a gestation of about a year, and stays with its mother for up to 14 months. One major calving area is at Península Valdés, Argentina. The calves are born in protected bays of this peninsula and the mother/calf pairs remain there until the calves are about four months old. During this time in sheltered waters, the suckling calves are gradually acquiring skills in a wide variety of activities.

No one has witnessed the birth of a Right whale calf, but like other whales they are probably born tail first and may be pushed to the surface for their first breaths of air. The newborn calf's tail, which shows fold marks from being doubled over in the mother's womb, is quite floppy at birth, but stiffens up quickly with use, and the calf is probably able to swim on its own within a few hours of birth.

Right whale calves must dive down to the underside of their mothers to nurse. The mother can probably squirt milk forcefully from her nipples into the calf's mouth. Other species have been reported to nurse their calves while lying on their sides, but this has not been observed for Right whales.

To begin with, the newborn calf simply swims beside its mother. It breathes in a jerky, awkward fashion, throwing its head up sharply to ensure that its blowholes clear the water before it inhales. Its mother, by contrast, comes up smoothly, often barely rippling the calm waters as she surfaces to breathe. After about three weeks the calf moves away from its mother's side for the first time. At first it hurries back to her, but later it makes a game of repeatedly leaving and approaching the mother.

The calf further develops the circling behavior when it learns to breach. In breaching the whale jumps to bring three-quarters of its body clear of the water, and then lands on its back with a huge splash. Young calves first experience the sensation of breaching while swimming quickly after their mothers in large waves. The upward thrust of the head to breathe combines with the rapid forward motion to throw the body out of the waves. Later, calves breach intentionally, several times during each circle out from the mother and up to 80 times or more in an hour.

Most early activity is centered around the mother—circling, touching, lying on her back. At other times the calf plays near the mother but does not pay her much attention. Rolling upside down is one such absorbing activity. The calf has learned to do this at the age of one and a half months, controlling its stability by flattening or rounding its lung-chest cavity. At first, it can only manage a quick complete roll, but with practice it is able to remain upside down for several minutes. Other behavior that does not center around the mother includes slapping a flipper or the tail flukes onto the water. These actions produce a large splash and a sharp report.

In play the calf learns and practices many behavior patterns that are important in adult life. Courting adult Right whales often roll upside-down to bring themselves belly to belly with a sexual partner. They stroke one another with their flippers and approach each other much as the circling calf does its mother. Adult whales slap their flippers and flukes as a defensive measure against Killer whales and an agitated mother may slap its flipper when separated from its calf.

As with most animals, the movements involved in play are combined in a different manner from their use in activity. Instead of concluding its approach with a roll underneath, as an adult would approach a potential mate, the Right whale calf may approach its mother, and hug her with its flipper, but then circle away and repeat its approach several times. Instead of slapping its flipper in the direction of a Killer whale or a

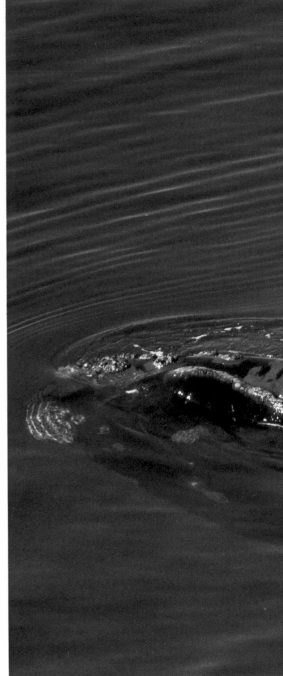

▲ **A close bond.** Mother and calf Southern Right whale stay together for up to 14 months, when the calf is weaned, and the mother leaves for the feeding grounds alone.

▶ **Shallow playground.** A Southern Right whale and her calf in the warm green-blue shallows off Argentina. On the beach are basking elephant seals.

◀ **Suckling and circling.** The calf has to dive beneath its mother to suckle, between visits to the surface to breathe (1). From about three weeks old, the calf begins to elaborate this into a game of approaching and leaving the mother (2). Tentative at first, the calf becomes more and more playful when it learns to roll onto its side. Now it makes quick careening corners, banking like an airplane, the pectoral flipper rising out of the water. The calf's repeated and increasingly complex circles and figures-of-eight incorporate rolling, putting the chin up against the mother's side, and slapping the water with the flipper.

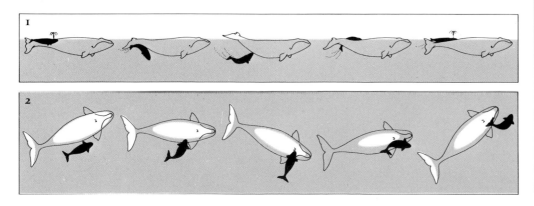

restlessness strengthens the calf's muscles for the long voyage ahead and gives the calf practice in staying beside its now more rapidly moving mother. Close contact with her is essential, not only for nourishment and protection but also because the calf gets hydrodynamic lift from the mother, much as a goose in a flock saves energy by flying beside and slightly behind another.

It is not known if the calves feed on plankton during their first southern summer on the feeding grounds, though they certainly do continue to nurse. Their mothers feed for the first time in the 4–6 months since their calves were born. Mothers save energy during the nursery period at Península Valdés by resting quietly in the shallows for about a quarter of the time spent there, but they also bear large costs at that time, supporting their calves' growth of 3ft (1m) a month, and their boisterous play (calves play up to 28 per cent of the time), on milk produced during that period. The summer feeding is crucial for the mothers if they are to rebuild their depleted reserves of the fat necessary to survive the calving season.

By the time the mothers return to Península Valdés with their yearling calves, after six months in deeper waters, they are beginning to wean them. If the calf strays from its mother's side she no longer goes to retrieve it. At this stage it is the calf which ensures that they remain together. It is remarkable that a female abandons her calf a full year before she will mate again. This suggests that she needs this year to replenish her resources in preparation for her next period of pregnancy and lactation. During the year before mating, the mother, unburdened by the demands of a calf, probably feeds intensively. Female Right whales are larger than males, and this probably reflects the need of the female to store large energy reserves which help her bear the cost of gestating and suckling her young.

There is conflict between the need of the mother to prepare physiologically to bear another calf, and the benefit that the calf will derive from continuing to get nourishment and protection from its mother. This conflict is resolved when the mother leaves the Valdés area after 2–8 weeks there. The calf stays in the sheltered waters, interacting on the fringes of groups of older sub-adults engaged in boisterous play, occasionally joining up with other yearlings, or playing quietly in the vicinity of adults. In late spring the yearling migrates to the feeding grounds, perhaps in the company of other whales. POT

competitor for a mate, the calf slaps its flipper onto its mother's back.

Though several dozen mother-calf pairs may be seen along a few miles of coastline, each pair is largely solitary, rarely interacting with other pairs in the area, with which they form a large loose herd. Also in the area, generally somewhat removed from the mothers and calves, are groups of up to 10 adults and sub-adults, often engaged in active social and sexual behavior. Mothers and calves tend to avoid these groups, keeping closer to the shore than the other whales in the area.

In mid-November the behavior of mother and calf changes suddenly, as they prepare to leave the sheltered lagoons for summer feeding grounds in mid-ocean. The calves cease their boisterous play and the mother-calf pairs begin to move quickly back and forth along the shores of the peninsula. This

# SEALS AND SEA LIONS

## ORDER: PINNIPEDIA
Three families: 17 genera: 33 species.

### Eared seals
Family: Otariidae.
Fourteen species in 7 genera.
Includes **Antarctic fur seal** (*Arctocephalus gazella*), **California sea lion** (*Zalophus californianus*), **Northern fur seal** (*Callorhinus ursinus*), **South American sea lion** (*Otaria flavescens*).

### Walrus
Family: Odobenidae
One species: **Walrus** (*Odobenus rosmarus*).

### True or Hair seals
Family: Phocidae.
Nineteen species in 10 genera.
Includes **Bearded seal** (*Erignathus barbatus*), **Crabeater seal** (*Lobodon carcinophagus*), **Grey seal** (*Halichoerus grypus*), **Harbor seal** (*Phoca vitulina*), **Harp seal** (*Phoca groenlandica*), **Leopard seal** (*Hydrurga leptonyx*), **Northern elephant seal** (*Mirounga angustirostris*), **Ribbon seal** (*Phoca fasciata*), **Ross seal** (*Ommatophoca rossi*), **Southern elephant seal** (*Mirounga leonina*), **Weddell seal** (*Leptonychotes weddelli*).

Few people have difficulty in recognizing a seal. A lithe, streamlined body with all four limbs modified into flippers is sufficient to assign any member of the group correctly to the order Pinnipedia, the seals in the broad sense. The word Pinnipedia refers to this modification and is derived from two Latin words: *pinna*, a feather or wing, and *pes* (genitive, *pedis*), a foot. The pinnipeds are thus the wing-footed mammals.

The Pinnipedia include three families—the Odobenidae, which today has only a single species, the walrus; the Otariidae, the eared seals, containing 14 species, and the Phocidae, the true seals, with 18 species (or possibly 19, if the Caribbean monk seal is not in fact extinct). The similarities between the Odobenidae and the Otariidae are sufficient to justify combining them into a superfamily: the Otarioidea. They are, however, quite distinct from the Phocidae, and most biologists today believe that the two groups arose separately from the carnivore stock: the eared seals about 25 million years ago and the true seals about 15 million years ago (see pp101, 113 and 119). The degree of relationship between pinnipeds and carnivores is a matter of debate. Some authorities believe its groups to be sufficiently related to place the pinnipeds within the Carnivora. Here we keep them separate.

The similarities between eared and true seals are more striking than the differences and it is these, in fact, that make recognition of a "seal" easy. The reason for this similarity is simple—all pinnipeds had to modify the basic mammalian pattern, which is designed for life on land, into a body form adapted to life in the three dimensional environment of water. Water is very much denser and more viscous than air. This meant that body form and locomotion methods had to change. Animals lose heat to water far more rapidly than they do to air; this meant that in order to avoid damaging losses of body

heat, pinnipeds had to develop strategies of heat conservation. Finally, because the oxygen dissolved in water is not available for respiration by mammals, the pinnipeds had to develop a suite of adaptations connected with maintaining activity while ventilating the lungs relatively infrequently—the whole comprising the physiology of diving.

These problems have confronted all three mammalian groups that have become aquatic. However, while the Cetacea (whales and dolphins) and Sirenia (manatees and sea cows) have severed all links with the land, the Pinnipedia find their food in the sea but are still tied to the land (or to ice) as a place where they must bring forth their young and suckle them. These two characteristics, offshore marine feeding and terrestrial birth, have left their mark on most aspects of the lives of pinnipeds.

▲ **Underwater acrobats.** All pinnipeds are agile and graceful in the water, less so on land. These are Australian sea lions.

► **The characteristic features** of the families of pinnipeds. (1) The Harbor seal (*Phoca vitulina*), a typical true seal, showing (1a) the sleek hair and lack of external ear flaps. True seals are cumbersome on land (1b), being unable to raise themselves by their foreflippers. (2) The Cape fur seal (*Arctocephalus pusillus*), a typical eared seal, showing (2a) the scroll-like external ear flaps and thick fur; the male shown here has a particularly thick mane. On land (2b) eared seals support themselves on their foreflippers and bring the rear flippers beneath the body. (3) The walrus (*Odobenus rosmarus*), showing (3a) its distinctive tusks, which on land (3b) are often used as levers.

**ORDER PINNIPEDIA**

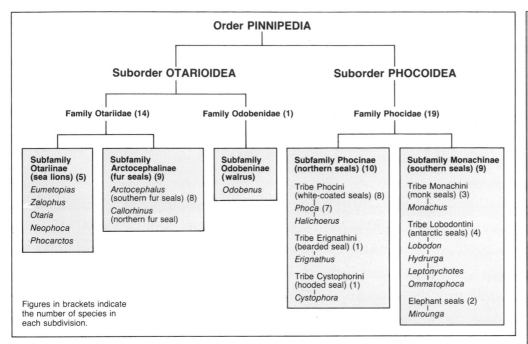

Order PINNIPEDIA

Suborder OTARIOIDEA

Suborder PHOCOIDEA

Family Otariidae (14)

Family Odobenidae (1)

Family Phocidae (19)

**Subfamily Otariinae (sea lions) (5)**
Eumetopias
Zalophus
Otaria
Neophoca
Phocarctos

**Subfamily Arctocephalinae (fur seals) (9)**
Arctocephalus (southern fur seals) (8)
Callorhinus (northern fur seal)

**Subfamily Odobeninae (walrus)**
Odobenus

**Subfamily Phocinae (northern seals) (10)**
Tribe Phocini (white-coated seals) (8)
Phoca (7)
Halichoerus
Tribe Erignathini (bearded seal) (1)
Erignathus
Tribe Cystophorini (hooded seal) (1)
Cystophora

**Subfamily Monachinae (southern seals) (9)**
Tribe Monachini (monk seals) (3)
Monachus
Tribe Lobodontini (antarctic seals) (4)
Lobodon
Hydrurga
Leptonychotes
Ommatophoca
Elephant seals (2)
Mirounga

Figures in brackets indicate the number of species in each subdivision.

## The Pinniped Body Plan

The sleek pinniped body is spindle-shaped and the head rounded, tapering smoothly into the trunk without any abrupt constriction at the neck. External projections have been reduced to a minimum. In the eared seals (sea lions and fur seals), the external ear flaps have been reduced to small elongated scrolls. It is these that have given the group its name, from the Greek *otarion*, a little ear. In the true seals and the walrus, external ears have been dispensed with altogether. In these two groups also, the testes are internal, while in all pinnipeds the penis lies in an internal sheath so that there is no external projection. The non-scrotal, internal testes of true seals are protected from sterilizing body heat by the flow of cool blood from a network of blood vessels in the hind flippers. Similarly, the nipples of pinnipeds (two in true seals, except for the Bearded seal and the monk seals, which have four, as do eared seals) are retracted and lie flush with the surface of the body. The mammary glands form a sheet of tissue extending over the lower surface and flanks, and even when actively secreting milk do not cause any projection on the body outline. The general contours of the body are smoothed by the layer of fatty tissue or blubber that lies beneath the skin, though as we shall see later, this has a more important role to play than just streamlining.

The flippers, of course, necessarily project from the body, though even they project much less than the limbs of most mammals. The arm and leg bones are relatively short and are contained within the body, the axilla (which corresponds to the armpit of

man) and crotch occurring at the level of the wrist (forearm in eared seals) and ankle respectively. However, most of the bones of the hand and foot are greatly elongated. The digits are joined by a web of skin and connective tissue, and this combined surface provides the propulsive thrust against the water in swimming.

The method of locomotion is different in eared and true seals, with the walrus intermediate between the two. Eared seals swim by making long, simultaneous sweeps of the foreflippers, "flying" through the water like a penguin, or rowing themselves along. The foreflippers form broad blades with elongated digits, the first being much longer than the others. The hindflippers appear to play no part in sustained swimming (except perhaps as a rudder), but in confined quarters or when maneuvering slowly the webs of the hindflippers may be expanded and they appear to play some role as paddles.

True seals, on the other hand, use their hindflippers almost exclusively for swimming. The locomotory movements are alternate strokes of the flipper, the digits being spread on the inward power stroke, so as to apply the greatest area to the water, and contracted on the recovery stroke. The movements of the flippers are accompanied by lateral undulations of the hind end of the body, which swings from side to side alternately with the flipper movements. Normally, the foreflippers are held close to the sides, where they fit into depressions in the surface. However, they may be used as paddles for positioning movements during slow swimming.

The walrus, which is a slow and cum-

THE PINNIPED BODY PLAN

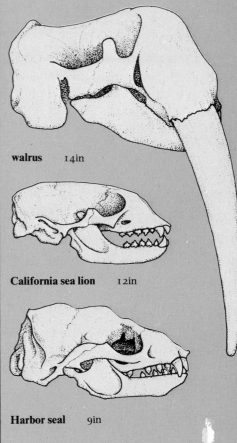

▼ **Skulls** of walrus, California sea lion (an eared seal) and Harbor seal (a true seal). The skulls of true and eared seals are generally similar, except for the region behind the articulation of the lower jaw.

**walrus**    14in

**California sea lion**    12in

**Harbor seal**    9in

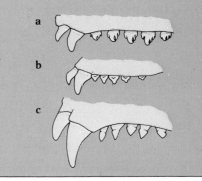

▼ **The teeth** of pinnipeds are more variable in number than those of most land carnivores. The teeth of the Crabeater seal (**a**) have quite elaborate cusps which leave only small gaps when the jaws are closed. This relates to its habit of feeding almost exclusively on the small crustacean, krill. In contrast, the Weddell seal (**b**), feeding on fish and bottom invertebrates, has far simpler teeth. The dental formula of both Crabeater and Weddell seals is I1/1 or 2, C1/1, P5/5, that of the South American sea lion (**c**) I3/2, C1/1, P6/5.

a
b
c

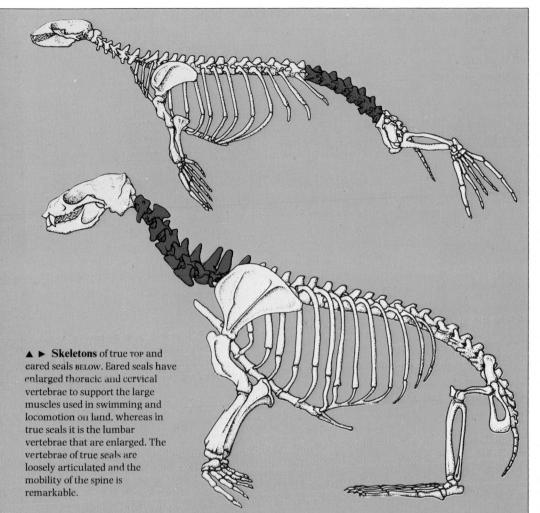

▲ ► **Skeletons** of true TOP and eared seals BELOW. Eared seals have enlarged thoracic and cervical vertebrae to support the large muscles used in swimming and locomotion on land, whereas in true seals it is the lumbar vertebrae that are enlarged. The vertebrae of true seals are loosely articulated and the mobility of the spine is remarkable.

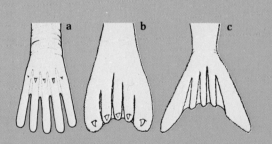

▲ **Hindflippers** of (a) a sea lion, (b) Harbor seal, (c) an elephant seal. In sea lions there are cartilaginous extensions to the digits and the nails are reduced to nonfunctional nodules. some distance from the edge. The Harbor seal, like all northern true seals, has large claws, but these are reduced in southern seals, like the elephant seals, which have fibrous tissue between the digits, increasing the flipper's surface.

▼ **Forelimbs** of pinnipeds and carnivores contrasted. Compared to the greyhound (a), both true seals (b) and eared seals (c) show broadening and elongation of the digits. In eared seals, the digits decrease in length serially from the first. The foreflippers of true seals are more variable: the fifth digit of northern true seals is not much shorter than the first but in the monk seals, shown here, the fifth is considerably shorter, while the other four are of similar length.

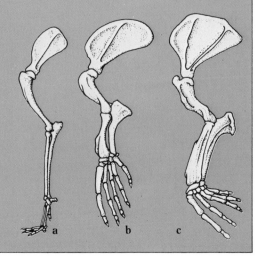

brous swimmer, uses its foreflippers to some extent but relies mainly on the hindlimbs for its propulsive power. The flippers are similar to those of eared seals, although the fore-flippers are shorter and more square.

Grooming, which is an important subsidiary function of the limbs, is generally carried out by the hindflippers in eared seals and by the foreflippers in true seals. How the Ross seal, which has practically no claws, grooms itself is a mystery.

The different swimming techniques of eared and true seals are reflected in their anatomy. The main source of power in the eared seal comes from the front end of the body, and it is here that the main muscle mass is concentrated. True seals, on the other hand, have their main muscles in the lumbar region. The muscles of the hindlimb itself are mainly concerned with orientation of the limb and spreading and contracting the digits, and play little part in applying the power.

On land, eared seals are much more agile than the other groups. When moving, the weight of the body is supported clear of the ground on the outwardly turned foreflippers and the hindflippers are flexed forwards under the body. The foreflippers are moved alternately when the animal is moving slowly, and the hindflippers advanced on the opposite side. Only the heel of the foot is placed on the ground, the digits being held up. As the speed of progression increases, first the hindflippers and then the fore-flippers are moved together, the animal moving forward in a gallop. In this form of locomotion, the counterbalancing action of the neck is very important, the body being balanced over the foreflippers. It has been suggested that if the neck were only half its length, eared seals would be unable to move on land. Walruses move in a similar, though much more clumsy, manner.

On land, true seals crawl along on their bellies, "humping" along by flexing their bodies, taking the weight alternately on the chest and pelvis. Some, such as the elephant seals, or the Grey seal, use the foreflippers to take the weight of the body. Grey seals may also use the terminal digits of the foreflippers to produce a powerful grip when moving among rocks. Other true seals, such as the Weddell seal, for example, make no use of the foreflippers. Ribbon and Crabeater seals can make good progress over ice or compacted snow by alternate backward strokes of the foreflippers and vigorous flailing movements of the hindflippers and hind end of the body, almost as though they were swimming on the surface of the ice.

## Heat Conservation

Because sea water is always colder, and usually very much colder, than blood temperature—approximately 99°F (37°C)—and heat is lost much more rapidly to water than to air, seals need adaptations to avoid excessive loss of heat from the body surface. One way of doing this is to reduce the area of surface. The streamlining of the seal's body, which has reduced projecting appendages, has already gone some way towards achieving this. Another important method is to take advantage of the relationship between surface and volume: for bodies of the same shape, larger ones have relatively less surface area. Seals have exploited this strategy to reduce heat loss, and seals are all large mammals in the literal sense, there being no small pinnipeds, as there are small rodents, insectivores or carnivores.

Another way to control heat loss is to insulate what surface there is. The layer of air trapped in the hair coat typical of mammals is an effective insulator in air. However, in water a hair coat is much less effective, since the air layer is expelled as the hair is wetted. Even so, by retaining a more or less stationary layer of water against the surface of the body it will have a significant effect. One group of pinnipeds, the fur seals, has, however, developed hair as a method of effective insulation. The coat of all pinnipeds consists of a great number of units, each composed of a bundle of hairs and a pair of associated sebaceous (oil) glands. In each hair bundle, there is a long, stout, deeply rooted guard hair and a number of finer, shorter fur fibers. In true seals and sea lions only a few (1–5) of these fibers grow in each bundle, but in the fur seals they comprise a dense mat of underfur. The fine tips of the fur fibers and the secretions of the sebaceous glands make the fur water-repellent, so that the water cannot penetrate to the skin surface.

Fur is an effective insulator, but it has the disadvantage that if the seal dives the air layer in the fur is compressed, by half its thickness for each 33ft (10m) depth, reducing its efficiency accordingly. Because of this, seals have developed another mode of insulation. This is a thick layer of fatty tissue, or blubber, beneath the skin, which also provides energy during fasting and lactation. Fat is a poor conductor of heat and a blubber layer is about half as effective an

## KEEPING COOL

▲ **The blushing walrus.** The skin of walruses becomes engorged with blood during hot weather, giving rise to a brick-red coloration. In contrast, old bulls, in which the natural pigmentation has faded, can appear deathly pale after immersion in cold water.

▼ **Flipper fanning.** In very warm conditions, seals fan their flippers to lose heat across their broad surfaces. These are California sea lions.

insulator as an equal thickness of fur in air. When in water, however, the blubber insulation is reduced to about a quarter of its value in air, but this is unaffected by the depth to which the seal dives. Seals commonly have in excess of 3–4in (7–10cm) of blubber, which effectively prevents heat loss from the body core. True seals have thicker blubber than eared seals.

In cold conditions, loss of heat from the flippers, which do not have an insulating covering, is minimized by reducing the flow of blood to them, only sufficient circulation being maintained to prevent freezing. Beneath the capillary bed, there are special shunts between the arterioles and venules known as arterio-venous anastomoses, or AVAs. By opening the AVAs more blood can be circulated through the superficial layers and heat can be lost when necessary.

Insulation which is effective in the water will also be effective in air, and a Weddell seal, for example, can comfortably endure an air temperature of −40°F (−40°C) on the ice. Skin surface temperatures, of course, may be much higher than the air temperature if the sun is shining. Most seals can thus easily tolerate cold climates, since almost any air temperature can be endured and water can never become much colder than about 28°F (−1.8°C). Pinnipeds are indeed characteristic of the polar regions, both north and south. However, not all pinnipeds live in cold climates, and for those in temperate or tropical regions (mainly eared seals and monk seals) a major problem is likely to be disposing of excess heat when out of the water. Monk seals in Hawaii avoid dry beaches on sunny days and, at the other extreme, Harbor seals in Nova Scotia take to the water when the air is below 5°F (−15°C).

Fur seals can suffer severely from heat stress after periods of activity. Heat can be lost only across the surface of the naked flippers. To do this, the AVAs are dilated, so that more blood is diverted through the superficial layer, and heat is then radiated away from the black surface of the flippers. This may be aided by spreading the flippers widely, fanning them in the air, or by urinating on them.

True seals have AVAs over the whole of the body. Blubber contains blood vessels, and a true seal can divert blood through to the skin surface and lose heat. Conversely, the system can be used to gain heat from radiation in bright sunshine, even at very low air temperatures. Walruses also have AVAs over their body surface and a herd of basking walruses may appear quite pink in

color because of the blood being diverted to the skin.

Periodically, it is necessary for any pinniped to renew its hair covering and the superficial layer of its skin. In eared seals, molt is a relatively prolonged process. The underfur fibers are molted first; in fur seals some of the molted fibers are retained in the hair canal. Guard hairs are molted shortly afterwards, but not all are lost at each molt. In true seals, molt is a much more abrupt process. In order that the necessary growth of new hair may take place, the blood supply to the skin has to be increased, which means also an increased heat loss. Because of this, most seals stay out of the water for much of the duration of the molt and some, such as elephant seals, may gather in large heaps, conserving heat by lying in contact with their neighbors.

## Diving
An air-breathing mammal in an aquatic environment must, as a first necessity, be able to prevent water from entering its lungs. Pinnipeds reflexly close their nostrils on immersion. The slits of the nostrils are under muscular control, and once immersed the pressure of the water will tend to hold them closed. Similarly, the soft palate and tongue together at the back of the mouth close off the buccal cavity from the larynx and esophagus when a seal needs to open its mouth under water, for example to seize prey.

Coupled with these adaptations is, of

▲ **A map of the molt.** During the molt, the skin of elephant seals resembles a map of the oceans they inhabit! Uniquely among seals, elephant seals shed the superficial layer of the skin in large flakes and patches, along with the rather scanty hair.

▼ **Hair bundles** of true seal LEFT and a fur seal RIGHT. In true seals the primary (guard) hair is accompanied by only a few secondary hairs, but in fur seals there may be 50 such fibers to each guard hair, giving a fiber density of up to 360,000 per sq in. This dense mat is supported by the shafts of the guard hairs, as in the pelt section BELOW.

course, the need to be able to hold the breath for extended periods. True seals have much better breath-holding capacities than eared seals, which seldom dive for more than five minutes or so. Despite this, the Cape fur seal has been shown to be able to hunt its prey below 330ft (100m), and the California sea lion has reached 240ft (73m) under natural conditions and 820ft (250m) after training. In comparison, true seals can dive for much longer periods. Elephant seals can stay submerged for at least 30 minutes and a Weddell seal has been timed in a dive lasting 73 minutes in the wild.

Breath-holding capacities can be increased by taking down more oxygen with each dive. Seals increase their rate and depth of breathing before diving, but they do not dive with full lungs, since this would create buoyancy problems. True seals exhale most of the breath before they dive. Sea lions, on the other hand, seem often to dive with at least partially inflated lungs. True seals have greater blood volume per unit body-weight than other mammals, that of the Weddell seal being about two-and-half times that of an equivalent-sized man. Additionally, the blood contains more oxygen-carrying hemoglobin, so that the oxygen capacity of the blood is about three times that of man. There are also greater concentrations of another oxygen-binding protein, myoglobin, in the muscles of seals. Myoglobin concentrations in the Weddell seal are about ten times that in man.

Even these increased oxygen stores would not be sufficient for prolonged diving unless there were associated physiological changes. When a seal dives, a complex response occurs, of which the most obvious component is a slowing of the heart-rate—the output of the heart drops to 10–20 percent of its pre-dive value and the blood flow is diverted largely to the brain. This enables the seal to use its available oxygen in the most economical manner, and the oxygen requirement of several organs, the liver and kidney for example, is significantly curtailed.

In the Weddell seal, under natural conditions, dives are usually fairly short, lasting less than 20 minutes, and metabolism is of the conventional aerobic (oxygen-using) kind, with carbon dioxide as the waste product. If dives longer than 30 minutes are undertaken the metabolism (except in the brain) becomes anaerobic (does not use oxygen) and lactic acid accumulates in the muscles as a waste product. Seals have considerable resistance to high concentrations of lactic acid and carbon dioxide in

their blood, but after such a dive there has to be a period of recovery, which leaves the animal incapable of further intense diving activity for some time. A 45-minute dive, for example, requires a surface period of 60 minutes. Consequently, long anaerobic dives are rare in nature.

Dives to great depth also involve the seals in problems relating to pressure. Weddell seals commonly dive to 1,000–1,300ft (300–400m), and have been known to reach 2,000ft (600m). At this depth, the pressure in the seal will be about 910lb per sq in (64kg per sq cm), compared to a pressure in air of 14lb per sq in (1kg per sq cm). As liquids are virtually incompressible, there will be little effect on most organs. However, where a gas space occurs this will be important. This is the case with the middle

▲ **The sleek lines** of a Galapagos sea lion underwater. Unlike true seals, which empty the lungs before diving, sea lions dive with some air in the lungs (note the bubbles here), which allows them to vocalize underwater. This ability is used by males in patrolling underwater territories. Although not such proficient divers as the true seals, sea lions have been trained to dive to 820ft (250m).

ear. The middle ear of seals is lined with a system of venous blood sinuses. When the seal dives, the increasing pressure causes the blood-filled sinuses to bulge into the ear, taking the place of the compressed air and matching the ambient pressure. By far the largest gas-space is in the respiratory system. When a seal dives it partially empties its lungs, but some air remains in the minute air sacs (alveoli) and air passages. As pressure increases, air is forced out of the lungs into the relatively non-absorptive upper airways, where there is less risk of nitrogen being absorbed and causing the condition known as "the bends" when the seal surfaces again. Despite this, repeated diving could raise nitrogen concentrations to a dangerous level, and it has been calculated that because of the depth and duration of some of their dives, the bends could be contracted from a single dive by a Weddell seal. As a last resort, collapse of the alveoli prevents high concentrations of nitrogen developing in the blood and tissues and thus avoids the bends.

## Senses

Pinnipeds have well-developed senses of sight, hearing and touch, but little is known about smell in these animals. Both eared and true seals produce strong odors in the breeding season and mothers identify their pups by scent, so it is likely that this sense is reasonably acute. A sense of smell would, of course, be of no value under water.

The eyes generally are large, and in some species, such as the Ross seal, very large indeed. Because of the absence of a nasolacrimal duct, which would remove tears, there is often the appearance of tears running down the face, a feature which evokes misplaced sympathy in many people. The retina is adapted for low-light conditions. It contains only rods (hence there is no color vision) and is backed by a reflective tapetum (as in cats) which reflects light back through the sense cells a second time. Pinnipeds can see clearly in both air and water. Because the cornea has no refractive effect when immersed in water, the lens has a stronger curvature than that of terrestrial mammals. In air, the pupil constricts to a vertical slit. This combines with a cylindrically, rather than spherically, curved cornea to avoid extreme accommodation for the change from water to air.

The hearing of seals is acute. Apart from the absence of the external ear flaps in the walrus and true seals and the modification associated with diving mentioned earlier, the structure of the ear is similar to that of most other mammals. Some seals produce click vocalizations under water, probably from the larynx, and it has been suggested that these are used in echolocation. The evidence for this is good for the Harbor seal, but attempts to demonstrate this in the California sea lion have not been successful. However, many seals are unable to use vision as a means of finding their food, for example in muddy estuaries or under ice in polar winters. There are many accounts of well-nourished seals chronically blind in both eyes. It is therefore clear that some means of locating prey, other than vision, must be present.

The whiskers of seals are usually very well developed and it is possible that these are used to detect vibrations in the water. The whiskers, or vibrissae, are smooth in outline in eared seals, the walrus, the Bearded and monk seals; they have a beaded outline in the others. The mystacial vibrissae, which emerge from the side of the nostrils, are the longest: up to 19in (48cm) in length in the Antarctic fur seal. Other vibrissal groups, above the nose and on the forehead, are usually shorter. Each whisker is set in a follicle surrounded by a connective tissue capsule richly supplied with nerve fibers. Their structure suggests that the whiskers would be most useful in detecting water displacements produced by swimming fish. Removal of the whiskers impairs the ability of Harbor seals to catch fish.

## Food and Feeding

When the pinnipeds first appeared, about 25 million years ago, they underwent a rapid species radiation. This was perhaps a response to the appearance of increased food

▲ **The stout whiskers** of a Galapagos sea lion, well displayed by this yawning bull. The whiskers may be used to detect disturbances of the water caused by the seal's prey.

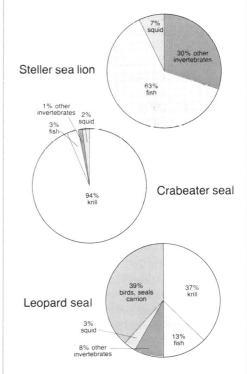

Steller sea lion
7% squid
30% other invertebrates
63% fish

Crabeater seal
1% other invertebrates
2% squid
3% fish
94% krill

Leopard seal
39% birds, seals carrion
37% krill
3% squid
8% other invertebrates
13% fish

▲ **The contrasting diets** of the Steller sea lion, Crabeater seal and Leopard seal.

of feeding the previous pup is completed. Usually this is four months or earlier after birth. After this, the blastocyst implants in the wall of the womb, develops a placenta and begins to develop normally. This phenomenon, known as delayed implantation, may serve to enable seals to combine birth and mating into a single period and avoid the potentially dangerous period spent ashore.

Some seals remain near their breeding grounds throughout the year, but most disperse, either locally or in some cases, such as the Northern fur seal, migrating for thousands of miles. During this period the seals are building up reserves to see them through the next breeding season. Juveniles and adolescents may follow the same pattern, or occupy different grounds from the adult seals. Unfortunately, we know very little about the life of seals at sea.

## Seals and Man

Seals and man have had a close relationship since primitive man first spread into the coastal regions where seals were abundant: the northern coast of Europe, the coast of Asia from Japan northwards, and arctic North America and Greenland. Seals were ideally suited to hunter-gatherers, in part as a result of the modifications that fitted them to an aquatic life. They were sufficiently large that the pursuit and killing of a single animal provided an ample reward, yet not so large that there were major risks involved. Their furry skins made tough and waterproof garments to keep out the elements. Beneath their skin was a layer of blubber, which besides its use as food with the rest of the carcass, could be burnt in a lamp to provide light and warmth during the long nights of the arctic winter.

Stone Age hunters have left records of

◀ ▲ **Splendid isolation.** Pinnipeds in general choose remote and inaccessible localities for breeding. Many breed on isolated rocks or islets where there are no natural predators, or on mainland coasts that are inaccessible from the interior, such as these Grey seals breeding on a cliff-bounded beach on the Cardigan coast, Wales LEFT. Other seals, like this breeding pair of Crabeater seals ABOVE, resort to seasonal pack ice. Ice has many advantages for a breeding seal. It affords immediate access to deep water, a virtually limitless area for breeding, and it is much easier for a seal to move over than sand or rock.

their association with seals in the form of engravings on bones and teeth and as harpoons, sometimes embedded in seal skeletons. In the Arctic, the Eskimos developed a culture which was largely dependent on seals for its very survival. They hunted Ringed seals, Bearded seals, walrus and what other species were available, developing a complex technology of harpoon and kayak to do so. Seal carvings figure importantly in Eskimo art.

North American Indians, from British Columbia southwards, hunted seals and sea lions. At the extreme tip of South America, in Tierra del Fuego, the Canoe Indians hunted fur seals, and when the European seal hunters all but exterminated these, the Indians starved.

Subsistence sealing as practiced by primitive communities, or by crofter-fishermen in Europe up to this century, made relatively little impact on seal stocks. The concept of investing in hunting equipment and engaging crews, with the object of securing as large a catch of seals as possible to be sold on a cash basis, introduced a new dimension into seal hunting. Harp seals were the first to be hunted in this way. Their habit of aggregating in vast herds at the breeding season made them vulnerable to the sealers. Hunting began in the early part of the 18th century. The Harp seal hunt, from a reduced stock, continues today (see pp134–135). Walruses were similarly hunted, mostly by arctic whalers, and their numbers were even more severely diminished (see pp116–117).

Eared seals have suffered equally, if not more, with fur seals being hunted avidly in both hemispheres. The Northern fur seal was first hunted in the late 18th century, perhaps $2\frac{1}{2}$ million being killed at the Pribilof Islands between 1786 and 1867. With the sale of Alaska by Russia to the USA, controls were placed on the sealing operations on shore. These were not, however, sufficient to prevent the drastic reduction of the stock, since sealing, which mainly took lactating females, began in 1886 and dealt the seals a severe blow. In 1911 the North Pacific Fur Seal Convention (the first international seal protection agreement) was signed, which banned open-sea sealing. Under careful management, the Pribilof stock of fur seals has recovered satisfactorily. Sealing continues today on one of the Pribilofs, St. Paul Island; the other island, St. George, is used as a research sanctuary.

In the Southern Hemisphere, fur sealing was combined with the hunting of elephant seals for their oil. Elephant seal stocks recovered in this century and formed the basis of a properly controlled and lucrative industry in South Georgia between 1910 and 1964. There is no commercial elephant sealing today. The Antarctic fur seal, almost exterminated in the 19th century, has now regained its former abundance (see pp 108–109).

Another early association between man and seals was competition between fishermen and seals. Seals damage fisheries in three main ways. To most fishermen the most conspicuous damage is that done to nets and the fish contained in them. Set nets are most affected and the damage can be serious when valuable fish, such as salmon, are being caught. A second form of damage is the toll taken by seals of the general stock of fish in the wild. This is difficult to calculate, for not only are the numbers of seals and the amount of fish they eat often unknown, but it is also difficult to discover how the amount of fish eaten by the seals affects the catch of the fishermen. Common sense suggests that the feeding activities of seals will reduce the catch of fish, but this is difficult to demonstrate in practice. Nevertheless, seals are often killed, or "culled," to reduce their impact on fisheries. The final form of damage to fisheries by seals is that caused by the seals acting as hosts for parasites whose larval stages occur in food fishes. The best known example of this is the Cod worm, a nematode worm which lives as an adult in the stomach of seals, predominantly Grey seals, and whose larvae are found in the gut and muscles of cod and other cod-like fish. When cod are much infested with Cod worm they may be valueless. Cod worm increased with increasing Grey seal stocks around the United Kingdom up to 1970, but though the seals have continued to increase, there has been no evidence of increase in the infestation rate.

Besides deliberate attempts to kill seals, either for their products, or because of the damage they do to fisheries, human activities may prove detrimental to seals in other ways. Purse-seining (fishing with large floating nets) and trawling operations often catch and drown seals. Discarded synthetic net fragments (which have a long life in the sea) and other debris may entangle seals.

Possibly the major impact fishing operations have on seals is the alteration of the ecosystem of which seals form part. However, there is no direct evidence that any commercial fisheries have adversely affected seal stocks. Seals can mostly turn to other species if one fish stock is seriously depleted by fishing. However, as man becomes ever more efficient in cropping the fish stocks, and widens the range of species caught, seals might have few alternatives.

Increasing industrialization in the Northern Hemisphere has led to the dump-

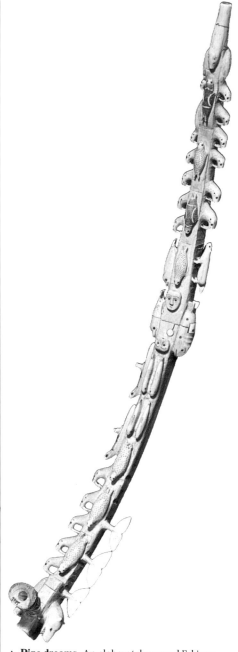

▲ **Pipe dreams.** An elaborately carved Eskimo ivory pipe probably from King Island, Alaska; 1870–1900. The pipe is carved from a walrus tusk and shows several of the species important to Eskimos: besides the walrus, there are two species of seal represented—the Ribbon seal and the Spotted seal.

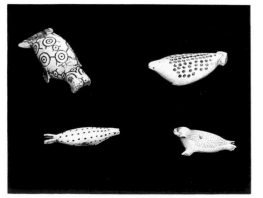

◀ **Eskimo artefacts.** The importance of seals and other sea mammals to the Eskimos is reflected in the many art objects that they carve from walrus ivory and the teeth of whales in the shape of the animals.

▲ **Cycle of conflict**—life history of the Cod worm, a pest that brings man into conflict with seals. The mature worm lives in the stomach of seals. The eggs, expelled from the seal in the feces, find their way, via a first larval stage in an invertebrate, to the second larval stage, which lives in the gut and muscles of cod, rendering them unfit for consumption.

▼ **Plastic torture**—an Antarctic fur seal with a plastic packing band cutting into its neck. The band is trapped by the backward pointing hairs and cuts into the hide.

ing of many biotoxic products in the ocean. Some of these are persistent and tend to accumulate in animals, like seals, at the top of the food chain. Pinnipeds accumulate organochlorine compounds, like DDT and PCB, mainly in the blubber, and heavy metals in the liver. The most convincing evidence for toxicity comes from north of the Baltic Sea where the population of Ringed scals has declined abruptly and the survivors show impaired reproduction (see pp 130–131).

Pollution by petroleum is a feature of many Northern Hemisphere coasts. Seals are often conspicuously contaminated by oil spills. However, they do not seem to suffer much from this. Unlike birds which preen, ingest oil and are poisoned, oiled seals make no attempt to clean their coats and thus rarely ingest oil. Fur seals, of course, might suffer heat loss from contaminated fur.

Habitat disturbance may affect seals. Reclaiming of productive shallow water areas, such as the Dutch polders, can deprive seals of their habitat. Recreational activities, particularly power-boating, can cause severe disturbance to seals at the breeding season. This is particularly serious for monk seals, which have a low tolerance of disturbance (see pp 136–137).

Seals, like most wildlife, are adversely affected by increasing human populations and industrialization. However, there is much real concern today for the welfare of seals, and though some species, such as the monk seals, are endangered, the great majority of seal stocks would seem assured of survival.                                    WNB

# EARED SEALS

**Family: Otariidae**
Fourteen species in 7 genera.
Distribution: N Pacific coasts from Japan to Mexico; Galapagos Islands; W coast of S America from N Peru, round Cape Horn to S Brazil; S and SW coasts of S Africa; S coast of Australia and South Island, New Zealand; oceanic islands circling Antarctica.

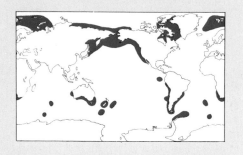

Habitat: generally coastal on offshore rocks and islands.

Size: head-to-tail length from 47in (120cm) in the Galapagos fur seal to 113in (287cm) in the Steller sea lion; weight from 60lb (27kg) in the Galapagos fur seal to 2,200lb (1,000kg) in the Steller sea lion.

Gestation: 12 months, including a period of suspended development (delayed implantation).
Longevity: up to 25 years.

Genus *Callorhinus*
One species: **Northern fur seal** or Alaskan fur seal (*C. ursinus*). Pribilof Islands, W Bering Sea, Sea of Okhotsk, Kuril Islands, San Miguel Island.

Genus *Arctocephalus*
Eight species: the southern fur seals. Southern Ocean, coasts of Australia and New Zealand, north to Baja California. Species include: **Antarctic fur seal** or Kerguelen fur seal (*A. gazella*), **Guadalupe fur seal** (*A. townsendi*), **South American fur seal** (*A. australis*)

Genus *Neophoca*
One species: **Australian sea lion** (*N. cinerea*). Islands off W Australia.

Genus *Phocarctos*
One species: **New Zealand sea lion** (*P. hookeri*). Islands around New Zealand.

Genus *Otaria*
One species: **South American sea lion** (*O. avescens*). Coasts of S America.

Genus *Eumetopias*
One species: **Steller sea lion** (*E. jubatus*). N Pacific.

Genus *Zalophus*
One species: **California sea lion** (*Z. californianus*). W coast of N America, Galapagos Archipelago.

On a sandy beach, a huge maned bull seal, head thrown back, bellows to proclaim his mastery, around him his harem of up to 80 females; beyond them, further groups, all presided over by a beachmaster—these are eared seals, all the species of which are gregarious, social breeders.

The living eared seals comprise the fur seals and sea lions. As a group, they are distinguished from the true seals by their use of the foreflippers as the principal means of propulsion through the water. Generally, most sea lions are larger than most fur seals, and have blunter snouts than those of the fur seals, which tend to be sharp. The flippers of sea lions tend to be shorter than those of fur seals. However, the most obvious difference is the presence of abundant underfur in the fur seals, and sparse underfur in sea lions. Nevertheless, it is clear that the two fur seal genera, *Callorhinus* and *Arctocephalus*, are less closely related to each other than *Arctocephalus* is to the sea lion genera, and the division which is sometimes made, into subfamilies Arctocephalinae and Otariinae, is unjustified.

Because the hindlimbs have not been greatly involved in aquatic locomotion, eared seals have retained a useful locomotory function on land, and they are comparatively agile. Circus sea lions can be trained to run up a ladder; more to the point, a bull fur seal can gallop across a rocky beach in pursuit of a rival. On broken terrain, a fur seal can progress faster than a man can run.

Eared seals are a more uniform group than the true seals, both in appearance and behavior. In all eared seals, males are substantially larger than females: up to five times heavier in the Northern fur seal. This disparity in size is rivaled among mammals only by the Southern elephant seal, in which the male may be up to four times heavier than the female, although both are very much heavier than the fur seals. Also, successful breeding males maintain a harem during the breeding season, a strategy known as polygynous breeding, as opposed to monogamous breeding, in which a male mates with only one female. We shall see that these two traits are in fact related. All eared seals are generalist feeders, there being no specialists as there are in true seals. No eared seal populations have adopted a freshwater existence, as have several true seals such as the Ringed and Baikal seals.

The 14 living species of eared seals are found today on the North Pacific coasts from Japan to Mexico; on the Galapagos Islands and on the western coast of South America, from northern Peru, round Cape Horn to southern Brazil; on the south and southwest coast of southern Africa; on the southern coast of Australia and the South Island, New Zealand; and on the oceanic island groups circling Antarctica. These locations tend to be cool- rather than cold-water areas (although the Northern fur seal, Steller sea lion and, particularly, the Antarctic fur seal all occur in regions of near freezing water), and eared seals are characteristic of temperate and subtemperate climates. There are no ice-breeding eared seals. Eared seals concentrate in areas where rising currents carry nutrients to the surface, feeding on a variety of open-sea and sea-bottom organisms, both fish and invertebrates—whatever food is most abundant and easy to catch. Many take their food, such as rock lobsters

▲ **The brush off.** This pair of New Zealand sea lions exemplifies the extreme sexual disparity in form found in most eared seals, with the shaggy mane of the bull making him look even larger than he is.

◄ **Seal spray.** The thick underfur of fur seals is prevented from becoming waterlogged by the oily secretions of the sebaceous glands and by the support given by the guard hairs. Nevertheless, the fur does hold a certain amount of water, as this Cape fur seal shows, spinning a halo of spray around itself.

and octopus, from the bottom of the sea. Australian fur seals have been caught in traps and trawls at a depth of 387ft (118m), but eared seals are probably relatively shallow feeders compared with true seals. Sometimes eared seals turn to warm-blooded prey. At Macquarie Island, the New Zealand sea lion feeds largely on penguins, and some Southern fur seals, often the subadult males, also take penguins. Steller sea lions occasionally take young Northern fur seals. The Antarctic fur seal is one of the few specialist feeders. It lives largely on Antarctic krill, which is the only food found to be taken by the breeding females (see pp108–109).

The amount of food consumed by eared seals is not easily determined. It varies from species to species, of course, and small animals need proportionately more food than large ones. Female Northern fur seals, and males under four years, need about 14 percent of their body weight of food a day, simply for maintenance purposes. Water

temperature greatly affects the food requirement, since, despite their fur coats, much energy is required to compensate for heat lost to the sea. Some fur seals in the Seattle Aquarium were fed just short of satisfaction on 26–27 percent of their body weight per day and grew normally without getting unduly fat.

The ancestors of the Otariidae diverged from the dog-like carnivore stock in the North Pacific Basin in the early Miocene or late Oligocene, about 25 million years ago. These small, primitive seal-like creatures, the Enaliarctidae, had teeth like those of typical carnivores, with carnassial teeth in the upper and lower jaws. They were probably coastal dwellers. Quite early on, the enaliarctids gave rise to a group, the Desmatophocidae, which had many otariid-like characteristics. These were larger animals with uniform teeth (unlike cats and dogs) and considerable modification of the ear region, associated with diving. It seemed that the desmatophocids had become adapted to an open-sea, rather than a coastal, life. *Allodesmus*, a desmatophocid that flourished in the middle and late Miocene, showed the sexual dimorphism (males larger than females), strong canines and teeth with marked growth zones associated with periodic fasting, that indicate that it had a polygnous breeding system very like that of the existing fur seals and sea lions. However, although the desmatophocids were a successful group, by the late Miocene (about 10 million years ago) they had disappeared. By that time, primitive walruses were abundant, having appeared in the early Miocene.

Meanwhile, some time in the early Miocene, the enaliarctids had given rise to the otariids—the eared seals. The earliest known otariid is *Pithanotaria*, known from several localities in California from about 11 million years ago. *Pithanotaria* was very small, somewhat smaller than the smallest living otariid, the Galapagos fur seal, and had a uniform dentition and bony processes about the eye sockets, both characteristic of modern otariids. However, its cheek teeth had multiple roots, and it did not show sexual dimorphism.

By 8 million years ago there were otariids in the North Pacific that showed an increase in body size and were clearly sexually dimorphic. Except for slight differences in some of the limb bones and the retention of double-rooted cheek teeth, these forms could easily be taken for modern sea lions. The Northern fur seal, *Callorhinus*, diverged from the main otariid stem about 6 million years ago, and soon afterwards otariids dispersed southwards to the Southern Hemisphere. There is no evidence that any otariid managed to follow the walrus ancestors through the Central American Seaway into the North Atlantic.

From 6 million years ago to about 2–3 million years ago there was little diversification in the otariid stock, which remained very similar to the existing genus *Arctocephalus*, the southern fur seals. In the past 2 million years, however, there was a sudden acceleration in the increase of size, the development of single-rooted cheek teeth and generic diversification. The existing five sea lion genera appeared from the arctocephaline stock in the last 3 million years or so.

Eared seals are all more or less social animals, tending to live in groups and to gather in aggregations, which may be very large during the breeding season. At their peak, the breeding haul-out of Northern fur seals at the Pribilof Islands represented perhaps the largest aggregation of large

mammals anywhere in the world. As already noted, male eared seals are polygynous, maintaining a harem of very many females, as do other socially-breeding pinnipeds, notably the elephant seals (see pp 132–133). The fact that similar behavior has evolved separately in the eared and true seals is believed to be related to the basic facts of life for seals, involving offshore marine feeding and birth on land.

Because seals have limited mobility on land, they seek out specially advantageous sites where the absence of terrestrial predators allows them to breed successfully. Such sites are relatively rare and space is often restricted, factors which tend to bring the females together. The males are more widely spaced because of their aggressive drive towards each other. This tendency of the females to clump and the males to space out means that some males will be excluded from a position among the females while the females will be drawn to the more successful males. Such behavior is believed to favor large size in the males, for two reasons. Firstly, males need to be powerful to defend their territories, and to have impressive features which they can use in threat displays and in courtship. Secondly, a successful male cannot relinquish his territory, by feeding in the water, until he has mated with as many females as possible; to do so requires a lengthy period of fasting, with reliance on a large store of blubber for energy (also, large animals need less energy per unit weight than do small animals). Thus the larger bulls will tend to be more successful—ie will produce more offspring, which will inherit the gross characteristics of the father.

▲ **Beach master.** A bull Subantarctic fur seal, surrounded by his harem of cows and their young still in their birth coats.

▶ **Representative sea lions and fur seals.** All species are sexually dimorphic, males being larger and generally darker in color than females. (**1–4**) Sea lions, which have broader muzzles than fur seals and lack underfur. (**1**) A male California sea lion (*Zalophus californianus*). (**2**) Female Steller sea lion (*Eumetopias jubatus*). (**3**) Female South American sea lion (*Otaria flavescens*). (**4**) Male New Zealand sea lion (*Phocarctos hookeri*). (**5–6**) Fur seals, which have thick coats that cause overheating on land. (**5**) Female South American fur seal (*Arctocephalus australis*). (**6**) Male Northern fur seal (*Callorhinus ursinus*).

▼ **Evolution** of sea lions and fur seals.

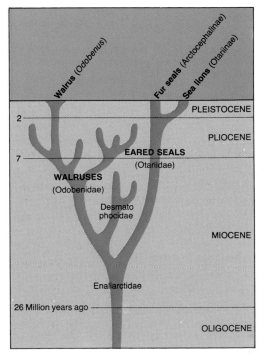

As a consequence of this course of evolution, an otariid breeding beach is a lively scene (see pp110–111). Bulls patrol their territorial boundaries, displaying frequently to neighbors. Most encounters between neighboring territorial bulls go no further than display and threat but actual fights are frequent when a newcomer attempts to establish a place on the beach. The development of a tough hide and a massive mane over the forequarters does something to lessen injuries, but even so serious wounds are common, and it is not unusual for a bull to die from his wounds. Many pups are trampled to death in these battles, but the great fecundity of the bulls is ample compensation for this. Because of the strain imposed by intense activity in territorial encounters and the long period of fasting (for example, 70 days in the case of the bull New Zealand fur seal), few males are able to occupy dominant positions on a breeding beach for more than two or three seasons.

The Antarctic fur seal shows a fairly typical annual pattern. During the winter, from May to October, the adults are at sea, and little is known of this phase of their life. In late October the breeding bulls begin to come ashore to establish territories. At this stage there is little fighting, as there is ample space on the beach. Later, as the beach fills up, boundary disputes are frequent and there is much fighting. The first cows arrive ashore 2–3 weeks later, pregnant from the previous year's mating. By the first week in December, 50 percent of the pups have been born, and 90 percent are born in a three-week period. Cows come ashore about two days before giving birth. For the next six days the mother stays with her pup, suckling it at intervals, and coming into heat again eight days after the birth. During this time the bulls are very active, fighting with neighbors and endeavoring to accumulate more cows in their territories. Though they cannot actively collect cows, they do their best to prevent cows already in their territory from leaving. This interception of cows that show signs of leaving brings the bull into contact with all the females coming into heat, when they become restless. Copulation follows once a receptive cow has been detected, and very soon after being mated the cow departs to sea on a feeding excursion.

There then follows a lactation period of about 117 days, during which the cow makes periodic returns to her pup to suckle it between feeding trips. There are on average about 17 of these feeding/suckling episodes, about twice as long being spent at

sea feeding as on shore suckling. While the cows are away the abandoned pups migrate to the back of the breeding beach, where they lie about in groups. A cow returning from a feeding trip comes back to the beach where she left her pup and calls for it with a characteristic pup-attraction call. The pup answers with its own call, which is recognized by the mother. She confirms recognition by smelling the pup, then leads it to a sheltered place, often on top of a clump of tussac grass, to feed it.

Eventually, weaning takes place. Surprisingly, in the Antarctic fur seal this occurs by the pup taking to the sea, so it is not present on the female's final return. Pups tend to take to the sea in groups, so weaning is more synchronized than birth. Consequently, late-born pups tend to have a shorter lactation period, and lower weaning weights,

▲ **Australian sea lions** on Kangaroo island, Australia. In the foreground, a mature female (yellowish belly), immature male (gray belly and black back but no mane), and in the background pups that have already molted to resemble females. Seals are present on this colony throughout the year and have become tolerant of human visitors.

◄ **New Zealand fur seal** ABOVE at Kangaroo Island, Australia. Note the scroll-like ears typical of eared seals.

◄ **Cape or South African fur seal** hauled out on a rock. Males of this species grow to be the longest of all fur seals.

► **Galapagos sea lion,** ABOVE a subspecies of the California sea lion, leaping from an old stone jetty.

► **New Zealand sea lion** mother nuzzles its pup on return from a feeding trip. Recognition of pups is by both scent and calls. The pup in the foreground belongs to another cow.

than those born earlier. Perhaps this grouping of pups is an anti-predator strategy, since Leopard seals are known to kill young fur seals.

The abruptly terminated lactation period of the Antarctic fur seal is not typical of eared seals. The only other species that shows it, the Northern fur seal, is also migratory, abandoning its breeding places completely in the winter. Most other eared seals will continue to feed their pups till the arrival of the next, alternating suckling and feeding trips. Some, indeed, will go further and can be seen suckling a pup and a yearling, or even with a two-year-old as well. This has been recorded, for example, in northern populations of Steller sea lions. The Galapagos fur seal is another species that may suckle its pup for 2–3 years, and it has been shown that the presence of an unweaned yearling or two-year-old inhibits the birth of a younger sibling. When a pup is born in these circumstances, it almost always dies in the first month if its older sibling is a yearling, or in about 50 percent of cases if it is a two-year-old.

Many of the eared seals were hunted almost to extinction in the 19th century, but the general picture in the 20th century has been one of recovery. The Juan Fernandez fur seal, considered extinct, was rediscovered in 1965, the Guadalupe fur seal, thought to have been exterminated in 1928, was rediscovered in 1954, and the Antarctic fur seal has made the most dramatic recovery of all, from near-extinction to a healthy population of between 700,000 and 1 million today (see pp108–109).

The South American fur seal has the longest continuous record of exploitation of any fur seal, the first skins coming from Uruguay in the 16th century; the seals on Isla de Lobos are still exploited under government control. The Northern fur seal has been heavily exploited at the Pribilof Islands since 1786, but in this century the population has been well managed and the stock is in good condition today.

Some seals are still harassed by fishermen, especially the California, South American and Steller sea lions, but, apart from unexplained declines, such as that of the South American sea lion in the Falklands (from 300,000 in the 1930s to 30,000 today), eared seals are now in a fairly healthy position. The Australian sea lion is perhaps symbolic of the improved relationship between seals and man: at Seal Bay, Kangaroo Island, the sea lions are so accustomed to human visitors that tourists can mingle with the seals on the beach. WNB

# Antarctic Renaissance

*The recovery of the Antarctic fur seal from near-extinction*

Reduced to only a few tens of individuals by fur hunters in the 19th century, after 75 years of protection the Antarctic fur seal is now well on the way to regaining its former abundance, numbered in millions. How has this happened?

Captain Cook was the first to discover the Antarctic fur seal, when he landed at South Georgia in 1775. By that time, sealing was in full swing at the Falkland Islands, so even if Cook had not announced his discovery, it is unlikely that sealers would have overlooked this rich resource. By 1800–1 fur sealing had reached a peak at South Georgia: 17 British and American vessels visited the island in that year and took 112,000 skins.

Sealing was wasteful at every stage. The sealers landed on the breeding beaches before the main body of seals arrived and took what they could find. Then they methodically slaughtered the seals as they arrived, taking preferentially the juvenile males and the breeding females, since these yielded the finest quality skins. The large harem bulls were usually avoided—their skins were inferior and they needed more salt for curing.

By 1822 the Scottish sealer James Weddell calculated that at least 1,200,000 fur seal skins had been taken at South Georgia, and the species was nearly extinct there. Meanwhile, however, another great refuge of the species had been discovered at the South Shetland Islands in 1819. Within three years, almost a quarter of a million seals had been taken and many thousands killed and lost, and the seals had been all but exterminated there too.

The fur sealers turned to killing Southern elephant seals for their blubber, meanwhile taking any fur seals they happened to find. Other island groups were searched and their seals hunted to virtual or actual extinction. There was a brief revival of sealing at South Georgia and the South Shetland Islands, which yielded a few thousand skins, but by the turn of the century the seals seemed to have disappeared entirely. The last recorded catch was in 1907 when an American whaler took 170 skins from South Georgia.

By this time, both South Georgia and the South Shetlands were regularly visited by modern steam whalers, and shortly afterwards government restrictions were placed on the killing of seals, fur seals being totally protected. Opportunities for sighting survivors were good, but it was 1916 before a single young male was found (and illegally shot) on South Georgia. Somewhere, probably on the islets and rocks just to the

northwest of South Georgia, a tiny remnant of the stock, perhaps as few as 50 animals, had managed to survive. In 1933 a party landed at one of these, Bird Island, and found 38 seals. Three years later, at the same place, 59 were found, of which 12 were pups.

The first proper scientific investigation of the recovery, in 1956, found a thriving colony at Bird Island that had produced at least 3,500 pups. Thereafter, regular visits were made. As numbers increased, it became increasingly more difficult to obtain accurate totals of the numbers of pups born, and indirect methods had to be used to estimate abundance. Between 1958 and 1972 the South Georgia population increased at 16.8 percent annually—a rate of

growth at which the population would double every $4\frac{1}{2}$ years! There are indications that the rate has slowed since then, but it still remains much higher than the rate of recovery of other species of fur seals enjoying similar protection. The present population of Antarctic fur seals (mainly at South Georgia) is estimated at between 700,000 and 1,000,000.

Such a spectacular recovery ought to have a visible cause and a likely one is to hand, in the equally spectacular decline of the baleen whales of the Southern Ocean, which commercial whaling has reduced to about 16 percent of their original biomass. Baleen whales and Antarctic fur seals both feed on krill, and the virtual removal of baleen whales around South Georgia must have reduced competition for food between the seals and whales.

Consumption of krill by baleen whales in the Antarctic has fallen from about 180 million tons to 33 million tons per year while the present population of Antarctic fur seals consumes about 1.2 million tons per year. Lactating fur seals, when making feeding excursions between bouts of suckling their pups would have benefited greatly from this reduced competition, perhaps improving the growth and survival of their pups, and their own chances of bearing pups in successive seasons.

Although the recovery has been mainly in South Georgia, fur seals are now found in increasing numbers in most of their old haunts. This is not simply a success story, however—success brings problems too. The present density of fur seals at the northwest end of South Georgia is in fact higher than has previously been recorded. At Bird Island, raised beach features which remained intact for many thousands of years are in places being eroded, as the constant passage of fur seals destroys the fragile vegetation cover that holds their gravels together. Tussac grass, which clothes the lower slopes behind the seal beaches, is a favorite place for the seals to bask, and repeated use denudes the tussac clumps, which die off to leave naked peaty stumps. Elsewhere, the grass is trampled and flattened. This is not just unsightly: it destroys the habitat of birds dependent on the tussac areas for nesting sites. These are mainly burrowing petrels, such as prions and Blue petrels, as well as the endemic Antarctic pipit. Destruction of the tussac may not only deprive the birds of their nest sites, but can also make them more vulnerable to predation by skuas. The seals also interfere with the breeding of Wandering albatrosses.

The interaction of the whales-seals-krill system has allowed an explosive recovery of the fur seals which conservationists generally will applaud, but the future of the fur seals will not simply be a return to the past. Conditions are very different now to the pre-exploitation days. The balance of an ecosystem is not simple, and while populations may prove very resilient when pressures are removed, there is no guarantee that former situations will be restored. WNB

### ANTARCTIC FUR SEALS ON BIRD ISLAND

▲ **Spectacular backdrop.** A beach breeding ground with large, maned males, smaller females and black pups.

▶ **Cows in clover,** or rather tussac, the thick clumped grass that clothes the lower slopes and beaches of breeding colonies. Here females bask among mature clumps, but lower down the beach SEE ABOVE overcrowding by seals has flattened the clumps, leading to severe erosion.

◀ **Chilly encounter.** A cow repels the advances of a bull during a snow storm.

# The Fight to Mate

*Breeding strategy of California sea lions*

Evenly spaced bursts of bubbles rising to the surface offshore of a California sea lion rookery indicate that, below, a male sea lion is patrolling his territory and barking underwater. These, the best-known of all sea lions, thanks to their performances in circuses and oceanaria, sometimes have territories that are mostly in the water, and males bark to warn intruders of their territorial boundaries.

The California sea lion is currently found in the eastern North Pacific from British Columbia to Baja California and in a separate population on the Galapagos Islands, near the Equator. Male sea lions are larger than females and maintain territories on the rookeries (pupping/mating sites) during the breeding season which lasts from May to August in California. Each male mates with as many females as possible. A successful adult male must defend his stretch of beach from all other males in order to maximize his mating success. Fighting occurs during the establishment of territories but is soon reduced to ritualized boundary displays. The displays include barking, head shaking, oblique stares and lunges at the opponent's flippers. These displays are most likely to occur on territorial boundary lines and can be used to plot the locations of individual territories on the rookery.

Ritualized fighting and large size are the two most important factors enabling the males to stay on their territories for long periods of time without feeding. For a male to maximize the numbers of his offspring he must remain on the rookery for as long as possible. Ritualized fighting uses less energy than does actual combat. Large size is not only an asset in combat but also confers a lower rate of energy expenditure and the ability to store abundant blubber. The blubber serves as a layer of insulation when the sea lion is in cold water and is its only source of food when it is on its territory.

Also important in the male sea lion's reproductive strategy is the timing of territory occupation. Ideally, territories should be occupied when the greatest number of receptive females are present. On average, there are 16 females for every territorial male and 2 females for every pup. In the Northern fur seal the females are receptive about five days after they have given birth. In this species, the males establish their territories before the females arrive on the rookeries in the Bering Sea. But in the California sea lion the females are not receptive until about 21 days after they have given birth. The fact that male California sea lions only hold their territories for an average of 27 days means that it is counterproductive for them to establish territories before the females arrive. In fact they do not even begin to set up territories until after the first pups are born. The number of territories on a rookery increases gradually and reaches a peak about five weeks after the peak of the pupping period.

The weather also affects the sea lions' breeding strategy. Temperatures of more than 86°F (30°C) occur during the breeding

▲ **Rookery on the rocks.** The breeding grounds or rookeries of California sea lions are often in very isolated and inhospitable locations.

▼ **Oblique aggression.** Ritualized gestures are used by territorial male California sea lions to maintain the boundaries of their territories after initial establishment. These take the place of fighting, allowing the males to save energy for mating. The individual gestures are performed in a variable order, but a typical sequence is: (1) head-shaking with barking as the males approach the boundary, followed by (2) oblique stares interspersed with lunges, and (3) more head-shaking and barking. During lunges, the males try to keep their foreflippers as far as possible from each other's mouths. The thick skin on the chest fends off potentially serious blows.

season, and while this is generally favorable to the pups, which have not yet fully developed their ability to regulate their body temperature, the territorial males may suffer. All sea lions have only a limited ability to regulate body temperature on land and normally cool off by entering the water. But for a territorial male to do this is to risk losing his territory. Therefore a successful territorial male must have access to water as a part of his territory. During hot weather territories without direct access to water cannot be defended.

Sometimes territories are mostly in the water. This often occurs at the base of steep cliffs where there is a little beach but still enough room for females to come ashore and give birth. Here, the males patrol their territories, barking underwater. It is possible that a male with a large portion of his territory under water would have an energetic advantage over one with most of his territory on land. What is certain is that any advantage a male can gain in order to leave more offspring will be exploited to the full.                                                    DKO

▲ **Water territories.** Where bull sea lion territories are in the water they maintain the boundaries by patrolling and barking.

# WALRUS

***Odobenus rosmarus***
Sole member of genus.
Family: Odobenidae.
Distribution: Arctic seas, from E Canada and
Greenland to N Eurasia and W Alaska.

Habitat: chiefly seasonal pack ice over
continental shelf.

Size: regionally-variable; smallest in Hudson
Bay, where adult males average 9.5ft (2.9m),
adult females 8.2ft (2.5m) in length and about
1,750lb (795kg) and 1,250lb (565kg),
respectively, in weight; largest in Bering and
Chukchi Seas, where adult males average about
10.5ft (3.2m), adult females 8.8ft (2.7m) in
length and about 2,670lb (1,210kg) and
1,835lb (830kg), respectively, in weight. Tusks
of Hudson Bay animals very short, averaging
about 14in (36cm) in adult males and 9in
(23cm) in adult
females; tusks of Bering-
Chukchi walruses
nearly twice as long,
averaging about 22in
(55cm) in adult males
and 16in (40cm) in
adult females.

Color: cinnamon brown to pale tawny, darkest
on chest and abdomen; immature animals
darker than adults. Surfaces of flippers hairless,
black in young animals, becoming brownish to
grayish with age. Hair sparse on neck and
shoulders of adult males.

Diet: mainly mollusks.

Gestation: 15-16 months, including 4-5
months of suspended development (delayed
implantation).

Longevity: up to 40 years.

Subspecies: 2 or 3. **Atlantic walrus** (*O. r.
rosmarus*); Hudson and Baffin bays to Kara and
Barents seas; males to 11.5ft (3.5m) long, with
length of tusks about 12 percent of head-to-tail
length. **Pacific walrus** (*O. r. divergens*); Bering
and Chukchi seas; males to 14ft (4.2m) long,
with length of tusks about 17% of head-to-tail
length. Males with "squarer" snout than
Atlantic walrus, and jutting chin. The name
*O. r. divergens* was originally assigned on the
basis of the tusks being more widely spread
than those of the Atlantic walrus; this
difference has never been confirmed. Walruses
of Laptev Sea intermediate in size; sometimes
considered as Atlantic, sometimes as Pacific,
occasionally as a separate subspecies (*O. r.
laptevi*).

THE image of the walrus, stout-bodied and
bewhiskered, with long white tusks, is as
symbolic of the Arctic as are ice and snow.
And rightly so, for walruses inhabit only the
Arctic Ocean and adjacent ice-covered seas.
Few other creatures have adapted so successfully to the pack-ice regime of the far
northern seas, and for that they are revered
by the maritime Eskimos, who see in them
many human attributes as well. Highly
social and gregarious, slow to mature and
reproduce, fiercely protective and gently
caring for their young, vocally communicat-
ive with each other, and long lived, walruses
are easy subjects to interpret in a human
way.

Walruses are also cherished by the
Eskimos as a major source of food and other
materials, on which these people have de-
pended for thousands of years. Farther
south, in Europe, Asia, and North America,
however, the main interest in walruses has
been for their ivory—the great white tusks,
second in size and quality only to those of
elephants. In the quest for that ivory and for
the thick hides and oil, Europeans nearly
eliminated walruses from the Arctic more
than 100 years ago.

Early descriptions of walruses drew attention to their resemblance to swine, in part
because of the tendency to huddle together,
sometimes one on top of another, and in part
because of the sparsely haired, rotund body,
about as large in circumference as in length.
In size, coloration, and general appearance,
however, walruses actually bear little resemblance to pigs. Outwardly they are most
similar to sea lions, except for their squarish
head and long tusks. Male walruses have a
pair of highly inflatable air sacs in the throat
which are used to produce special sounds
during courtship and as an aid to floating
while resting at sea.

When on land or ice, walruses stand and
walk on all four limbs. The heels of the
hindflippers are brought in under the rump
for support, and the toes are turned forward
and outward; the palms of the forelimbs
support the trunk, and the fingers are
turned outward and back.

In water, the walrus propels itself almost
exclusively by means of the hindlimbs, the
forelimbs being used mainly as rudders. This
sculling with the hindlimbs is an adaptation
for bottom-feeding, in which a slow, meth-
odical pace is more advantageous than high
speed.

One of the principal anatomical peculiar-
ities of the walrus is the skin, 0.8-1.6in
(2-4cm) thick, which is thrown into creases
and folds at every joint and bend of
the body. This thick skin is a protective
"armor", guarding against injury by the
tusks of other walruses. Everywhere but on
the flippers, the skin is covered by coarse
hair about 0.4in (1cm) long, which imparts
a furry to velvety texture to the body surface
of females and young males; adult males
(bulls) tend to be sparsely haired and to have
nearly bare, knobby skin on the neck and
shoulders. That knobby skin is up to 2in
(5cm) thick, for added protection, and it

**▲ Walrus haul-out.** Walruses are extremely gregarious, hauling out in vast aggregations, normally on ice, but when not available they select rocky islands as here at Round Island, Alaska.

**◄ Lord of the floe.** A male walrus on a floe in the Bering Sea in spring. At this time of the year male and female populations are entirely separate, the females having migrated north to the Chukchi Sea.

**▷    A pile of walruses** OVERLEAF. In restricted locations, walruses are quite happy to haul out onto other walruses. Note the contrast between the basking pink herd and the pale individual emerging from the sea.

imparts a distinctive appearance which clearly separates the bulls from all other animals. The folds of the skin are infested by blood-sucking lice which seem to cause some irritation, for walruses often rub and scratch their skin.

The walrus's nearest living relatives are the fur seals, with which it evolved from bear-like ancestors, the Enaliarctidae, in the North Pacific Ocean about 20 million years ago. Early walruses were similar in appearance to modern sea lions, and from about 5–10 million years ago they were the most abundant and most diverse pinnipeds in the Pacific Ocean. Some of those early

forms were fish-eaters, but some had already changed their diet from fishes to mollusks and other bottom fauna. With that change in diet, they gradually changed in appearance and behavior. Probably in that connection, the change from forelimb to hindlimb propulsion took place, and the tusks began to enlarge.

Between 5 and 8 million years ago, some of these bottom-feeding walruses with tusks made their way into the North Atlantic Ocean, through what was then an open passage, known as the Central American Seaway, in what is now Costa Rica and Panama. Subsequently, they flourished in the North Atlantic, while all of those in the North Pacific died out. Within the past million years, those in the Atlantic invaded the Arctic, and some made their way back to the Pacific via the Arctic Ocean as recently as 300,000 years ago.

Walruses today feed primarily on bivalve mollusks—the clams, cockles, and mussels that abound on the continental shelves of northern seas. They also eat about 40 other kinds of invertebrate animals from the sea floor, including several species of shrimps, crabs, snails, polychaete and priapulid worms, octopus, sea cucumbers, and tunicates, as well as a few fishes; occasionally they even eat seals.

To locate their food, walruses probably rely more on touch than on any other sense, for they feed in total darkness during the winter and in murky waters or at depths where penetration of light is very poor most of the rest of the time. Their sense of touch appears to be most powerfully developed on the front of their snout, where the thin skin and about 450 coarse whiskers are highly sensitive. The upper edge of the snout is armored with tough, cornified skin and is apparently used for digging, pig-fashion, to unearth many of the small clams and other invertebrates lying at shallow depths in the bottom mud. Those buried deeper in the sediments are believed to be excavated by means of jetting water into their burrows. The ability of walruses to squirt large amounts of water under high pressure from their mouth is well known to zoo keepers. The old hypothesis that walruses dig clams with their tusks is now known to be incorrect; the tusks are primarily "social organs," like the antlers of deer and the horns of sheep. They become worn not from digging but from being dragged along in the mud and sand, while the walrus moves forward excavating its prey with the snout and oral jet.

A few females first breed at 4 years and a

few as late as 10 years of age; the average is 6 or 7 years. Males are much slower to mature, for they may not take part in breeding until they are physically as well as sexually mature. For most males, that development requires about 15 years. Full maturity is necessary for breeding because the bulls are highly competitive for mates, and only those that are large enough in body and tusk size are capable of competing successfully.

Mating takes place in January-February, probably in the water, during the coldest part of the winter. At that time, the adult females (cows) and young congregate in traditional breeding areas, forming into herds of 10–15 animals which travel and feed together. Several such herds may coalesce when they haul out onto the ice to rest, between feeding bouts. Each herd is followed by one to several bulls, which mostly remain in the water, nearby. These bulls engage incessantly in vocal displays, consisting of set sequences of repetitive "knocks" and "bells" made underwater, and shorter sequences of "clacks" and "whistles" at the surface. Like the songs of birds, these repetitive calls probably serve to attract mates and to repel potential competitors. The bell-like sound is apparently produced by using one of the inflatable sacs in the throat as a resonance chamber and is used only in sexual display. The normal sounds of walruses are barks of variable pitch.

The female gives birth to a single calf in the spring of the following year, usually in May. Because of the long pregnancy, females cannot breed more often than at two-year intervals, and the intervals become longer with age. For this reason, the walrus has the lowest rate of reproduction of any pinniped and one of the lowest among mammals in general.

The calf at birth is about 3.6ft (1.1m) long and weighs about 130–140lb (60–65kg). It has a short, soft coat of hair, pale grayish flippers, a thick white mustache, and no visible teeth. It feeds only on milk for the first 6 months, but begins to eat some solids by the end of that time.

After one year, the calf has approximately tripled in weight and has developed tusks 1in (2.5cm) long. For another year, the calf remains with its mother, dependent on her for guidance, protection and milk, while gradually developing its ability to bottom-feed and range independently. At 2 years of age, it separates from the mother, who then gives birth to another calf.

After weaning, the young walruses con-

## Why do Walruses have Tusks?

In both male and female walruses, the upper canine teeth develop into great "tusks." These serve many functions, from ice-choppers to defensive weapons, but their primary role lies in the establishment of the bearer's status within walrus society. In any herd, the largest walrus with the largest tusks tends to be the dominant one. Simply by adopting postures that display the size of its tusks, the dominant animal can move unchallenged into the most comfortable or advantageous positions, displacing subordinates which have shorter tusks. If the dominant walrus encounters another with tusks of comparable size, however, their confrontation may escalate from visual displays to stabbing with the tusks. Eventually one of the combatants concedes defeat by turning away and withdrawing. Such contests occur in males and females but they are more intense between bulls in the breeding season.

The social value of the tusks extends beyond the competition for dominance. By their size and shape, the tusks convey much information about the sex and age of their bearer. For about the first year and a half after birth, young walruses have no visible tusks, since their canine teeth do not emerge through the gums until 6–8 months of age, and they are covered by the ample upper lip for another year thereafter. Hence, any small animal with no tusks is immediately recognizable by all others as young and dependent, and its larger companion is tentatively identifiable as an adult female.

At all ages, the tusks of females tend to be rounder in cross section, shorter in length, as well as more slender and more curved than those of males. In old age, the tusks of both sexes tend to be stout but shortened and blunted by fracture and abrasion. A human observer can identify the sex and approximate age of a walrus from its tusks, so other walruses are probably at least as perceptive.

Occasionally, a walrus emerging from the water onto an ice floe uses its tusks as a fifth limb, jabbing the points into the ice and heaving the body forward. Tales of this behavior led the 18th-century zoologist Brisson to give the walrus the generic name *Odobenus*, a contraction of the Greek words *odontos* and *baenos*, meaning literally "tooth-walk." The tusks are sometimes also used to break breathing holes in the ice.

tinue to associate and travel with the adult females. Gradually, over the next 2–4 years, the young males break away, forming their own small groups in winter or joining with larger herds of bulls in the summer. Seasonal segregation of sexes appears to take place to some degree in all walrus populations, but it is most clearly expressed in the Bering-Chukchi region. There, most of the bulls congregate in separate haul-out and feeding areas in the Bering Sea during the spring, while the cows and most of the immature animals migrate northward into the Chukchi Sea. They remain separated in this way throughout the summer; then as the cows come southward again in the fall, the bulls apparently meet them in the vicinity of the Bering Strait and accompany them to the wintering-breeding areas in the Bering Sea. At that time, the immature males move off separately to spend the winter in other parts of the pack ice, outside the breeding areas. By segregating in this way, Pacific walruses distribute their impact on the food supply and minimize the potential conflict between adult and adolescent males in the breeding season.

Walrus populations throughout the Arctic were severely depleted during the 18th, 19th, and 20th centuries by commercial hunters from Europe and North

▲ **Slaughter on the ice.** The walrus is still vital to the economies of the Eskimos, but stocks may not be sufficient to sustain exploitation.

▶ **Walrus engraving on a whale's tooth.** The Eskimos' reliance on sea mammals is symbolized by this representation of walrus hunting drawn on a Sperm whale's tooth.

◀ **Versatile tusks.** The walrus's tusks are primarily social organs, used in dominance disputes (1). Such encounters are usually ended by the less bulky or strong walrus turning away (2). Walruses sometimes use their tusks simply to prop the head up (3). The tusks also function as a fifth limb when emerging from the water onto ice (4).

America, who sought the animals principally for their tusks, skins and oil. At that time, little was known about the biology and ecology of walruses, hence there was little scientific basis for managing the hunters by regulating their catch. The North Atlantic population is about 30,000 individuals; these stocks were the first to be depleted, were reduced to the lowest numbers and have never recovered. The Bering-Chukchi population, although depressed twice to about 50 percent of its former size, appa-

rently rebounded each time within a 15–20 year period, the latest being from about 1960 to 1980; it now numbers about 260,000. There are less than 10,000 walruses in the Laptev Sea. Currently, about 6–7 percent of the western North Atlantic population and 2–4 percent of the Bering-Chukchi walrus populations are killed annually.

For several thousand years, walruses have been the mainstay of numerous Eskimo communities from eastern Siberia and Alaska to eastern Canada and Greenland. In recent years, management of walruses as a natural resource in the USSR, Canada and Greenland has recognized aboriginal subsistence as the first consideration, after that of survival of the walruses themselves. The North Atlantic stocks are so low that they may not be able to bear continued exploitation by the Eskimos, while the high level of the North Pacific stock has opened the way for renewed consideration of potential commercial use.   FHF

# TRUE SEALS

**Family: Phocidae**
Nineteen species in 10 genera.
Distribution: generally in polar, subpolar and temperate seas, except for the monk seals of the Mediterranean, Caribbean, and Hawaiian regions.

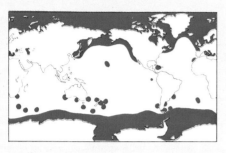

Habitat: land-fast ice, pack ice and offshore rocks and islands.

Size: head-to-tail length from 50in (117cm) in the Ringed seal to 193in (490cm) in the male Southern elephant seal; weight from 100lb (45kg) in the Ringed seal to 5,300lb (2,400kg) in the male Southern elephant seal.

Gestation: 10–11 months, including 2.5–3.5 months of suspended development (delayed implantation).
Longevity: up to 56 years.

## Genus *Monachus*
Three species: **Caribbean monk seal** (*M. tropicalis*). **Hawaiian monk seal** (*M. schauinslandi*). **Mediterranean monk seal** (*M. monachus*).

## Genus *Lobodon*
One species: **Crabeater seal** (*L. carcinophagus*).

## Genus *Leptonychotes*
One species: **Weddell seal** (*L. weddelli*).

## Genus *Hydrurga*
One species: **Leopard seal** (*H. leptonyx*).

## Genus *Ommatophoca*
One species: **Ross seal** (*O. rossi*).

## Genus *Mirounga*
Two species: **Northern elephant seal** (*M. angustirostris*). **Southern elephant seal** (*M. leonina*).

## Genus *Erignathus*
One species: **Bearded seal** (*E. barbatus*).

## Genus *Cystophora*
One species: **Hooded seal** (*C. cristata*).

## Genus *Phoca*
Seven species: smaller northern seals. Species include: **Baikal seal** (*P. sibirica*), **Harbor seal** (*P. vitulina*), **Harp seal** (*P. groenlandica*), **Ribbon seal** (*P. fasciata*). **Ringed seal** (*P. hispida*). **Spotted seal** (*P. largha*).

## Genus *Halichoerus*
One species: **Grey seal** (*H. grypus*).

A SEAL laboriously humping across the ice, unable to raise itself by means of its foreflippers, is, moments later, plunging to 2,000ft (600m) and staying underwater for over an hour—true seals are wonderfully adapted to diving, but at the expense of agility on land. Despite the extreme refinement of their physiology to equip them for diving, they are still not fully emancipated from their otter-like ancestors of some 25 million years ago. The tie to land or ice for birth and nurture of their young sets the basic pattern of their lives.

Unlike eared seals (but like otters), true seals swim by powerful sideways movements of their hindquarters. The trailing hindlimbs are bound to the pelvis so that the "crotch" is at the level of the ankles and the tail scarcely protrudes. The long, broadly webbed feet make very effective flippers but are useless on land. The forelimbs, unlike those of eared seals, are not strongly pro-pulsive; they are buried to the base of the hand and are used for steering in the water and, sometimes, to assist in scrambling on land or ice. The northern true seals have evolved more powerful arrangements of muscle attachments along the spine, whereas antarctic species may have longer, more mobile foreflippers.

Respiration and circulation in true seals are adapted to one overwhelming purpose; that of spending long periods of time underwater. The Weddell seal is a supreme diver, with dives of 2,000ft (600m) to its credit.

Anatomically, the 18 living species of true seals fall into two subfamilies. The southern seals, or Monachinae, include the tropical Hawaiian and Mediterranean monk seals (another monk seal, the Caribbean monk seal, is thought to be extinct, see pp 136–137), the Northern and Southern elephant seals, and the Antarctic seals (Crabeater, Leopard, Ross and Weddell

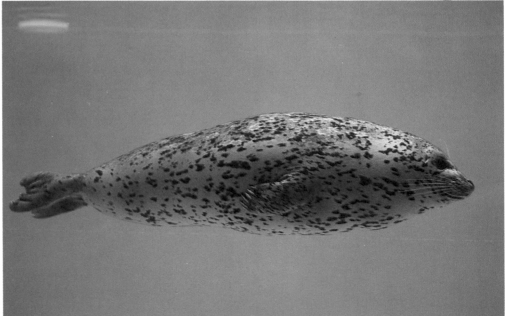

▲ ▶ **Red balloon/Black hood.** The Hooded seal has two bizarre forms of nasal display. The lining of one nostril can be forced out through the opposite nostril to form a red bladder ABOVE. Alternatively, the whole of the black hood, an enlargement of the nasal cavity, can be inflated RIGHT.

◀ **Clumsy on land, sleek in water.** ABOVE The Weddell seal is one of the largest species of true seal, but its head is extremely small, seeming to be tacked on as an afterthought. BELOW The Harbor seal, a small seal, assumes an efficient torpedo-like shape in the water.

▼ **The evolution of true seals.**

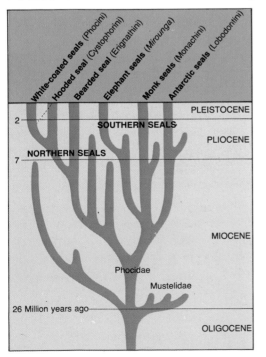

seals), as three distinct tribes. The northern seals, or Phocinae, also have three tribes: for the Bearded seal, the Hooded seal, and for the remaining, primitively ice-breeding seals: the Baikal, Caspian, Grey, Harbor, Harp, Ringed and Spotted seals.

Although now largely found in high latitudes of both Northern and Southern Hemispheres, the true seals probably originated in warm waters, where the monk seals still live. All of the northern seals except the Harbor seal breed on ice, the Harbor seal breeding as far south as Baja California (the Grey seal can breed on land or ice). Of the southern seals, the Northern and Southern elephant seals breed respectively from California to Mexico and in the temperate to subantarctic parts of the Southern Ocean. The four Antarctic seals breed on ice and occur generally south of the Antarctic Convergence at 50°–60°S.

The most obvious differences between species are in size and the relative sizes of the sexes. Some populations of Ringed seals reach weights of only about 110lb (50kg), whereas a fully grown male Southern elephant seal may be 50 times heavier. In most species, males and females are of similar size. The females of southern seals, especially the monk seals, the Leopard and Weddell seals, tend to be larger than the males, whereas the males of some northern seals—the Grey, Hooded and elephant seals—are much larger than the females; these large males also have heavy, arched skulls and nasal protuberances for aggressive displays. The size disparity is most marked in the Southern elephant seal, in which the male can be more than three times the weight of the female.

The fossil record has recently yielded many new insights into the evolution and spread of the true seals. Their origin in the North Atlantic region is certain, and their derivation from otter-like ancestors in Europe or western Asia is highly probable. The oldest, mid-to-late Miocene fossils (12–15 million years ago) of eastern USA and Europe are assignable to the modern tropical and northern seal groups.

Evidently the monk seals arose near the Mediterranean, where they still occur, and crossed to the Pacific through the Caribbean and the open (until 3.5–4 million years ago) Central American Seaway. They may have soon after crossed to Hawaii, for the isolated monk seal there is, in bone structure, more primitive than any living and many fossil seals. Ancestral elephant seals from the same Atlantic tropical seal stock, made the same crossing and invaded the Southern Hemisphere via the west coast of South America, leaving behind the more primitive northern species.

Analyses of fossils from eastern USA and Europe, along with recent finds in Argentina, Peru and South Africa, suggest that the tropical ancestors of the antarctic seals likewise entered the Southern Ocean along western South America, but also possibly along eastern South America and West Africa. Such multiple invasions may help account for the present diversity of antarctic true seals in the absence of geographical barriers in the Southern Ocean.

The Bearded seal, although a northern

seal in terms of bone structure, is linked with the tropical seals by its less-developed pelvic and ear regions, by the presence of four mammae (two in other northern seals), and by the dark lanugo. The Hooded seal, formerly classed with the elephant seals, is clearly a true northern seal, perhaps the remnant of a more primitive ice-breeding group in the North Atlantic.

The remaining northern seals evidently had a common ancestor, as they all have 32 chromosomes (34 in all other true seals), a similar bone structure and a clearly ice-adapted white lanugo. Seals of the latest Miocene, some 10 million years ago, in southern Europe, included forms allied to the modern Ringed seal and were possibly ancestors of the other northern seals. The Caspian and Baikal seals may thus be relics of a more extensive inland distribution of such seals well before the Pleistocene (about 2 million years ago).

True seals are unknown as North Pacific fossils much before the early Pleistocene (about 7 million years ago), and the ancestral Spotted and Ribbon seals, the latter closely related to the Atlantic Harp seal, must have arrived from the north after the submergence of the Bering land bridge, some 3.5 million years ago. A form like the Spotted seal (once classed as a race of the Harbor seal) is a plausible ice-breeding ancestor of the Pacific Harbor seal, which may have returned as a land-breeding form

to the Atlantic during a warm period. The Grey seal alone among this primitively ice-breeding group has no Pacific counterpart.

Although some fossil seals are possible ancestors and intermediates in the evolution of modern seals, some clearly are not. Perhaps the most unusual is a recently discovered form from Peru, *Acrophoca longirostris*, related to the antarctic seals, but curiously long-snouted, like a dolphin. Nevertheless, the true seals do not seem to have undergone the "bursts" of evolutionary diversification that occurred among the eared seals in the North Pacific.

Aquatic life restricts seals to a diet of relatively small or soft food, hence the array of premolars and molars, for cutting and crushing, which is found in terrestrial carnivores, is reduced to rows of uniform teeth, usually five. Most seals are somewhat opportunistic, with few obvious specializations for feeding.

Where several species inhabit the same area, some differentiation is apparent. In the Okhotsk and Bering seas, the Ringed seal breeds on land-fast ice or heavy pack (drift-

of true seals have been extensively documented. Ages of sexual maturity vary somewhat unexpectedly, being later in small species like the Ringed and Caspian seals than in the large antarctic species or the huge elephant seals. Early maturity may be a disadvantage in species, like the Harbor and Ringed seals, that disperse in complex, near-shore environments where land (or ice) predation is a threat and where learning about surroundings is essential for safe reproduction. Although both sexes of the Grey and elephant seals (see pp132–133) are fertile when quite young, males are incapable of securing mates until they are much larger, some years later.

Although species differences remain, females of the Baikal, Ringed, Harp, Harbor and elephant seals have all been shown to mature earlier in populations reduced by exploitation. This has been attributed to increased food availability or reduced social interaction, but the mechanisms are not known. A remarkable decrease in mean age of first reproduction by female Crabeater seals, from more than 4 years in 1945 to less than 3 years in 1965, was associated with a vast "release" of its krill food base through depletion of the great whales (see pp 128–129).

Reproductive seasons may be set by female receptivity at optimal times for rearing young or fostering their independence; males are often potent long before and after. Occasional newborns occur as much as six months outside the normal season, and have been attributed to young mothers whose cycles had not been set. Most females of a species reproduce at about the same time, although populations at higher latitudes may be later. Grey seals show marked regional differences in timing and choice of breeding sites. Extreme local variability occurs among Harbor seals in western North America, where nearby populations may differ by up to four months, perhaps from "drift" in this relatively nonseasonal region.

Mean lactation periods are 1–2 weeks in pack-ice seals and up to 11–12 weeks in the Ringed and Baikal seals, which suckle their young in snow "caves" on the fast ice (see pp130–131). The difference seems related to stability and protectiveness of the nursery. Pups of Weddell seals on fast ice and of Harbor and Monk seals on land are weaned when about 5–6 weeks old, whereas those of the elephant and Grey seals (in which the males mate on land with as many females as they can) are weaned at 3–4 weeks, perhaps an evolutionary response to pre-emptive

▲ **True seals from northern and southern oceans.** (1–6) Northern seals. (1) Hooded seal (*Cystophora cristata*). (2) Ringed seal (*Phoca hispida*). (3) Grey seal (*Halichoerus grypus*). (4) Harp seal (*Phoca groenlandica*). (5) Bearded seal (*Erignathus barbatus*). (6) Ribbon seal (*Phoca fasciata*). (7–12) Southern seals. (7) Ross seal (*Ommatophoca rossi*). (8) Weddell seal (*Leptonychotes weddelli*). (9) Crabeater seal (*Lobodon carcinophagus*). (10) Leopard seal (*Hydrurga leptonyx*). (11) Southern elephant seal (*Mirounga leonina*). (12) Hawaiian monk seal (*Monachus schauinslandi*).

ing) ice and feeds on small fish and planktonic crustaceans, while the Spotted and Ribbon seals use somewhat lighter pack ice and feed respectively on shallow-water fishes and deep-water fishes and squids. The Bearded seal, which also inhabits this region, is unique among true seals in feeding on bottom-dwelling mollusks and shrimps; its teeth are worn down quite early in life.

Under fast ice around Antarctica, the Weddell seal eats fishes, and in the pack ice the Ross seal subsists on deep water squids, the Leopard seal mainly on seals and penguins (see pp138–139), and the Crabeater seal (see pp136–137) lives mostly on krill, which it strains through its many-pointed teeth. Competitive interactions may be intense in confined waters like the Gulf of St. Lawrence, where Grey and Harbor seals are resident, Ringed seals rare and local, and Harp and Hooded seals present during the breeding season.

Since the discovery, in the mid-20th century, of a method of age determination from layers in their teeth, the basic patterns of growth, reproduction and survival rates

males (see pp132–133). Pups of most species increase in weight on average 2.5–3.5-fold during lactation and the Baikal seal, with a lactation of 8–10 weeks, is said to grow 5.5-fold. The blubber of females is transferred to the pup as very rich, fatty milk. For example, the fat content of Harp seal milk increases from around 23 percent at the start of lactation to more than 40 percent at the end, with a complementary decline in water content. As the female fasts while lactating, the decreasing water content may be important in maintaining her water balance. Abandoned or prematurely weaned pups may become dwarfed adults. Pups are occasionally adopted, and some male pups of Northern elephant seals may solicit an unrelated "nurse" after being weaned normally, thereby gaining unusual weight and, possibly, adult fitness.

Copulation is on land in elephant and Grey seals and normally in water among all others. In all species, mating evidently occurs soon after, and sometimes shortly before, pups are weaned, so gestations are 10–11 months. However, the period of active embryonic growth is only 6.5–8 months. This delay in implantation and growth of the embryo has the consequence that males compete for females when they are localized and restrained by maternal duties, and at the same time adjusts the rate of fetal growth to the feeding and physiological capacities of the females.

Although some true seals have been casually reported to mate with a single partner, males of all species are probably at least opportunistically promiscuous and some mate with very many females. Individual male elephant seals (see pp132–133) may control access by others to spontaneously clumped females (misleadingly called "harems"), or dominant males may be spaced among continuously distributed females. Females may incite male combat by vocalizing and by trying to escape from attempted matings; this is probably done to assess paternal fitness, giving a more dominant male opportunity to displace the original one. Some male Grey seals in Britain may patrol true territories of 100sq mi (260sq km) or more, excluding other males and sometimes thwarting the departure of females, whereas on a Nova Scotia beach spaces used by males are flexible and overlapping (ie not territorial), and males copulate with nearby females as these become receptive. Although such behavior varies within species, what does not vary is the fact that only a proportion of males is successful; in the Southern ele-

phant seal, for example, the effective sex-ratio may locally exceed 100 females to 1 male.

Among species that mate in water, underwater territoriality has been suspected or confirmed in some. Male Weddell seals display in, and aggressively defend, narrow stretches of water, up to 650ft (200m) long, under females congregated with young along ice cracks. Individual male Ringed seals (see pp130–131) may use ice holes as much as 0.6mi (1km) apart, excluding other males, but not females. Male Harbor seals may patrol waters off restricted stretches of shoreline, and bite wounds suggest that they too are territorial. Although Crabeater, Grey, Hooded, and Spotted seals are said to form "families" of male and female with young, the males are merely awaiting receptivity of females for mating. The females are aggressively defended, but may be abandoned once mated, as males leave to seek other matings.

The fact that the difference in size between males and females is generally small among species that mate in water suggests that agility and speed may be more advantageous than brute size in males of such species. Exceptions are the large males of Hooded seals and Grey seals. The large size of the male Hooded seal suggests that they, like the Grey seal, may once have been land-breeders.

The social behavior of most species has been little studied outside the breeding season. Species may be basically solitary, aggregating merely because of clumped food or resting places, or may interact in truly social ways. Harbor seals in Quebec were shown to reduce their individual rates of scanning for danger when in larger groups. The navigational skills of Harp seals may be enhanced when they migrate in herds. Weaned young Crabeater seals may gather for protection from Leopard seals. Group "herding" of fishes has been mooted in Grey and Northern elephant seals.

Only the monk seals are truly endangered as species (see pp136–137). Isolated populations or subspecies of other seals are rare or declining. Female Ringed and Grey seals in the inner Baltic show pathological sterility, attributed to pollutants (see p131). There may be fewer than 200 Ringed seals remaining there, isolated in Lake Saima, Finland, although the population of 10,000 or so in Lake Ladoga, USSR, seems secure under restricted hunting. The distinctive Harbor seal of the Kuriles, with some 5,000 individuals, is protected in the USSR, but some are killed in northern Japan. Some lake populations of Harbor seals in northern Canada have been reduced and possibly eliminated.

By contrast, most populations of seals are probably stable or increasing, some after heavy exploitation in the past. A striking example is the Northern elephant seal, which has increased from fewer than 100 in 1912 to some 50,000 today.

Although the killing of young Harp seals in eastern Canada is repugnant to many, research on, and management of, this population in recent years have been more thorough than for almost any other wild mammal, and recent evidence indicates slow increase under current quotas (see pp 134–135). The White Sea herd is managed less scientifically but probably more conservatively. The scientific basis for killing young Hooded seals in the North Atlantic is much more tenuous. Commercial hunting by Soviet sealers of several species in the Bering and Okhotsk seas was sharply curtailed after overexploitation in the 1960s. Hunting of Baikal and Caspian seals has also been recently reduced on the basis of stock assessments.

Seals are also killed for subsistence and commerce in skins by aborigines in northern regions and, on a smaller scale, by coastal peoples elsewhere. Although subjected to scientific scrutiny only in some regions, notably northern Canada, Alaska and Greenland, there is no evidence of any but localized declines in the populations.

Bounties and culls by authorities have been used to reduce populations of seals perceived as threats to fishermen. Today, apparently only Grey seals in Britain, Iceland, Norway and Canada are subject to such controversial controls, although other seals are shot without official sanction.    IAM

▲ **Bobbing like corks,** a group of adult Grey seals swim in a bay of the Orkney Islands. Although seals spend much of the year at sea, very little is known of this aspect of their lives.

◄ **Face-to-face confrontation.** Two male Grey seals dispute a boundary at Sable Island, east of Nova Scotia. This is one of the few sites where Grey seals breed on sand.

► **Resplendent lanugo.** A dewy-eyed Grey seal pup, still in its creamy-white birth coat, awaits its mother's return. The lanugo is molted after 2–3 weeks and replaced by a coat similar to that of the adult.

# THE 19 SPECIES OF TRUE SEALS

Abbreviations: HTL = head-to-tail, straight-line length. wt = weight.
E Endangered. ? = information unconfirmed or unknown.

## Mediterranean monk seal E
*Monachus monachus*

Main population in Aegean and E
Mediterranean seas, also in SW Black
Sea, C and W Mediterranean, Adriatic
Sea, and Atlantic around Madeira, the
Canaries, and Spanish Sahara.
Population 500–700. Male HTL about
100in; wt about 570lb. Female HTL
106in; wt 660lb. Coat: dark above,
gray below, sometimes with large
white area. Newborn with black
lanugo. Female first young and male
age of maturity unknown. Longevity
unknown. Births May–November,
peak September–October, generally
now in caves and grottos in sea cliffs.
Lactation 6 weeks? Males possibly
polygynous, mating in water; social
structure unknown, although
somewhat gregarious. Diet: fishes and
octopus, some quite large.

## Caribbean monk seal E
*Monachus tropicalis*

Last reliable sighting in 1952;
probably extinct. Historically in
Florida Keys, Bahamas, Greater and
Lesser Antilles, Yucatan, on offshore
islets and atolls. HTL about 85in; wt
about 440lb? Coat: dark above and
light below, the latter less extensive in
females? Newborn with dark lanugo.
In form, evidently closer to
Mediterranean monk seal than to
Hawaiian monk seal. Reproductive
characteristics and longevity
unknown. Births in December. Other
features of life history unknown.

## Hawaiian monk seal E
*Monachus schauinslandi*

Breeds regularly on 6 atolls of the NW
Hawaiian Islands and comes ashore
on 3 others, but rarely elsewhere.
Population 500–1,000. Male HTL
about 82in; wt about 375lb.
Female HTL about 90in; wt about
550lb. Coat: dark above, pale below.
Newborn with dark lanugo. Like *M.
tropicalis*, but perhaps the most
primitive of all phocids in structure of
posterior *vena cava*, of ear region of
skull, and in the unfused bases of the
tibia and fibula. Female first young
about 5 years, male maturity
unknown. Longevity: 30 years.
About two-thirds of adult females give
birth each year in January–August,
on beaches. Lactation 6 weeks. Males
may harass females with pups, but
mate later in water. Diet: fishes,
cephalopods.

## Crabeater seal
*Lobodon carcinophagus*

Distributed throughout antarctic pack
ice, most abundantly near the broken
periphery in the southern winter, in
residual ice nearer the continent in
summer. Has strayed as far north as
Heard Island, S Africa, Uruguay, N
New Zealand, S Australia.
World population 15 + million?
Both sexes HTL 92in; wt
about 485lb. Coat: uniform, usually
pale gray, sometimes darker;
immature darker and may be
somewhat mottled. Often heavily
scarred from fights with other
Crabeaters and Leopard seals.
Newborn with brownish or grayish
lanugo. A rather slender, small-
headed species. Cheek teeth
elaborately multicuspid for straining
macroplanktonic food. Female first
young 2.3–4.5 years, according to
year and region. Male maturity about
4.5 years. Longevity: male 30 +
years, female 36 years. Births on pack
ice in September–October. Lactation 4
weeks? Males form "triads" with
female and pup, sequestering female
until she is ready to mate on the ice.
Generally non-gregarious, but young
may form (protective?) groups. After
breeding, continue to use ice floes to
rest and as escape from Killer whales
and Leopard seals. Diet:
predominantly krill, also some fishes,
squids.

## Weddell seal
*Leptonychotes weddelli*

The most southerly seal, breeding in
fast ice around Antarctica and on
islands north to S Georgia. Has
strayed as far north as Uruguay, Juan
Fernandez Island, N New Zealand, S
Australia, Kerguelen. World
population about 1 million? Male HTL
98in; wt 859lb. Female HTL
106in; wt 992lb. Coat: gray, darker
above, mottled with black, gray and
whitish blotches. Newborn with
brownish-gray lanugo. Canines and
two large, protruding incisors often
worn from "sawing" at ice holes.
Female first young about 3 years,
male maturity about 4 years, but
probably breeding successfully only
when older. Longevity: male 21
years, female 25 years. Births on fast
ice, rarely on islands, mid-September
to early November. Lactation 5–6
weeks. Adult females along ice cracks
are spaced in relation to holes for
access to water. Adult males vocalize,
display and fight under the ice along
such cracks to mate in elongated

"territories," or may simply prevent
access to breathing holes by other
males. Adults later join immatures at
edges of fast ice and rest on ice floes,
rarely land. Diet: mostly fishes (some
large), cephalopods, some krill,
bottom invertebrates (secured by
deep-diving).

## Leopard seal
*Hydrurga leptonyx*

Found generally near the fringes on
the antarctic pack ice and around
subantarctic islands. May show
periodic dispersal northward; has
strayed as far north as Sydney,
Australia, Rarotonga in the Cook
Islands, S Africa, Tristan da Cunha,
N Argentina. World population about
500,000? Male HTL 110in; wt about
720lb. Female HTL 118in; wt about
815lb. Coat: dark gray above, pale
below, with light and dark spots on
throat, shoulders and sides. Newborn
with lanugo resembling adult pattern.
Bodies elongate, heads large and jaws
massive, set with saw-like cheek
teeth. Female first young about 6
years, male maturity about 5 years.
Longevity: male 23 + years, female
26 + years. Births in
November–December on loose pack
ice, occasionally on islands. Lactation
4 weeks? Males not seen with females
and young on ice. Female may only
reproduce in alternate years? Usually
found in association with Crabeater
seals and large colonies of penguins,
which form prey; diet also includes
fishes, some krill.

## Ross seal
*Ommatophoca rossi*

Found sparsely and patchily
throughout Southern Ocean. Has
strayed to Heard Island. World
population 100,000–220,000? HTL
about 80in?; wt about 395lb?,
with little sexual difference? Coat:
dark above, silvery-white below, with
light and dark flecks, and with light
and dark stripes from chin to chest
and sometimes along sides of neck.
Lanugo of newborn has pattern
similar to adult coat. A thick-necked,
short-muzzled, large-eyed species,
with long foreflippers. Incisors and
canines sharp and recurved to secure
slippery prey, but cheek teeth small,
often loose or missing. Female first
young about 4 years, male maturity
about 4 years. Longevity: male 21
years, female 19 years. Births in
November on pack ice. Lactation
period unknown. Males make trilling
sounds with larynx. Non-gregarious,

patchy distribution probably related
to preference for more productive
waters, not for very dense pack ice as
previously supposed. Diet: mainly
squids, some fishes and occasionally
bottom invertebrates.

## Northern elephant seal
*Mirounga angustirostris*

Breeds on islands from central
California to central Baja California,
mostly on the Channel Islands; some
recently on mainland sites. After
breeding and molting, disperses
northward, a few as far as S Alaska.
World population about 55,000. Male
HTL about 165in; wt about 5,000lb.
Female HTL about 122in; wt about
2,000lb. Coat: silvery when young,
becoming darker above with age.
Newborn with black lanugo. Males
become corrugated and heavily
scarred in thick-skinned neck region,
and develop pendulous, inflatable
enlargement of nasal cavity. Canines
very large, cheek teeth peg-like, but
sometimes with cusps and double
roots. Female first young about 4
years, male maturity about 4.5 years,
sexually competent when 9–10 years
old. Longevity: male and female 14
years. Births on islands mid-December
through January. Lactation 4 weeks.
Females group on beaches after
smaller number of large males
establish dominance hierarchies by
vocalizations, displays, combat. A
single male may mate with up to 80
females in a season. After breeding
season, largely offshore. Diet: bottom
and mid-water fishes, some squids.

## Southern elephant seal
*Mirounga leonina*

Breeds mostly on islands both sides of
Antarctic Convergence, in 3 separate
groups, perhaps subspecies (another
group eliminated on Juan Fernandez
Island): 1) S Georgia, Falkland,
Gough, S Shetland islands, islands
and mainland of Antarctic Peninsula,
Patagonia north to Valdes Peninsula;
2) Kerguelen, Heard, Marion, and
Crozet islands; 3) Macquarie and
Campbell islands. Scattered births
found elsewhere, north to S Africa,
S Island of New Zealand, Tasmania,
Tristan da Cunha. Migrates to
Antarctic mainland and has strayed
north to S Australia, Mauritius and
Rodriguez Island, Uruguay, Peru,
N New Zealand. World population
about 650,000. Male HTL 193in; wt
5,291lb (S Georgia). Female HTL 118in;
wt 1,500lb (S Georgia). Male HTL
167in (Macquarie Island).

Female 104in (Macquarie Island). Coat: silvery when young, darker with age, especially in female. Newborn with black lanugo. Adult males with thick, scarred neck shield, proboscis less developed than in Northern elephant seal. Skull generally more massive than in Northern elephant seal, and cheek teeth never (?) cuspid or double-rooted. Female first young 4.2 years at S Georgia, 5.6 years at Macquarie Island, male maturity about 4 years, sexually competent at 9+ years at S Georgia, 8+ years at Macquarie Island. Longevity: male 20 years, female 18 years. Births on shore, occasionally shore ice, late September and October. Lactation 3–3.5 weeks. Breeding behavior as in Northern elephant seal, but single males may defend "harem" of up to 50 females, or "share" much larger aggregations, in which the sex ratio may reach 300 females to each male, with some male exchanges during the season. After breeding, disperse widely, molting ashore in January–April. Diet: fishes (often large), squid.

## Bearded seal
*Erignathus barbatus*

Circumpolar in relatively shallow arctic and subarctic waters, south to S Labrador, S Greenland, N Iceland, White Sea, Hokkaido, Alaska Peninsula. Has strayed to Tokyo Bay, Cape Cod, N Spain. World population 0.6–1 million? Atlantic subspecies *E. b. barbatus* weakly distinct from *E. b. nauticus*, found from W Canadian Arctic to central Siberia. HTL both sexes 87–90in, wt 518–573lb in various localities; HTL 79in, wt 419lb in Okhotsk Sea. Coat: gray above, rarely with few faint spots. Newborn lanugo dark brown, often with light spots on back and head. Four mammae (2 in other northern seals); large crinkled whiskers. Skull with deep jaw, teeth rudimentary and often missing when older. Female first young 6.5–7.2 years, various regions, male maturity 5.5 years Bering Sea. Longevity: male 25 years, female 31 years. Births on pack ice mid-March to late April. Lactation 2 weeks. Males "sing" underwater during the breeding season. Solitary individuals rest on ice floes when available, some on land in Okhotsk Sea. Diet: bottom-dwelling mollusks, crustaceans, sea cucumbers and fishes.

## Hooded seal
*Cystophora cristata*

Breeds in Gulf of St. Lawrence; northeast of Newfoundland; in Davis Strait; northwest of Jan Mayen Island; occasionally near White Sea. Migrates in summer mainly to waters off Greenland, with large molting region in Denmark Strait. Has given birth on land in Norway, Maine, and strayed to N Alaska, Florida, S Portugal. World population 250,000–400,000? Male HTL about 98in; wt about 880lb. Female HTL 87in; wt 705lb. Coat: both sexes gray with large black blotches and spots and black heads. Pale lanugo shed before birth, the newborn silvery with dark back. Mature male can inflate "hood" on snout and force nasal membrane through either nostril as red "balloon." Skull heavy, with 2 lower, 4 upper incisors, large canines and peg-like cheek teeth. Female first young about 4.5 years, male maturity about 5 years but mating only when older. Longevity: male 34 years, female 35+ years. Loose aggregations of females give birth mid-March to early April on old, heavy ice floes. Lactation 10–14 days. Female and pup attended by one male, rarely more, which uses "hood" in aggressive displays and calls under water. Rests on ice, rarely land, at other seasons. Diet: deepwater fishes, eg redfish, Greenland halibut, and squid.

## Harbor seal
*Phoca vitulina*
Harbor or Common seal.

In N Atlantic, Murmansk to outer Baltic and N France, UK south to E Anglia, S Ireland, Faeroes, Spitsbergen, Iceland, SE and W Greenland, Canadian Arctic south to Cape Cod; in N Pacific region from Bristol Bay, Pribilof, Aleutian, Commander islands, south to central Baja California and Hokkaido. Has strayed to Florida and Azores. World population 300,000–400,000? Male HTL 63–67in; wt 242–264lb. Female HTL 59–61in; wt 176–198lb (most of range); in Kurile Islands and Hokkaido, the distinctive subspecies *P. v. stejnegeri* is larger and more sexually dimorphic (male HTL about 79in; wt about 408lb; female HTL 67in; wt 264lb). Coat: varies from pale to dark gray, and ringed; *P. v. stejnegeri* all (?) dark. Whitish lanugo shed before birth, occasionally soon after. Dog-like face with teeth set obliquely in jaws. Large male

*P. v. stejnegeri* with more arched skulls. Female first young 4.8–6.2 years, male maturity 4.8–5.9 years, in various populations. Longevity: male 26 years, female 32 years. Births on land January–September in wide range, generally late spring. Rests on islets, rocks, sandbars, sometimes ice, generally in inshore waters. A few freshwater populations in E and N Canada; wanders up rivers elsewhere. Adults relatively sedentary, young dispersing. Diet: migratory, bottom-dwelling and open-sea fishes, some invertebrates.

## Spotted seal
*Phoca largha*

Separate populations in Bering and Chukchi Seas, Okhotsk Sea to Hokkaido, Tartar Strait, Peter the Great Bay, Po Hai and N Yellow Sea. Some geographical variation in this range. World population about 400,000? Male HTL 61in; wt 198lb. Female HTL 59in; wt 176lb (Bering and Okhotsk Seas); some 4in longer and 33lb heavier near Hokkaido and in Peter the Great Bay. Coat: typically light gray, darker above, with many small, dark spots, as in light form of Harbor seal. Born with whitish lanugo. Unlike closely related Harbor seal, teeth set straight in jaws. Female first young about 5 years, male maturity about 4.5 years. Longevity: male 29 years, female 32 years. Births in mid-February to April, latest in north, on ice floes near margin of pack ice in Bering Sea, closer to shore elsewhere. Lactation 3–4 weeks. Male, female and pup in "triads" scattered widely on ice. Moves to coasts in summer, resting on land and sometimes entering rivers. Diet: migratory and shallow-water bottom fishes, some invertebrates.

## Ringed seal
*Phoca ( = Pusa) hispida*

Circumpolar in arctic and subarctic waters, breeding south to White Sea, Norway, N Iceland, S Greenland, N Gulf of St. Lawrence, Alaska Peninsula, S Sakhalin, with isolates in inner Baltic and nearby Lakes Ladoga, Saima. Has strayed to S Portugal, C California, N Japan. World population 3.5–6 million? Much variation in body and skull measurements expressed as 7–8 subspecies, most doubtful. Male HTL 49–59in; wt 143–209lb. Female HTL 46–54in; wt 99–176lb (various populations). Large fast-ice and small pack-ice forms in Canadian

Arctic, Okhotsk and Bering–Chukchi Seas may result from differing lengths of lactation period and local population traditions. Coat: silvery to dark gray below, darker on back, with rings on sides and back. Born with white lanugo. Short muzzle, with fine, cuspid teeth. Female first young 5.8–8.3 years, male maturity 7.1–7.4 years, various populations. Longevity: male 43 years, female 40 years. Births March–April in snow lairs over breathing holes in fast ice, sometimes in open on pack ice. Lactation up to 2.5 months in fast ice, shorter in unstable ice. Males call underwater and may be "territorial." Rests on ice, rarely land. Diet: inshore: polar cod, bottom-dwelling crustaceans; offshore: planktonic crustaceans, some fishes.

## Baikal seal
*Phoca ( = Pusa) sibirica*

Lake Baikal (USSR), mainly in deeper parts. Population about 70,000. HTL 48in; wt 159lb (mean of both sexes). Coat: silver-gray, darker above, and unspotted. Born with white lanugo. Skull foreshortened, with large eye sockets. Claws on foreflippers heavier than in Ringed and Caspian seals, for keeping holes open in freshwater ice? Female first young 5.3 years, male maturity about 5 years. Longevity: male 52 years, female 56 years. Births in late February to early April in solitary snow lairs, as in Ringed seal. Lactation 8–10 weeks. Diet: largely deep-water fishes.

## Caspian seal
*Phoca ( = Pusa) caspica*

Caspian Sea, concentrating in north during breeding season, and in cooler, deeper middle and south of the lake during summer. Population about 450,000. HTL about 49in; wt 121lb (both sexes). Coat: gray, darker on back with fine dark spots. Newborn with white lanugo. Skull like Ringed seal's. Female first young 6.8 years, male maturity 6.6 years. Longevity: male 47 years, female 50 years. Aggregations of females give birth in late January to early February on pack ice north of Kulaly Island. Lactation 2 weeks. After ice melt, occasionally remain on islets and rocks. Diet: wide range of small fishes, crustaceans.

CONTINUED ▶

## Harp seal

*Phoca ( = Pagophilus) groenlandica*

Discrete populations breed off NE Newfoundland and in Gulf of St. Lawrence, around Jan Mayen Island and near mouth of White Sea, summering in Kara and Barents Seas and in waters off Greenland and the Canadian Arctic Archipelago. Has strayed to Mackenzie Delta, Virginia, Scotland and France. World population 2.6–3.8 million. HTL 67in; wt 286lb (mean both sexes in NW Atlantic, slightly larger elsewhere). Coat: light gray with dark brown spots in juveniles, some subadult males becoming very dark, developing dark, U-shaped "harp" on back of gray adult, more slowly and less contrastingly in female. Newborn with white lanugo. A rather slender, active species, with small, cuspid teeth. Female first young 5.5 years in NW Atlantic, about 5 years in White Sea, male maturity 4 years in White Sea. Longevity: male 29 years, female 30+ years. Gregarious females give birth among hummocks near middle of large floes, mid-February to March in White Sea, slightly later at Jan Mayen Island and in NW Atlantic. Lactation 9–12 days. Females then join underwater aggregations of vocalizing, displaying males for mating. Migrate and spend summer in sometimes large and fast-moving groups, sometimes resting on ice. Diet: capelin and other fishes, shrimps and krill (especially by young seals) in south; polar cod, planktonic amphipods in north.

## Ribbon seal

*Phoca ( = Histrophoca) fasciata*

Breeds in Bering and Okhotsk Seas, with populations from the former summering in Chukchi Sea. Has strayed to Beaufort and E Siberian Seas, S Hokkaido, C California. World population about 180,000? HTL 63in; wt 209lb (both sexes; little geographical variation). Coat: in young silvery, dark above, becoming uniformly darker with age, except for distinct bands around neck, hind torso and each foreflipper. Born with whitish lanugo. Skull foreshortened, with small teeth, large eye sockets. Female first young 3.3 years in Okhotsk Sea, 3.8 years in Bering Sea; male maturity 3.1 years in Okhotsk Sea, 3.5 years in Bering Sea. Longevity: male 31 years, female 23 years. Births on heavier pack ice than for Spotted seal, mainly in early April. Lactation 3–4 weeks. Males not seen with scattered females and pups. Stay offshore after melt. Diet: open-sea fishes, shrimps, cephalopods in deeper water; the young eat krill.

## Grey seal

*Halichoerus grypus*

Three populations distinct in breeding seasons and, weakly, in form are: *H. g. grypus* in NW Atlantic from S Greenland (formerly?) and S Labrador to Massachusetts; *H. g. atlanticus* in NE Atlantic from Spitsbergen (formerly) and Murmansk coast to S Iceland, UK, S Ireland; *H. g. balticus* in inner Baltic. Has strayed to New Jersey, S Portugal, N Labrador. World population 120,000–135,000. Male HTL 84in; wt 595lb; female HTL 72in; wt 309lb (Northumberland). Male HTL 90in; wt 727lb; female HTL 79in; wt 375lb (Nova Scotia). Coat: male heavily dark-spotted, sometimes black, female gray, darker above, with black spots and blotches below. Born with whitish lanugo. Snout elongate and arched, especially in adult male, which also develops heavy, scarred neck region. Large peg-like teeth. Female first young 5.5 years in UK, 5.0 years in Nova Scotia, male maturity about 6 years in Scotland, 4.2 years in Nova Scotia, but does not mate until about 8–10 years old. Longevity: male 31 years (43 in captivity), female: 46 years. Births on land in NE Atlantic group during September–December, on pack ice in Baltic during February–March, and on land or ice in NW Atlantic in January–February. Lactation 2–2.5 weeks. Males territorial or aggressive but mobile among grouped females, perhaps polygynous on ice. At other seasons, often on offshore islets and rocks. Diet: migratory, open-sea and bottom fishes (often large specimens), some invertebrates.

IAM

► **Elephant of the oceans.** The massive nose of the Northern elephant seal leaves no doubt as to how it got its name. Elephant seals show the most extreme disparity in form between male and female to be found in true seals. The nasal protuberance of the males is the primary organ of sexual display.

# The Krill-eating Crabeater

*The world's most abundant large mammal*

The Crabeater seal is a creature of superlatives. It numbers 15–40 million, which is at least equal to the total for all the other pinnipeds combined (the total weight of the population is about four times or more that of all other pinnipeds combined); it occupies a range of up to 8.5 million sq mi (22 million sq km), the maximum extent of the antarctic pack ice, but as the pack ice contracts in summer it is confined to six residual pack-ice regions totalling 1.6 million sq mi (4 million sq km); it feeds on the swarming Antarctic krill, the abundance of which has been estimated at 500–750 million tons, and which is possibly the most abundant animal species, by weight.

The Crabeater seal is a key species in the Southern Ocean and there is evidence that it has now overtaken the baleen whales as the major consumer of krill, possibly eating up to 160 million tons a year. As the commercially sought baleen whales declined during this century due to over-hunting by man (see pp74–75), certain other krill-feeding birds, seals and whales have increased. In the case of the Crabeaters, the body growth-rates appear to have accelerated so that they mature earlier: at 2.5

years now compared with 4 years in 1950; this, together with the fact that up to 94 percent of mature females may be pregnant at any one time, and a life span of up to 39 years, indicates an expanding population.

Despite their huge overall population, Crabeater seals are fairly sparsely distributed. During the summer, recorded mean group sizes are 1.3–2.2; the densities are 5–18 per sq mi (2–7 per sq km) and they haul-out during the day, with maximum counts around midday. They feed mainly at night when krill are nearer the surface.

The Crabeater pupping season lasts for 4–6 weeks and is highly synchronized, with a peak in early to mid-October. Until recently, very little was known about their breeding behavior because of the difficulty of reaching their breeding populations in the remote southern pack ice, but in 1977 an expedition set out with this objective.

The basic social unit is the mother and the milk-coffee-colored, furry pup, which select a hummocked floe and remain together for no more than a few weeks until the pup is weaned, growing from 55lb (25kg) to 264lb (120kg) solely on the mother's milk. They are joined by an adult male to form a

▲ **Jaws agape,** a young Crabeater seal displays its elaborately cusped teeth used for straining krill from the sea, its principal and almost exclusive food.

▶ **Not a nuclear family.** This triad of male, female and pup Crabeaters is not quite what it seems. The male is not the father of the pup, is aggressive to both mother and pup and is merely waiting for the opportunity to mate with the female when the pup has been weaned. Prior to mating, the male drives the mother away from the pup.

▼ **Basking Crabeaters** on an ice floe. The Crabeater seal is almost exclusively a creature of the antarctic pack ice. The spotted animal in the foreground is a Weddell seal.

triad which persists until the pup is weaned. These groups are usually separated by 0.6–1.2mi (1–2km). On average, the female is slightly larger than the male and drives him away from the pup with an aggression that fades as the pup grows and her own condition weakens. The male is very aggressive and persistent in trying to stay with the female, and the pup is weaned when the male becomes dominant and drives the female away from it. Other males occasionally approach the family group over the ice, when a fight ensues lasting up to six minutes. The mated pairs are very obvious because the female's back is red where she has been bitten by the male and the rear half of her body is very thin. Mating occurs, it is thought, on the floe, a few days after weaning. Soon the pairs break up and solitary females are seen. As a result of fights with both males and females the old male Crabeaters are heavily scarred about the head and neck.

Many Leopard seals (see pp138–139) occur in the leads (the channels of open water between the floes) and these prey on the Crabeaters. They bob up to look over the surface of floes, turning their heads from side to side in a sinister, questing way. Leopard seals have been seen eating weaned Crabeater pups in the water; one chased a yearling Crabeater with great speed and energy—three times the Crabeater exploded from the water onto a floe, hotly pursued by the Leopard seal, which made a supreme effort but just failed to catch it and gave up the chase. However, young weaned pups must be easy prey for they do not swim with such agility. Leopard seals preferentially take weaned Crabeaters in the spring, but as these pups grow throughout the summer and become more experienced, the probability of escape increases, although up to 84 percent of those escaping receive wounds, which are visible as parallel scars on most adults. When the new crop of weaned Crabeaters appears the Leopard seals switch to this easier prey. The age-composition of the Crabeater population reflects high mortality in the first year, but subsequently annual mortality is relatively low.

Such predation may have played an important role in the evolution of Crabeater behavior, resulting in mating on the floes (although this has yet to be confirmed), because pre-mating behavior underwater would presumably attract these predators and possibly Killer whales. It may also explain widely dispersed family groups, because fewer larger groups would be more vulnerable to predation.     RML

# Birth in a Snow-cave

## The lairs of the Ringed seal

As the winter pack ice thickens and snow builds up around pressure ridges in the ice, pregnant Ringed seals dig upwards with their foreflippers from the water below, to create a lair or snow-cave. Here the pup is born and spends the first one or two months. This behavior is unique among seals.

The Ringed seal is only about half the size of other true seals. The name derives from its distinctive coat pattern of dark spots surrounded by a white ring, scattered over the gray-brown fur. It is one of the most numerous and successful of northern true seals, with a circumpolar distribution, although the Baltic population is declining.

During the winter, Ringed seals live on land-fast ice, although pack ice may sometimes be used as long as it is well-consolidated and stable. In early winter, they use the open leads and cracks in the ice for access to the air, but as the ice thickens they must claw at the ice with their fore-flippers to maintain breathing holes. Around these holes, the accumulating snow is excavated to form a small cave. Both sexes excavate hauling-out lairs, but the pupping lairs, perhaps up to three within 330ft (100m) of each other, are constructed by females alone. This complex of birth lairs probably provides alternative refuges to which a female can move her pup if danger threatens.

The lair is thought to give the pups some protection from predation by Polar bears, Arctic foxes and man. But the lairs are quite conspicuous, and predation rates by Arctic foxes on newborn pups may be as as high as 58 percent. It may be that the benefit the lair confers in keeping the pup warm until its insulating blubber is laid down may outweigh this risk of predation.

In the Baltic, pups are born from late February to late March, about one month earlier than in the Canadian Arctic. Each female's single pup bears a white fluffy coat and weighs about 11lb (5kg). Pups are suckled for 6–7 weeks. It is possible that the female feeds during this time; otherwise the demands of lactation and her own body requirements might deplete her blubber stores too quickly. Females lose up to 40 percent of their body weight during the spring and early summer.

Females become receptive towards the end of the lactation period, and mating occurs under the ice. Little is known of their sexual behavior because of the difficulties of observation beneath the ice, but the Ringed seal appears to be very similar in many ways to the much larger Weddell seal of the Antarctic. Male Weddell seals defend under-

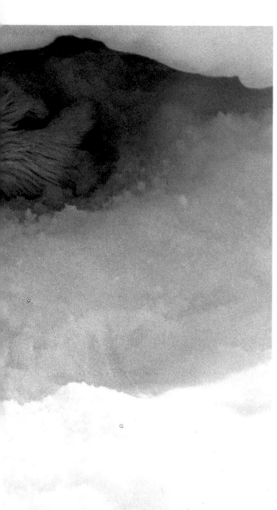

water territories and are thought to exhibit a limited form of polygyny, in that they try to prevent access to the females by other males. Male Ringed seals often carry wounds which could well be the result of territorial disputes within a similar social system. However, the sex ratio of adult Ringed seals is equal and birth lair complexes are widely spaced, so it is unlikely that males could defend more than one at a time.

The only time that Ringed seals haul out in large numbers on the ice is immediately after pupping. In the spring sunshine, the ice begins to crack and seals butt and scratch at the snow roof of their haul-out lairs to make an exit. A few mothers may still be suckling their pups, but most of the adults laze on the ice for days or more at a time, doing very little except scratching and being vigilant for predators. The molt occurs during this time on the ice surface, and the seals scratch incessantly. Sun-bathing is also important, in that high skin temperatures help the molting process. The pups have already molted within their lairs, shedding their white birth coat for the first adult coat.

As the ice melts, the seals disperse, adopting an open-sea existence for the short arctic summer. They feed intensively to replace their depleted blubber. By mid-fall thin ice covers the bays and the annual cycle begins again.

In the Canadian Arctic, the Ringed seal is the most numerous marine mammal, but the Baltic population has declined markedly during this century. Because of the difficulties of counting seals in their lairs, estimates of numbers can only be crude, but it appears that a population once numbered in hundreds of thousands is now reduced to about 10,000. Overhunting has been a major cause of decline, but now the species is fully protected.

Recently, a more insidious threat has been implicated—pollution by organochlorine compounds, in particular polychlorinated biphenyls (PCBs). The reproductive rate of Ringed seals in the Baltic has declined sharply: in the Canadian Arctic 80–90 percent of mature females are pregnant in one year, but in the Baltic the figure is now less than 25 percent. Associated with this lack of fertility are abnormalities of the female reproductive tract which have been linked with high levels of PCBs in seal tissue. As fertility has declined, so has the age of maturity. Baltic Ringed seals of both sexes now mature at 3 years of age, whereas 40 years ago the age of maturity was 5. Such a change often occurs when a population declines, thus easing competition for food. A direct causative link between PCBs and reduced fertility remains to be established, but the decline in the population of Ringed seals in the Baltic is giving cause for serious concern. SSA

▲ **Pup peering out of a lair.** The pups spend up to two months in the lair before being weaned.

◀ **Birth in a snow-cave.** The Ringed seal exploits the build-up of snow around pressure points in the ice to hollow out a lair in which to give birth.

▶ **Adult Ringed seal** on Lake Saima, Finland, showing the distinctive markings: pale rings scattered over a dark gray coat. The population of this isolated subspecies (*P. h. saimensis*) is estimated at 100–120 individuals and they give birth on ice but not in ice lairs.

# Beach Warfare

*Sexual conflict among Northern elephant seals*

"The battle between the sexes" which is a perennial subject for cartoonists and humorists is a serious and fascinating study for evolutionary biologists, and nowhere is it more vivid than within the society of Northern elephant seals.

The most striking thing about elephant seals is that males and females look and act differently. The disparity in size is so marked that it would be understandable to mistake the sexes for different species. Males are at least three times the weight of the females and they have two outstanding secondary sexual characteristics: a pendulous, elephantine proboscis and a thick shield of wrinkled tissue on the neck and chest. They engage in bloody fights for the dominant status which confers access to groups of females. The few males that achieve the highest status monopolize mating. The alpha male (the dominant of dominants) alone may inseminate 100 females in one breeding season and four times that number in his lifetime.

This is what is known as a polygynous mating system. The male is a father in only the genetic sense, for males exhibit no paternal behavior. Females look like a larger version of the juveniles and, unlike males, they are gregarious, gathering together in groups or harems of up to 1,000 individuals to give birth and nurse their young. Virtually all adult females give birth to a single pup annually throughout their lives. If a female starts reproducing early, at three years old, and lives long, to 14 years, she may produce a maximum of 12 pups in her lifetime.

From the moment that females appear on the sandy island beaches of California and Mexico where they breed, they are hounded by males eager to mate with them. Males not only pursue receptive females, they direct their attention to females that do not want to mate and are not yet capable of being inseminated. These include pregnant females, females giving birth and nursing females.

Male courtship is direct, aggressive and relentless. Without preliminaries, a male moves directly to the side of a female, puts a foreflipper over her back, bites her on the neck, pulls her strongly to him, and attempts to copulate. If the female protests or attempts to move away, as is usually the case, the male pins her down by slamming the full weight of his head and forequarters on her back one or more times and bites her more vigorously.

In these sexual disagreements, the outcome is usually bad for the female. Mount-ing is harmful for pregnant females: it disrupts the mother-pup bonding process in females giving birth and it interrupts feeding and causes mother-pup separation when nursing mothers are involved. Moreover, in their single-minded efforts to chase subordinates out of the harem or to evade a superior, males trample over pups in their path. Up to 10 percent of the pups born in one season may die in this way. After a four-week nursing period, at the end of which mating occurs with a high ranking male in the harem, females face a more serious peril as they attempt to return to sea. They must run the gauntlet of several peripheral males surrounding the harem. These males intercept departing females and compete fiercely to mate with them. In their zeal to outdo each other, males sometimes injure and kill females inadvertently. All that a female can do in these disagreements is to make it difficult for young, low-ranking males to mate. Females protest vocally at all attempts to mate with them. This signals to all males in the vicinity that a female is being mounted. If a male dominant to the mounter is nearby, he chases him off and usually continues the sexual assault himself.

Clearly, mating in this species is not a cooperative venture where two individuals combine efforts to produce an offspring. Rather, the impression is that the large males dominate the smaller females and selfishly take what they want, being constrained only by energy limitations or by each other. Females do the best they can under the circumstances. How has this strategy evolved?

The differences in form and behavior between the sexes, and their conflict, so apparent in this species, evolved in part because of the disparity in reproductive potential between them. Gestation severely constrains productivity of females and sets the stage for two entirely different reproductive strategies: one emphasizes quantity and the other quality of offspring produced. For males, the mating game is to gain membership of an exclusive breeding club. A one-year membership is all that is needed to hit the genetic jackpot, although a male may retain dominant status for up to four years. However, the club has stringent entrance requirements such as great size, fighting ability and sexual prowess, and since a male must become a member or he doesn't breed, he is compelled to take risks to increase his chances. For example, newly weaned male pups risk injury by attempting to steal milk from nursing females in the harem. If successful, they may double their

**▲ Battle for dominance.** Rearing their necks, two bull Northern elephant seals strive for mastery of a segment of a breeding beach. The neck, which is toughened, and the huge nasal protuberance bear the brunt of these attacks.

**◄ Irony of reproduction.** In his selfish urge to mate, a lumbering bull elephant seal has trapped a pup between himself and the cow. Many pups are crushed to death by the bulls, but not normally their own kin.

weight and obtain additional nutrients important in development at a time when other weaned pups are losing weight and energy reserves. This early advantage usually leads to increased size in adulthood, which in turn is linked to fighting success and social rank achieved. Female pups do not attempt to steal milk because the potential benefits do not outweigh the risks. The female strategy is to work hard to ensure the survival of the limited number of pups she produces. There is no jackpot here but a small steady flow of winnings.

Why, then, is the difference in size between males and females more extreme in the Northern elephant seal than in any other seal? We can only speculate on this, but it may be that the distribution (in this case, clumping) and relative abundance of resources (either food or suitable breeding sites, or both) provide an opportunity for males to monopolize large numbers of females at these sites, and inter-male competition for the females (requiring great strength and endurance) consequently becomes intense. BLeB

# Culling the Whitecoats
## The controversial fate of the Harp seal

The Harp seal is the most numerous pinniped of the North Atlantic Ocean, despite periods of overexploitation. It inhabits the fringes of the pack ice and undergoes extensive migrations necessitated by the seasonal freezing and melting of the ice. The coats of the young—"whitecoats"—have been highly prized and the Harp seal's fecundity has allowed a substantial cull to be taken every year without diminishing the population.

Harp seals are divided into three stocks, pupping in the White Sea, near Jan Mayen Island east of Greenland, and on both sides of Newfoundland. These give birth respectively in late February, late March, and late February to mid-March (in each area, this is the time when daytime melting of the leads begins).

At the time of reproduction in early spring, adult females form aggregations of several tens of thousands on close, one-winter pack ice, which they reach from the leads of open water. They maintain an individual distance, displaying to each other with head pointed vertically, and snarling. The ice may drift at 1mph (1.5km/h) or more and have a subsequent life of a few weeks only; a premium is therefore placed on rapid development, and the whitecoat grows from 18lb (8kg) at birth to 77lb (35kg) at 10–14 days when it is weaned. It then starves for several weeks and sheds its lanugo before beginning to enter the water to feed on krill and small fish. The adult males rest in groups within the whelping patches, but are aggressive to each other and extremely vocal underwater amongst the ice floes. Mating takes place, mainly in the water, when the pup is weaned. Development of the embryo is arrested at an early stage and then resumes in late July or August. At the time of mating, the adults leave the ice floes and the pups soon begin to enter the water among the loose ice floes and start to feed.

The animals haul out on pack ice again about a month after whelping, and are then not aggressive to each other and are highly aggregated. The immature animals and adult males begin to molt, starting in late March at Newfoundland, and the females arrive later, in late April at Newfoundland, after a phase of fattening which follows the heavy drain of food reserves due to lactation.

Each stock of Harp seals probably originally numbered 3 million animals. Each was subject to heavy hunting, beginning in the 18th century, when a number of north European nations, engaged in taking Bowhead whales, added a catch of Harp seals in the spring months. The people living around the White Sea in arctic Russia, and the early settlers of Newfoundland, started sealing from shore and from small craft in order to find a source of revenue in the winter months when fishing was not possible. Although ice and storms protected the seals from rapid overexploitation, each stock eventually became depleted, the Newfoundland stock twice (in the mid-19th and mid-20th centuries, with a phase of recovery between). The hunting of all three stocks has now been controlled by the governments of Norway, the USSR, Denmark (for Greenland) and Canada. Protective measures have included, in succession: a prohibition against shooting adult females at the whelping patches, a closing date for hunting of molters and, finally, a quota on the killing of pups. These measures have allowed recovery of the White Sea herd to a present level of 0.75 million or more, and of the Newfoundland herds to 1.5 million or more, though Norway has kept the Jan Mayen herd at about 0.25 million animals in order to prevent excessive predation by Harp seals on its important fishery for capelin in the Barents Sea. Present pup production at Newfoundland is estimated from capture-recapture tagging at about 400,000 and a recent catch of 180,000, mostly pups and young immatures, is believed to be allowing an increase of the

▲ **Death of a whitecoat.** The Harp seal population is no longer in danger from exploitation, so the case against culling rests on its intrinsic unpleasantness.

▼ **Pack-ice patrol.** Harp seals in an open lead between the pack ice of the Gulf of St. Lawrence, Canada. Harp seal migrations follow the freezing and melting of the pack ice.

▲ **Tearful, large eyes** and creamy coat of a Harp seal pup show just why there is so much public resistance to the practice of clubbing them to death. Even if it is allowed to survive, this stage of life is very short: weaning takes 10–14 days and the birth coat is shed a few weeks later.

population at about 5 percent per annum.

The principal goal of the hunt in recent decades has been pups of all stages, especially the young, fast-haired whitecoats and the fully-molted "beaters," valuable for their hair coats and oil. While a controlled kill of young seals gives a higher production than a kill of the biologically more valuable adults (especially the females), and killing of the pups can be humane, public reaction has set in against the killing of the attractive whitecoats in the presence of their mothers. Public opinion moreover has been skillfully manipulated by confusing the issue of humane killing with the alleged overexploitation of the herds, which is no longer a valid issue, as discussed above. The sealers, who include northern hunters and fishermen-hunters, therefore face economic deprivation at a time when successful management of the seal herds has been achieved, a distressing irony.                    DES

# The Rarest Seals

*Saving the imperiled Monk seals*

Monk seals are the only pinnipeds that live in warm, subtropical seas. Of the three species, the Caribbean monk seal is probably extinct; the two remaining species are both imperiled, such that rapid action is required to save them. Overall, numbers have declined by half within the last 30 years because of human interference. There are estimated to be about 500 Mediterranean monk seals, and the number of Hawaiian monk seals may be closer to this than to the figure of 1,000 often quoted.

The Hawaiian monk seal has been described as a "living fossil." Certain anatomical characteristics of the species (eg the bony structure of the ear) are at a more primitive stage developmentally than those found in seal fossils dating back some 14.5 million years (man's first upright ancestors appeared only about 3 million years ago). Over 15 million years ago, the ancestors of today's Hawaiian monk seals left a population of Atlantic-Caribbean seals in the North Atlantic Ocean and swam halfway across the Pacific, through a long-gone channel, the Central American Seaway, separating North and South America, to the Hawaiian Islands.

The Mediterranean monk seal may have given rise to the mythical nymphs and sirens, who lay on the rocks and sang a song so enchanting it lured passing sailors to their doom, and Aristotle's description of it is the first record of a pinniped.

The Hawaiian monk seal colonizes six of the nine atolls and islands that make up the Leeward Hawaiian islands, a low, fragmented chain of coral and rock islets that extends for over 1,000mi (1,600km) northwest from the main Hawaiian islands. Sealing expeditions in the 19th century reduced the population, and later expeditions for guano, feathers and whales further disturbed their environment. However, the species remained isolated from permanent human settlements until World War II, when US naval bases were established.

Monk seals are sensitive to any human intrusion into their habitat, particularly during reproductive periods. Nursing is interrupted, the vital mother-pup bond may be broken, and pup-mortality rates rise. Some 39 percent of pups born at one of the Leeward Islands during a study in the late 1950s died before weaning, most likely from malnutrition after nursing was disrupted. When disturbed, pregnant monk seals may leave their sheltered beach pupping-grounds for exposed sand-spits.

Shark attacks and disease also take their toll. As many as 60 seals died at Laysan Island (the largest of the Leeward chain) in 1978, possibly from ciguatera, a form of fish poisoning thought to originate with infected microorganisms. Ciguatera outbreaks may follow the destruction of coral reefs, such as that caused by extensive harbor dredging in recent years at Midway Atoll.

Unlike the Mediterranean monk seal (whose fate is in the hands of at least 10 countries bordering the Mediterranean and northeast Atlantic) conservation of the Hawaiian monk seal comes under the jurisdiction of just one country. In 1976, the United States government declared the monk seal to be an endangered species. All but two of the Leeward Islands are protected

▼ **Frolicking in the Mediterranean.** Mediterranean monk seals in an idyllic scene from an old print. The modern reality though is far from idyllic. With the increased human presence around the Mediterranean, seals no longer congregate on rocks or beaches. Instead, they shelter and give birth in sea-caves, usually with underwater entrances. Even here, pregnant females are vulnerable to disturbance. Aborted fetuses have been discovered outside cave entrances and newborn pups in caves must contend with sudden flooding during storms. One of the largest Atlantic colonies (at Cap Blanc, consisting of possibly more than 50 seals) was destroyed in 1978 when the cave in which it had found refuge collapsed.

▲ **Exotic contrast.** The Hawaiian monk seal presents a contrast in setting to the other true seals, but its tropical paradise is no more secure than that of the Mediterranean monk seal. The establishment of American naval bases in World War II probably led to the disappearance of one large colony (at Midway Atoll between 1958 and 1968); others appear to be following in its wake: 1,200 seals were counted at the Leeward islands in 1958, less than 700 in 1976. There may now be as few as 500 Hawaiian monk seals.

under the Hawaiian Islands National Wildlife Refuge, and some breeding areas have been placed off-limits. In 1980, the United States National Marine Fisheries Service appointed a 12-member Monk Seal Recovery Team to review all available information on the species and to develop a management program to ensure that future disturbance is kept to a minimum. Despite such measures, the monk seal's future is by no means assured. Population growth is hampered by a low rate of reproduction and high pup mortality. During a four-year observational study, 136 pups were born at Laysan Island, of which 15 died or disappeared before weaning and two were stillborn. Only females older than six years produced offspring. The pregnancy rate of the Hawaiian monk seal has been estimated at 56 percent, over a two-year period.

A proposal has been made to establish a large commercial fishery in the waters surrounding the islands. This would lead to further disturbance of breeding females, seals might become entangled in fishing gear, and would be viewed as competitors for prey species also claimed by man.

Halfway across the world, a similar situation exists. The Mediterranean monk seal survives in tiny, scattered colonies, with the greatest numbers found in the Aegean Sea

and along the adjacent Turkish coast. Although once hunted commercially (primarily during the 15th century), the species is now too rare to support sealing, but human pressures persist. Since the 1950s, increased affluence has led to a burgeoning tourist industry, a rapidly expanding human population and the development of the Mediterranean as one of the world's most intensively fished seas.

The Mediterranean monk seal's decline is due mainly to the loss of suitable breeding and resting habitat. A possible solution would be the creation of international coastal marine parks devoted to year-round protection. Such sanctuaries would have to take into account the needs of fishermen and tourists for, clearly, they are not going to abandon this ancient coast. Financial compensation for the fishermen and education for those catering for the tourists are required. If conservation sites are provided for the monk seal which enable it to survive, this will also help a number of endangered species of birds, some endangered and indeed almost unknown plant species, as well as those habitats in which they dwell. Immediate and effective action by the USA and those European countries within whose boundaries the monk seal occurs can provide a future for the species.                    KR

# Hunter of the Southern Ocean

*The predatory Leopard seal*

A slender body, spotted like a leopard, a way of craning its neck in an almost reptilian pose, a gaping mouth, and its habit of preying on penguins and other seals, have given the Leopard seal a sinister reputation. There are even stories of explorers reportedly attacked on the ice by Leopard seals. Recent evidence has shown that this reputation is exaggerated.

The largest of the antarctic seals, the Leopard seal is the only seal that regularly preys on warm-blooded animals. Throughout its circumpolar distribution, the Leopard seal is generally closely associated with the edge of the pack ice, but it frequently hauls out on islands near the continent in summer, when the ice melts, and on subantarctic islands during the winter months, when the ice sheets expand.

The Leopard seal is largely solitary, to the extent that it is more likely to haul out on the ice next to a Crabeater seal, its prey, than

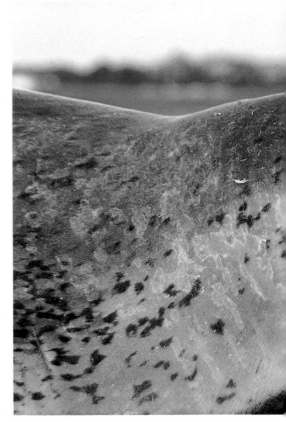

with another Leopard seal. It is an opportunistic predator, feeding on a wide variety of prey, including krill (37 percent), fish (13 percent), squid (8 percent), as well as penguines (25 percent), other seabirds (3 percent), and seals (8 percent). It is an active predator only in the water; on land it is quite cumbersome and certainly no threat to man unless closely approached.

The proportions of large and small prey in the diet undoubtedly vary according to their seasonal and distributional availability and the maturity of the Leopard seal. Young Leopard seals are dependent largely upon krill initially. The manner in which Leopard seals feed on krill is unknown, but they probably seek out krill swarms and gulp mouthfuls of water containing krill, which are then strained through the sieve-like rows of the ornately shaped post-canine teeth.

Only larger and older Leopard seals ap-

◀ **Built like a tank,** the leopard seal is paradoxically both thick-set and reptilian.

◀**Jaws.** BELOW LEFT The impressive gaping mouth of the Leopard seal leaves no doubt about its ability to seize large prey such as other seals. Its teeth, however, are very similar to those of the Crabeater seal, which it sometimes eats, in being adapted for catching the small crustacean, krill.

▼ **Predator and prey at rest.** Out of the water, leopard seals are too cumbersome to catch penguins, a fact which enables the two species to coexist, apparently peacefully, on an ice floe.

pear to take larger prey. Although spectacular, predation on penguins in the vicinity of rookeries is seasonal and appears to be the speciality of just a few seals; these individuals may have quite different diets from the bulk of the Leopard seals distributed on the pack ice. Even in the vicinity of rookeries, the mobility of swimming penguins makes them elusive prey.

When preying on penguins, Leopard seals attack from below and presumably by surprise. Accordingly, in the vicinity of penguin rookeries, the seals tend to patrol the deeper inshore waters where penguins are more vulnerable to this mode of attack, rather than the shallow, sloping beach areas. Even when a penguin is captured, the seals often have difficulty in killing and devouring their prey. Penguins repeatedly escape their captors, although sometimes the seals may be "playing" with their quarry in a cat-and-mouse fashion. Leopard seals cannot ingest a whole adult penguin, so portions of flesh are torn from the body by vigorously thrashing the victim about. Once the body skin is ripped open, only the fleshy body parts are normally eaten, leaving the legs, flippers, head, and much of the inner skeleton. Nonetheless, a fair amount of feathers is ingested.

The Leopard seal is unique among seals in habitually feeding on other seal species. Such an attack has never been witnessed, but the high frequency (55 percent) of attack-scarring on Crabeater seals, together with the observed high frequency of seal remains in Leopard seal stomachs, taken from pack-ice areas, indicates a fairly high level of predation. The majority of the seals preyed upon are young animals, but freshly scarred older seals attest to the fact that all age classes are vulnerable. In addition to the Crabeater, seal prey species include the Weddell seal, the pups of elephant seals, fur seals, and presumably also the Ross seal. Unlike the other true seals (but like the eared seals), the Leopard seal has elongated foreflippers which give it an advantage in speed and maneuverability in the water and on land.

The characteristic scarring on Crabeater seals resulting from Leopard seal attacks consists of slashes, up to 12in (30cm) long, often in parallel pairs, coursing tangentially across the body. Once thought to be caused principally by Killer whales, it now appears that they result from the evasive rolling action which often enables Crabeaters to escape from Leopard seals. When a Crabeater is caught, only the skin and attached blubber are eaten.          AWE

# SEA COWS AND MANATEES

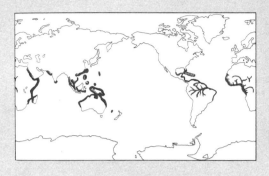

## ORDER: SIRENIA

Two families: 2 genera: 4 species.
Distribution: tropical coasts of E Africa, Asia, Australia and New Guinea; southeastern N America, Caribbean and northern S America; River Amazon; W African coast (Senegal to Angola).

Habitat: coastal shallows and river estuaries.

Size: head-to-tail length from 3.3–13ft (1–4m) in the dugong; 7.7–15ft (2.5–4.6m) in manatees; weight 500–2,000lb (230–900kg) in the dugong; 770–3,550lb (350–1,600kg) in manatees.

## Dugong
Genus *Dugong*
One species: **Dugong** (*Dugong dugon*)

## Manatees
Genus *Trichechus*
Three species: **West Indian manatee** (*Trichechus manatus*), **West African manatee** (*Trichechus senegalensis*), **Amazonian manatee** (*Trichechus inunguis*).

---

ALTHOUGH the Sirenia have a streamlined body form like those of other marine mammals which never leave the water, they are the only ones which feed primarily on plants. The unique feeding niche of the Sirenia is the key to understanding the evolution of their form and life history, and possibly explains why there are so few species in this order.

Current theories suggest that, during the relatively warm Eocene period (54–38 million years ago), a sea cow (*Protosiren*), closely related to the ungulates and descended from an ancestor shared by elephants, fed on the vast seagrass meadows found in shallow tropical waters of the west Atlantic and Caribbean. This was the ancestor of the modern manatees and dugongs. After the global climate cooled, during the Oligocene (38–26 million years ago), these seagrass beds retreated. The manatees (family Trichechidae) appeared during the Miocene (26–7 million years ago), a geological period which favored growth of freshwater plants in nutrient rich rivers along the coast of South America. Unlike the seagrasses, the floating mats of grasses found in the rivers of South America contain silica, an abrasive defense against herbivores, which causes rapid wearing of the teeth. Manatees have an unusual adaptation which minimizes the impact of wear: worn teeth are shed at the front and are replaced at the back throughout life.

Today, there are only four sirenian species: one dugong and three manatees. A fifth species, Steller's sea cow, was exterminated by humans in the mid-1700s. Adapted to the cold temperatures of the northern Pacific, Steller's sea cow was a specialist, feeding on kelp, the dense marine algae which became abundant after the retreat of the seagrass beds.

Sirenians are non-ruminant herbivores (like the horse and elephant and unlike sheep and cows), and they do not have a chambered or compartmentalized stomach. The intestines are extremely long—over 150ft (45m) in manatees—and between the large and small intestines there is a large mid-gut cecum, with paired blind-ending branches. Bacterial digestion of cellulose occurs in this hind part of the digestive tract and enables them to process the large

▶ **The sirenians.** The body of sirenians is similar to that of other sea mammals, but more stocky, due to the presence of large blubber stores. They have only foreflippers, the hindlimbs having been lost, leaving a vestigial pelvic girdle. The head is large, with small eyes and pinpoint ear openings. There is a pair of valved nostrils on the top of the head. (**1**) Steller's sea cow (*Hydrodamalis gigas*), extinct since 1768, was the largest species, with a tough bark-like skin. (**2**) Amazonian manatee (*Trichechus inunguis*), feeding on floating vegetation and showing the rounded tail typical of all manatees. It also has a white belly patch and no nails. (**3**) West African manatee (*Trichechus senegalensis*), showing the strong bristles on very mobile lips typical of sirenians. (**4**) West Indian manatee (*Trichechus manatus*) carrying vegetation with its flippers. Sirenians are well adapted to feeding on aquatic plants; dense bones serve as ballast and the dextrous forelimbs can dig into hard sediments to free submerged vegetation. This manatee has vestigial nails. (**5**) Dugong (*Dugong dugon*) showing the tail with a concave trailing edge. The dugong has no nails and its nostrils are placed further back than those of manatees.

---

Abbreviations: HTL = Head-to-tail length; wt = Weight; [EX] Extinct; [V] Vulnerable; [*] CITES listed.

### West Indian manatee [V]
*Trichechus manatus*
West Indian or Caribbean manatee.

Southeastern N America (Florida), Caribbean and northern S America or Atlantic coast to central Brazil. Shallow coastal waters, estuaries and rivers. HTL 12–15ft; wt 3,527lb. Skin: gray-brownish and hairless; rudimentary nails on foreflippers. Gestation: approximately 12 months. Longevity: 28 years in captivity, probably longer in the wild.

(Two subspecies—*T. m. manatus* and *T. m. latirostris*—have been proposed for the S and N American coastal population and the Caribbean populations respectively, but such a division is probably not justified, because detailed comparative studies of the two groups have not yet been made.)

### West African manatee [V]
*Trichechus senegalensis*
West African or Senegal manatee.

W Africa (Senegal to Angola). Other details, where known, similar to West Indian manatee.

### Amazonian manatee [V]
*T. inunguis*
Amazonian, South American manatee.

Amazon river drainage basin in floodplain lakes, rivers and channels. HTL 8–10ft; wt 660–1,102lb. Skin: lead-gray with variable pink belly patch (white when dead); no nails on foreflippers. Gestation: not known but probably similar to West Indian manatee. Longevity: grater than 30 years.

### Dugong [V]
*Dugong dugon*
Dugong or Sea cow or Sea Pig.

SW Pacific Ocean from New Caledonia, W Micronesia and the Philippines to Taiwan, Vietnam, Indonesia, New Guinea and the northern coasts of Australia. Indian Ocean from Australia and Indonesia to Sri Lanka and India, the Red Sea and south along the African coast to Mozambique. Coastal shallows. HTL 3–13ft; wt 507–1,984lb.

Skin: smooth, brown to gray, with short sensory bristles at intervals of 0.75–1in. Diet: sea grasses. Gestation: 13 months (estimated). Longevity: to more than 55 years.

### Steller's sea cow [EX]
*Hydrodamalis gigas*

Bering and Commander (Komandorskiye) Islands. HTL to about 26ft; wt to 13,000lb. Diet: algae (kelp).

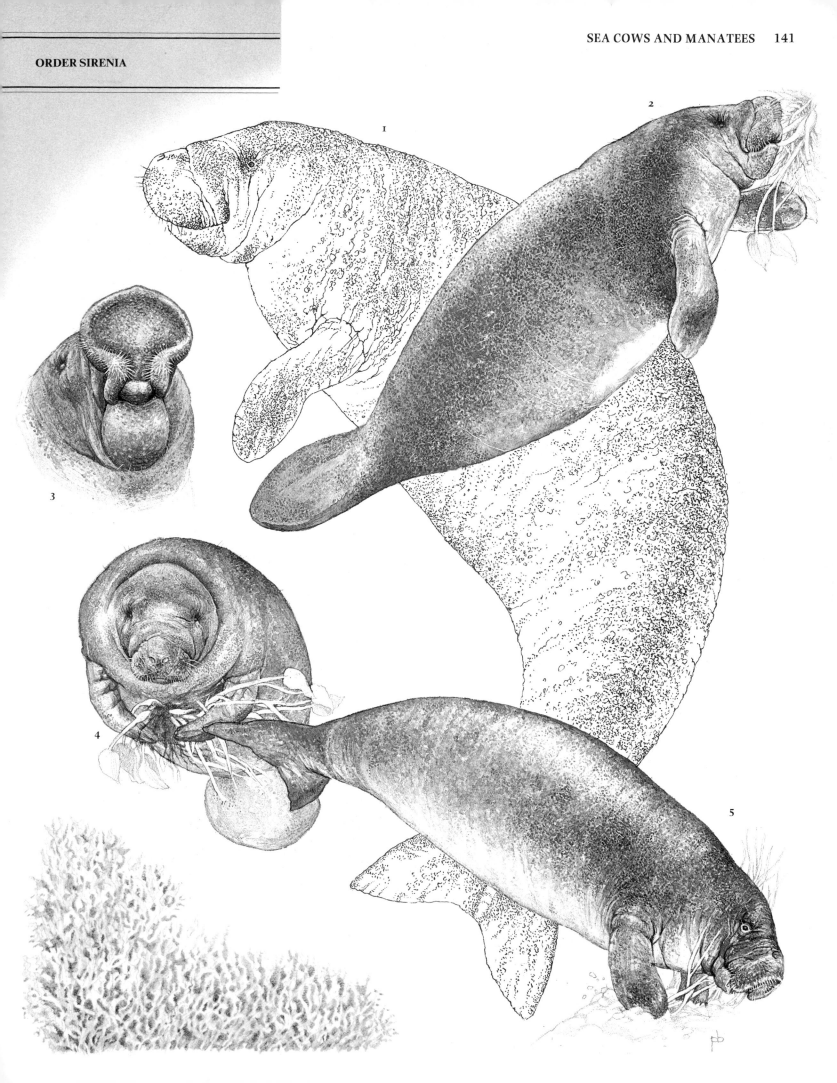

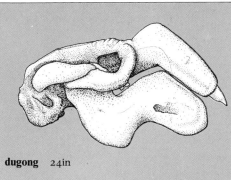

dugong   24in

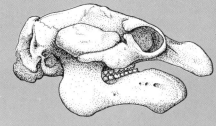

West Indian manatee   26in

▲ **Skulls** of dugong and West Indian Manatee. The angle of the snout is more pronounced in the dugong, which also has a pair of short "tusks" (projecting incisor teeth). Both manatees and dugong only have teeth at the back of the jaw, but in manatees the teeth move forward in the jaw and are then lost.

volume (8–15 percent of their body weight daily) of relatively low-quality forage required to obtain adequate energy and nutrients.

Sirenians expend little energy: for manatees, about one-third that of a typical mammal of the same weight. Their slow, languid movements may have reminded early taxonomists of mermaids—sirens of the sea. Although they are capable of more rapid movement when pursued, in an environment without humans they have little need for speed, having few predators. Living in tropical waters, sirenians can afford to have a low metabolic rate, because little energy is expended in regulation of body temperature. Marine mammals which inhabit deeper, colder water require extra energy to add to a thick layer of blubber which functions as insulation, and as an energy store during periods of scarcity of food supply. Sirenia also conserve energy by virtue of their relatively large body size. The cold-tolerant Steller's sea cow weighed about 5–6 times as much as contemporary topical sirenian species.

The large body size dictated by the requirements of nutrition and temperature regulation is associated with traits seen in other large mammalian herbivores as well as large marine mammals. The life span is

long (a 33-year-old manatee is still doing well in captivity), and the reproductive rate is low. Females give birth to a single calf after about a year's gestation, calves stay with the mother for 1–2 years and sexual maturity is delayed (4–8 years). Consequently, the potential rate of increase of population is low. It is possible that rapid reproduction brings no advantage where the renewability of food resources is slow and there are few predators.

Sirenians have few competitors for food. In contrast to the complex division of food resources by grazing and browsing herbivores seen in terrestrial grasslands, the only large herbivores in seagrass meadows are sirenians and sea turtles. Marine plant communities are low in diversity compared with terrestrial communities and lack species with high-energy seeds which facilitate niche subdivision by herbivores in terrestrial systems. It is not surprising that dugongs and manatees dig into the sediments when they feed on rooted aquatics; over half of the mass of seagrasses is found in the rhizomes, which concentrate carbohydrates. In contrast, the cold-blooded sea turtles subsist by grazing on the blades of seagrasses without disturbing the rhizomes, and appear to feed in deeper water. Thus sea turtles probably do not compete signifi-

▲ **Surface browsing.** An Amazonian manatee feeding in a tangle of water weeds. It is this feeding habit which has been used to advantage to clear congested waterways.

◄ **Docile duo.** West Indian manatees are placid, slow-moving creatures.

▷ **Manatee mother and calf** OVERLEAF West Indian manatees are slow breeders and the suckling period in West Indian manatees is 12–18 months. The cow-calf bond is the only strong social relationship among manatees, and throughout the period of dependency calves stay very close to females.

▼ **Sea-grass browser.** A West Indian manatee feeding on sea grasses in shallow water.

cantly for food taken by sirenians.

The four sirenian species are geographically isolated. Dugongs occupy tropical coastlines in east Africa, Asia, Australia and New Guinea. The West African manatee and the similar West Indian manatee have been isolated long enough to become distinct, since their supposed common ancestor migrated to Africa across the Atlantic Ocean. Each can occupy both saltwater and freshwater habitats. The Amazonian manatee apparently became isolated when the Andes mountain range was uplifted in the Pliocene (2–5 million years ago), changing the river drainage out of the Amazon basin from the Pacific to the Atlantic Ocean. Amazonial manatees are not tolerant of salt water and occupy only the Amazon River and its tributaries. JMP/GBR/DPD

Docility, delicious flesh and a low reproductive capacity are not auspicious characteristics for an animal in the modern world. **Manatees** have all three and are consequently among the most threatened of aquatic mammals. They are the only fully aquatic freshwater herbivores, and this role, rather like that of an aquatic cow, has given rise to the names *vaca marinha* (sea cow) in Spanish-speaking countries and *peixe-boi* (fish cow) in Portuguese.

Manatees have the typical sirenian body form and are distinguished from dugongs mainly by their large, horizontal, paddle-shaped tail, which moves up and down when the animal is swimming. They have only six neck vertebrae, unlike all other mammals, which have seven. The lips are covered with stiff bristles and there are two muscular projections that grasp and pass the grasses and aquatic plants that they feed on into the mouth.

The eyes of manatees are not particularly well adapted to the aquatic environment, but their hearing is good, despite the tiny external ear openings, and often alerts them to the presence of hunters. They do not use echolocation or sonar, and may bump into objects in murky waters; nor do they possess vocal cords, but they do communicate by vocalizations, which may be high-pitched chirps or squeaks. How these sounds are produced is a mystery. Taste buds are present on the tongue, and are apparently used in the selection of food plants, and also in the recognition of other individuals by "tasting" the scent marks left on prominent objects. Unlike the toothed whales, manatees still possess the parts of the brain concerned with a sense of smell, but since they spend most of their time underwater with the nose valves closed this sense may not be used.

A unique feature of manatees is a constant horizontal replacement of their molar teeth. When a manatee is born, it has both premolars and molars. As the calf is weaned and begins to eat vegetable matter, it seems that the mechanical stimulation of the teeth, by chewing, starts a forward movement of the whole tooth row. Now teeth entering at the back of each row push the row forward through the jawbone, at a rate about $\frac{1}{25}$in per month, until its roots are eaten away and it falls out. This type of replacement is unique to manatees.

As aquatic herbivores, manatees are restricted to feeding on plants in, or very near, the water. Occasionally, they feed with their head and shoulders out of water, but normally they feed on floating or submerged grasses and other vascular plants. They may eat algae but this does not form an important part of the diet. The coastal West Indian and West African manatees feed on sea grasses which grow in relatively shallow, clear marine waters, as well as entering inland waterways, rivers, lakes etc, to feed on freshwater plants. Amazonian manatees are surface feeders, browsing floating grasses (the murky Amazon waters inhibit the growth of submerged aquatic plants). The habit of surface feeding may explain why the downward deflection in the snout of Amazonian manatees is much less pronounced than that of the bottom-feeding West Indian and African manatees. Some 44 species of plants and 10 species of algae have been recorded as foods of the West Indian species, but only 24 species for the Amazonian manatee.

Many of the manatees' food plants have evolved special anti-herbivore protective mechanisms—spicules of silica in the grasses, tannins, nitrates and oxalates in other aquatics—which reduce their digestibility and lower their food value to the manatee. The constant replacement of teeth in manatees is an adaptation to the abrasive spicules of silica in the grasses or rooted plants. Microbes in the digestive tract may be able to detoxify some of the plants' chemical defenses.

Manatees can store large amounts of fat as blubber beneath the skin and around the intestines, which affords some degree of thermal protection from the environment. Despite this, in the Atlantic Ocean manatees generally avoid areas where temperatures drop below 68°F (20°C). The blubber also helps them to endure long periods of fasting: up to six months in the Amazonian manatee during the dry season, when aquatic plants are unavailable.

Manatees are extremely slow breeders: at most they produce only a single calf every two years, and calves may be weaned at 12–18 months. Although young calves may feed on plants within several weeks of being born, the long nursing period probably allows the calf to learn from its mother the necessary migration routes, foods, and preferred feeding areas. In highly seasonal environments such as the Amazon and probably at the northern and southern extremes of manatee distribution, the availability of food dictates when the majority of manatee females are ready to mate and this, in turn, results in a seasonal peak in calving. The reproductive biology of male manatees is poorly known, but it is not uncommon for a receptive female to be accompanied by 6–8 males and to mate with several of these within a short time. The age of attainment of sexual maturity of manatees is not known, but based on size it must be between 5 and 8 years of age.

Direct observation and radio-tracking studies have shown that manatees are essentially solitary but occasionally form groups of a dozen or more (see pp148–149).

All three species of manatees are considered by the IUCN to be threatened as a result of both historical and modern overhunting for their meat and skins, as well as more recent threats such as pollution, flood-control dams and high-speed pleasure craft. They are protected under the Convention on International Trade in Endangered Species of Fauna and Flora (CITES), and legally in most countries where they exist, but most underdeveloped countries lack sufficient wardens to implement practical measures such as sparing females. In Florida, signs and posters have been used

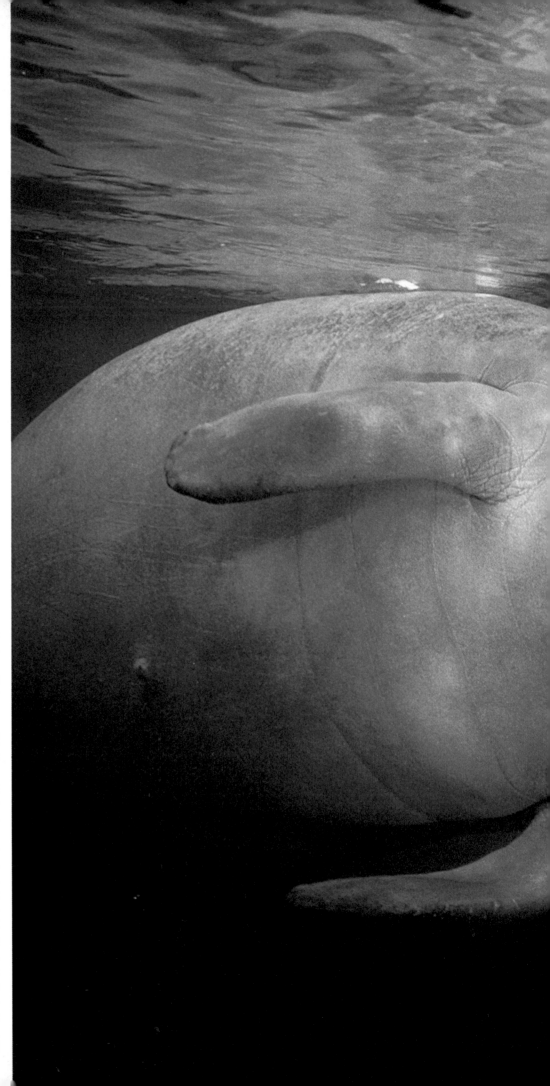

with some success to warn boaters about the presence of manatees in inland waterways, and manatee-proof flood-control structures have been developed.

Manatees have long been appreciated by man for their savory meat, oil for cooking and their tough hide, but now a more hopeful use is being found for them: that of clearing weeds in irrigation canals and the dams of hydroelectric power stations. It is thus possible that their gentle herbivorous life-style might survive in an aggressive world.                                    RB

A gentle marine herbivore, the **dugong** has not had a happy relationship with man. Although seafarers' accounts of mermaids are associated with sirenians, and coastal peoples throughout the dugong's range have a rich mythology associating humans and dugongs, hunting for meat, oil and tusks has decimated or exterminated most dugong populations.

The dugong is distinguished from the manatees by its tail, which has a straight or slightly concave trailing edge. A short, broad trunk-like snout ends in a downward facing flexible disk and a slit-like mouth.

For the zoologist, the dugong is uniquely interesting: it is the only truly sea-dwelling vegetarian among mammals, the manatees being at best venturers into the sea.

Dugongs feed on seagrasses—marine flowering plants which sometimes resemble terrestrial grasses and are distinct from seaweeds (which are algae). Seagrasses grow on the bottom in coastal shallows and dugongs generally feed at depths of 3–16ft (1–5m). The food they most prefer is the carbohydrate-rich underground storage roots (rhizomes) of the smaller seagrass species. These they dig from the bottom, hence the alternative name "sea pig".

Dugongs appear to "chew" vegetation mainly with rough horny pads which cover the upper and lower palates. Adults of both sexes have only a few peg-like molar teeth, located at the back of the jaws. Juveniles also have premolars, but these are lost in the first years of life. Adult male dugongs have a pair of "tusks": incisor teeth which project a short distance through the upper lip in front of the mouth and behind the disk. The uses to which these stubby tusks are put are not clear, but a few observations suggest that the males use them to guide their slippery mates during courtship.

While the preferred feeding mode of the dugong is pig-like, the name "sea cow" is not always a misnomer. At Shark Bay, Western Australia, low winter temperatures

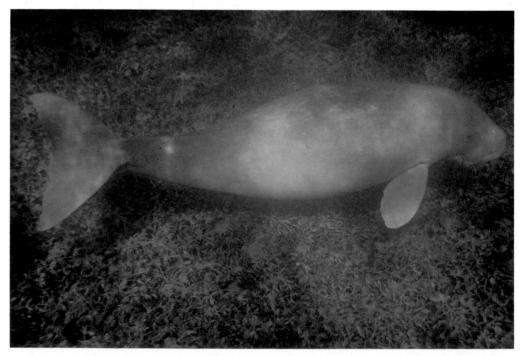

▲ **A sun-dappled dugong** rises to the surface to breathe. They need to do this every 40–70 seconds when feeding and at intervals of 2–3 minutes when resting. The sharp angle of the snout is particularly noticeable here.

◄ **The dugong's tail,** well displayed here, is its most distinctive feature for identification, having a concave trailing edge, unlike that of the manatees, which is rounded.

drive the herds from their summer feeding grounds and their choicest food plants. After their migration of over 100mi (160km) to the warmer waters of the western bay, they feed during the winter months by browsing the terminal leaves of *Amphibolis antarctica*, a tough-stemmed, bush-like seagrass.

In both feeding modes, the dugong's foraging apparatus is the highly mobile horseshoe-shaped disk at the end of the snout. Bristles on the surface of this disk vary from fine and hairlike to coarse, stiff, and recurved. Pressed into the sea bottom, or moved along the *Amphibolis* canopy, the edges of the disk flare outward while waves of contraction pass along its surface, producing a precisely controllable rake-conveyor system that extracts food items and passes them backwards to the mouth with its horny grinding pads.

Despite the special interest that dugongs have for zoologists, little is known about their behavior and ecology. Dugongs are not easily studied. The waters in which they are found are generally turbid, and dugongs combine shyness and curiosity in a way that frustrates close observation. When disturbed, their flight is rapid and furtive; only the top of the head and nostrils are exposed as they rise to breathe. When underwater visibility is adequate, and they are approached cautiously, they will come from 330ft (100m) or more to investigate a diver or a small boat, probably alerted at first by their extremely keen underwater hearing. Normal behavior stops until their investigation of the person is complete, then they swim off, frequently on a zigzag course that keeps the visitor in view with alternate eyes.

Their curiosity suggests that as adults, at least, they have few predators. Although they display more overt curiosity in this way than do dolphins, for example, there is little basis for rating them as highly intelligent. Dugongs have relatively smaller and less complexly structured brains than do whales and dolphins, and their greater tendency to approach and investigate objects visually may simply be due to the dugong's apparent lack of echolocation apparatus. Known dugong calls are limited to faint squeaks.

Large size, tough skin, dense bone structure, and blood which clots very rapidly to close wounds seem to be an adult dugong's main means of defense. Calves remain close to their mothers, probably using the mother's bulky body as a screen and shield. When undisturbed, feeding dugongs surface to breathe at intervals of less than a minute. Specialized for life in shallow waters, their ability to stay submerged is limited, as are their speed and endurance when pursued. Wherever men hunt them, they are no match for rifles, outboard motors and large-mesh nylon nets.

Female dugongs become reproductively mature at 8–18 years. The long gestation is followed by nearly two years of suckling the single young, during which the calf maintains close and persistent contact with its mother. A female, though she may live for up to 50 years, is likely to produce no more than five or six offspring over an average lifetime. Little is known about parental care, but the location of the two teats, just behind and below the pectoral flippers, shows that tales of mother dugongs cradling their nursing young in the flippers are wholly imaginative: a young dugong suckles lying beside its mother, behind her flipper and often belly up.

Dugongs may be found singly, as cow-calf pairs, or in herds of up to several hundred. So little is known about their behavior and means of communication, no conclusions can be drawn about social relationships.

The only close relative of the dugong surviving into historic times was Steller's sea cow. This giant sea cow (three times as large as the dugong) differed most strikingly in its cold-water habit and its diet (algae). Further, its jaws were toothless and in contrast to that of the bottom-rooting dugong, its mouth was directed forwards (appropriate for browsing on tall-growing kelps). The flippers were stump-like, with stiff bristles on the "soles" which were used to maintain position as it fed in rocky shallows. Fossil evidence suggests that some 100,000 years ago its range extended along northern Pacific coasts from Japan to California.

At the time of its discovery, by a shipwrecked Russian exploring party in 1741, Steller's sea cow was restricted to the shores of two subarctic Pacific islands, each 30–60mi (50–100km) long. Like the dugong, it fed in inshore shallows where it was vulnerable to hunters in small boats. The survivors of the shipwreck discovered the sea cow's vulnerability and edibility out of dire necessity, and over the next quarter century, parties of fur-hunters found it convenient to winter on the two islands in order to exploit the easily accessible food supply. By 1768 no more of the giants could be found, and several isolated dugong populations appear to have suffered similar fates. Even though a few dugong herds as numerous as those of Steller's sea cow at the time of its discovery still exist, the story of the extinction of the dugong's huge relative has an obvious moral.                    PKA

# The Manatee's Simple Social Life

*Scent marking in an aquatic mammal*

Each October, more than 100 West Indian manatees arrive at Crystal River on the central west coast of Florida, in retreat from falling water temperatures in the Gulf of Mexico. At Crystal River, some individuals begin to rub on prominent submerged logs and stones. The manatees use the same 1–3 traditional rubbing sites year after year. If an object disappears, they use a new object close to where the old one was located. Why do they do this?

Preliminary observations show that females rub more frequently than males, and the regions of the body that are rubbed often are areas where glandular secretions may occur. In decreasing order of frequency, these are their genitals, the area around their eyes, their arm pits and their chin. Manatees may use rubbing posts to scratch themselves and thus remove external parasites, but there may be additional functions. Perhaps females leave a chemical message on a rubbing post that communicates their presence and reproductive condition to other manatees, especially males? This would allow the widely roaming males that pass through a female's home range to go directly to a traditional rubbing post and detect (by taste or smell) any messages left by the resident female. Females would thus be able to advertise their reproductive state to a large number of males, resulting in a large mating herd and a wide selection of mates.

West Indian manatees do not form cohesive social groups, but can be found in unorganized groups at warm-water sources in winter or during mating activities. They are found in warm coastal waters from Brazil to the southeastern USA, where the only significant populations are found in Florida, with its temperate but mild climate. In winter, manatees in Florida escape low water temperatures (less than 68°F; 20°C) either by a southerly migration or by taking refuge in the warm-water outfalls from hydroelectric plants.

Individuals may form loose, transient associations on summer ranges, which may be of importance in establishing movement patterns that later become habitual. In addition to extensive seasonal movements, manatees travel long distances within seasons. This is especially true of males, which are more likely to encounter receptive females by traveling circuits of great length. During the receptive period, which may last up to two weeks, a female attracts a mating herd of 5–17 unrelated males that escort her closely. A constant and sometimes violent pushing and shoving occurs in

▲ **Manatees frolicking** at Crystal River, Florida. Receptive females attract groups of males which engage in pushing and shoving contests, probably to establish breeding rights. Sometimes all-male cavorting groups of 3–10 animals gather.

◄ **The mangled tail** of a manatee injured by a boat's propeller. Florida's heavy boat traffic inflicts severe damage on manatees; most individuals have distinctive patterns of scars which enable them to be recognized.

mating herds. This is probably a relatively unorganized contest of stamina and strength, in which males may establish a rank order for copulation rights, and females may choose particular males with which to copulate. Females probably remain receptive for a relatively long period of time in order to gather many males into their mating herds and thus increase their choice of potential mates.

Other research on communication is being carried out at Blue Spring Run on the St. Johns River, a warm water refuge for about 30 manatees. Here, the work focuses on observing recognizable individuals from the shore while eavesdropping on them with a hydrophone coupled to a tape recorder. Radio-tracking has also been used to record their movements in the dark, tannin-stained waters of the river. In keeping with their relatively simple social lives, manatees do not use elaborate courtship displays, loud, long-distance calls or song-like signals or other intricate social behavior characteristic of territorial mammals. Their calls are relatively short in duration, not particularly loud, and are generally issued as single notes that to the human ear resemble squeals, whines, or grunts. These sounds are used for short-range communication and are designed to convey information on the mood or intentions of the calling manatee through changes in such qualities as pitch, loudness, duration and harshness.

During basic maintenance activities such as resting, feeding or traveling, manatees often call less than once every ten minutes. There is no evidence that calling rates are higher in dark water than in clear water. Calling is most conspicuous between cows and calves, and duet-like sequences often occur between the two, involving production of sounds every two or three seconds for periods of up to several minutes at a time. These sequences usually occur when the pair rejoins after drifting apart, during disturbances, or when a calf is soliciting nursing.

Much of what is being learned about social organization and communication in manatees depends on our ability to recognize individual animals. It is sad that we are only able to do this because most manatees have distinctive patterns of scars inflicted by boat propellers. Indeed, collisions with boats constitute the largest identifiable source of mortality: in one sample, 24 percent of animals for which a cause of death was determined. Florida's abundant boat traffic has other detrimental effects on manatees: boat traffic can interrupt mating activities and a tremendous amount of sound pollution from boat engines occurs, which can disrupt communication by vocal signals. Although we are beginning to piece together details about the underwater social lives of these mammals, in Florida, where the human population is burgeoning and development is proceeding at a rapid pace, prospects for their future seem dim.   GBR/TJO

▲ **Behavior of manatees.** The West Indian manatee lacks any cohesive social organization, with the exception of the mother-offspring relationship during the period of calf dependency (2). Other assemblages are either aggregations at concentrated resources such as food or warm water, or are ephemeral with no consistency in composition, such as mating herds and all-male cavorting groups. Despite the lack of continuity in social groupings, manatees exhibit frequent social interactions that are characterized by simple gestures, such as "kissing" (1) and physical contact. Manatees sometimes lie on their backs on the bottom (3). The use of rubbing posts (4), where only one animal need be present at a time, is an extreme case of animals achieving interactions through probable chemical communication without intricate gestures or social groupings.

# Managing the Manatee

*Conservation of Amazonian manatees*

*Mixira*, the meat of the Amazonian manatee cooked in its own blubber, is a valuable food in tropical regions, where it stays fresh for months. Once an abundant and staple item of the diet of the indigenous peoples, it became a commercially valuable food with the arrival of the first European colonists in Brazil, the missionaries who, believing the manatee to be a fish, recommended it as an alternative to fish for the Friday meal.

Commercial exploitation then became intense, starting with Dutch merchantmen who, in the 1600s, sent up to 20 ships yearly to Europe filled with manatee meat. Yet by 1755 it was difficult to fill a single ship. In more recent times, about 200,000 animals were killed over the period 1935–1954, mainly for their skins, and this resulted in the near extinction of many local populations. It is difficult to find large numbers of the Amazonian manatee anywhere today.

A major project to study the biology of Amazonian manatees and to initiate management plans was started at the National Research Institute for the Amazon (INPA) in 1976. The first challenge was to raise newborn, orphaned manatee calves, and the work has since grown to encompass studies of the ecology of captive animals, distributional studies of wild animals, and the use of manatees as agents for control of aquatic weed in reservoirs.

The eleven manatees hand-reared since 1976 have been excellent subjects for studies on physiology, nutrition and behavior. It was discovered that manatees do not reduce their heart-rate during diving, as most marine mammals do, but they increase the frequency slightly before each breath. This increase, of some 8–10 beats per minute, serves to evacuate the end-products of respiration from the tissues to the lungs. Frightened manatees, however, can reduce the heart-rate from a normal 40–50 beats per minute to about 8 beats per minute while submerged. Under these circumstances, the peripheral circulation is closed, allowing the oxygenated blood to flow only to the vital organs, the brain, heart and lungs. The rest of the body remains active, but does not use oxygen (anaerobic respiration).

The metabolic rate of manatees is one of the lowest known for any mammal, about one-quarter that of humans, which may help to explain their excellent diving ability: they use much less oxygen per minute

▶ **Captured manatee in boat.** Immediately after capture, each manatee is transported by canoe to a small lake where they remain for up to several months. They are then transported to the hydroelectric dam, where they are used as natural weed-control agents.

▶ **Transporting manatees.** BELOW The 620mi (1,000km) journey between the catching area on the remote Japurá river and the town of Santarém is made using an empty boat hull, lined with canvas, towed alongside a research boat. Up to 20 manatees at a time have been transported in this way.

▼ **The blunt snout** of the Amazonian manatee is less angled than that of the West Indian manatee. This reflects their different feeding habits: surface browsing in the Amazonian and bottom browsing in the West Indian.

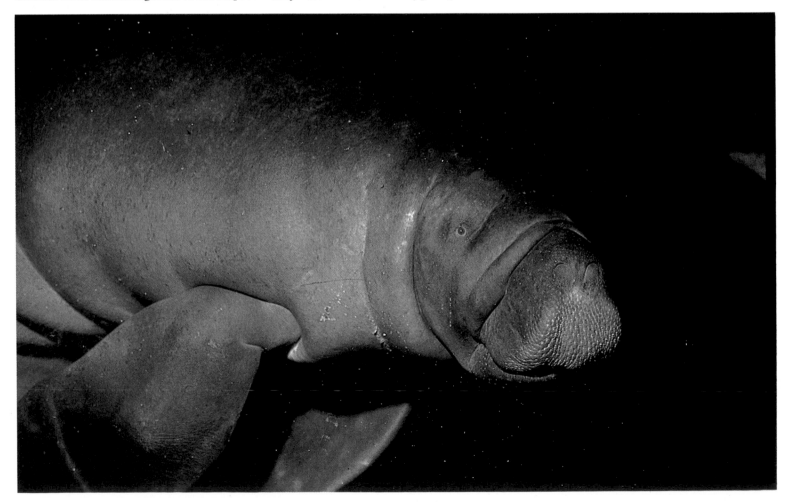

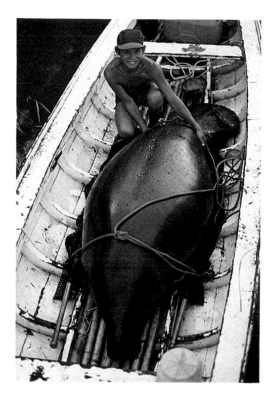

compared with other animals. A low metabolic rate is not without its drawbacks, since it implies a poor ability to regulate temperature. At water temperatures below 72°F (22°C), their body temperature, normally between 96.1 and 97.0°F (35.6–36.1°C), drops at an alarming rate, eventually resulting in death. Average water temperatures in the Amazon vary only 3–4° annually, with an average of 84°F (29°C). In captivity, manatees consume about 8 percent of their body weight daily in aquatic plants, spending 33 percent of the day feeding, 17 percent resting and 50 percent swimming slowly.

Radio-tracking of Amazonian manatees has shown that they move about 1.7mi (2.7km) per 24 hours and are active by day and night. As the water rises, they prefer the newly flooded areas where the aquatic vegetation which they feed upon is most lush. Subadults tend to group together in twos or threes, whereas adults seem to prefer a more solitary existence. Occasionally, however, an adult will move up to 6.2mi (10km) or

more and spend a day or two with another individual before unerringly returning to the original home site. How these animals navigate under the extensive floating meadows of the Amazon is not known.

Field studies of wild Amazonian manatees have shown that for six months they inhabit flooded areas of the Amazon basin, feeding on the luxuriant Amazon grasses, and for the remaining six months they migrate to deepwater lakes. Here they endure a prolonged fast, from 4–6 months, depending on the timing of the floods, but are at least safe from stranding and the attention of human hunters. However, during one prolonged dry season, even the deepwater lakes became shallow and several thousand were killed by hunters.

Mating takes place during the flood season and considerable food reserves are required to sustain the females through the fasting portion of the year-long pregnancy. Births occur in the following flood season when sufficient food is available to support the female during milk production.

Pressure on the manatee population has been eased by stopping the commercial sale of manatee meat, by the emigration of many of the riverine inhabitants to urban centers and by the introduction of nylon gill fishing nets from which large manatees can easily escape. Young calves still get trapped in these nets and attempts are now being made to encourage fishermen to release them immediately. Since 1977, five Nature Reserves have been created in the Brazilian Amazon, all of which contain manatees.

The most promising development in manatee conservation is their use as an ecological agent in tropical manmade reservoirs. Such lakes rapidly become overgrown with floating weeds which increase evaporation by up to six times, kill fish, and corrode the metal parts of turbines through the production of hydrogen sulfide gas on decomposition; the weeds also reduce light penetration which is essential for the growth of phytoplankton on which fish feed, impede navigation and block the turbine outlets. Introduction of manatees can control these weeds, allowing the recycling of nutrients into the water instead of from plant to plant, which in turn increases fish production. These managed manatee stocks will be invaluable for the study of the species in the future, and controlled exploitation of the meat and hides may even be possible. In addition, their potential economic value in reservoirs has stimulated a much greater national interest in the protection of the species. RB

# BIBLIOGRAPHY

The following list of titles indicates key reference works used in the preparation of this volume and those recommended for further reading. The list is divided into two categories: general mammalogy and those titles relevant to sea mammals.

## General

Boyle, C. L. (ed) (1981) *The RSPCA Book of British Mammals*, Collins, London.

Corbet, G. B. and Hill, J. E. (1980) *A World List of Mammalian Species*, British Museum and Cornell University Press, London and Ithaca, N.Y.

Dorst, J. and Dandelot, P. (1972) *Larger Mammals of Africa*, Collins, London.

Grzimek, B. (ed) (1972) *Grzimek's Animal Life Encyclopedia*, vols 10, 11 and 12, Van Nostrand Reinhold, New York.

Hall, E. R. and Kelson, K. R. (1959) *The Mammals of North America*, Ronald Press, New York.

Harrison Matthews, L. (1969) *The Life of Mammals*, vols 1 and 2. Weidenfeld & Nicolson, London.

Honacki, J. H., Kinman, K. E. and Koeppl, J. W. (eds) (1982) *Mammal Species of the World*, Allen Press and Association of Systematics Collections, Lawrence, Kansas.

Kingdon, J. (1971–82) *East African Mammals*, vols I–III, Academic Press, New York.

Morris, D. (1965) *The Mammals*, Hodder & Stoughton, London.

Nowak, R. M. and Paradiso, J. L. (eds) (1983) *Walker's Mammals of the World* (4th edn), 2 vols, Johns Hopkins University Press, Baltimore and London.

Vaughan, T. L. (1972) *Mammalogy*, W. B. Saunders, London and Philadelphia.

Young, J. Z. (1975) *The Life of Mammals: their Anatomy and Physiology*, Oxford University Press, Oxford.

## Sea Mammals

Allen, K. R. (1980) *Conservation and Management of Whales*, Butterworths, London.

Bonner, W. N. (1980) *Whales*, Blandford, Poole.

Bonner, W. N. and Berry, R. J. (eds) (1981) *Ecology in the Antarctic*, Academic Press, London.

Ellis, R. (1983) *Dolphins and Porpoises*, R. Hale, London.

Gaskin, D. E. (1972) *Whales, Dolphins and Seals*, Heinemann Educational Books, London.

Gaskin, D. E. (1982) *The Ecology of Whales and Dolphins*, Heinemann, London.

Harrison Matthews, L. (1978) *The Natural History of the Whale*, Weidenfeld & Nicolson, London.

Harrison Matthews, L. (1979) *Seals and the Scientists*, P. Owen, London.

Herman, L. M. (1980) *Cetacean Behavior: Mechanisms and Functions*, John Wiley & Sons, Chichester.

King, J. E. (1983) *Seals of the World*, Oxford University Press, Oxford.

Martin, R. M. (1977) *Mammals of the Seas*, Batsford, London.

Ridgeway, S. H. and Harrison, R. J. (eds) (1981) *The Handbook of Marine Mammals*, vols I & II, Academic Press, London.

Slijper, E. J. (1979) *Whales*, Hutchinson, London.

Watson, L. (1981) *Sea Guide to Whales of the World*, Hutchinson, London.

Winn, H. E. and Olla, B. L. (1979) *The Behavior of Marine Mammals*, vol 3, *Cetaceans*, Plenum, New York.

# GLOSSARY

**Adaptation** features of an animal which adjust it to its environment. Adaptations may be genetic, produced by evolution and hence not alterable within the animal's lifetime, or they may be phenotypic, produced by adjustment on the part of the individual and may be reversible within its lifetime. NATURAL SELECTION favors the survival of individuals whose adaptations adjust them better to their surroundings than other individuals with less successful adaptations.

**Adaptive radiation** the pattern in which different species develop from a common ancestor (as distinct from CONVERGENT EVOLUTION, the process whereby species from different origins became similar in response to the same SELECTIVE PRESSURES).

**Adult** a fully developed and mature individual, capable of breeding, but not necessarily doing so until social and/or ecological conditions allow.

**Aerobic** deriving energy from processes that require free atmospheric oxygen, as distinct from ANAEROBIC processes.

**Air sac** a side-pouch of the larynx (the upper part of the windpipe), used in some primates and male walruses as a resonating chamber in producing calls.

**Alloparent** an animal behaving parentally toward infants that are not its own offspring; the shorthand jargon "HELPER" is most commonly applied to alloparents without any offspring of their own and it can be misleading if it is used to describe any non-breeding adults associated with infants, but which may or may not be "helping" by promoting their survival.

**Alveolus** a microscopic sac within the lungs providing the surface for gaseous exchange during respiration.

**Amphibious** able to live both on land and in water.

**Amphipod** a CRUSTACEAN of the invertebrate order Amphipoda. Includes many freshwater and marine shrimps.

**Anaerobic** deriving energy from processes that do not require free oxygen, as distinct from AEROBIC processes.

**Antarctic Convergence** the region between 50°–55°S where the antarctic surface water slides beneath the less-dense southward-flowing subantarctic water.

**Aquatic** living chiefly in water.

**Arteriole** a small artery (ie muscular blood vessel carrying blood from the heart), eventually subdividing into minute capillaries.

**Arterio-venous anastomosis (AVA)** a connection between the ARTERIOLES carrying blood from the heart and the VENULES carrying it back to the heart.

**Axilla** the angle between a forelimb and the body (in humans, the armpit).

**Baleen** a horny substance, commonly known as whalebone, growing as plates from the upper jaws of whales of the suborder Mysticeti, and forming a fringe-like sieve for extraction of plankton from seawater.

**Bends** the colloquial name for caisson disease, a condition produced by pressure changes in the blood as a diving mammal surfaces. Too rapid an ascent results in nitrogen dissolved in the blood forming bubbles, which cause excruciating pain.

**Benthic** the bottom layer of the marine environment.

**Binocular** form of vision typical of mammals in which the same object is viewed simultaneously by both eyes; the coordination of the two images in the brain permits precise perception of distance.

**Biomass** a measure of the abundance of a life-form in terms of its mass, either absolute or per unit area (the population densities of two species may be identical in terms of the number of individuals of each, but due to their different sizes their biomasses may be quite different).

**Biotic community** a naturally occurring group of plants and animals in the same environment.

**Blastocyst** see IMPLANTATION.

**Blowhole** the opening of the nostril(s) of a whale, situated on the animal's head, from which the "spout" or "blow" is produced.

**Blubber** a layer of fat beneath the skin, well developed in whales and seals.

**Breaching** leaping clear of the water.

**Brindled** having inconspicuous dark streaks or flecks on a gray or tawny background.

**Cephalopod** a member of an order of mollusks including such marine invertebrates as squid, octopus and cuttlefish.

**Cerebral cortex** the surface layer of cells (gray matter) covering the main part of the brain, consisting of the cerebral hemispheres.

**Cetacea** mammalian order comprising whales, dolphins and porpoises.

**Chromatin** material in the chromosomes of living cells containing the genes and proteins.

**Class** taxonomic category subordinate to a phylum and superior to an order (see TAXONOMY).

**Clupeid** a bony fish of the family Clupeidae, including herrings and similar fish, with soft fin-rays, a scaly body and four pairs of gills.

**Convergent evolution** the independent acquisition of similar characters in evolution, as opposed to possession of similarities by virtue of descent from a common ancestor.

**Copepod** a small marine CRUSTACEAN of the invertebrate order Copepoda.

**Crustaceans** members of a class within the phylum Arthropoda typified by five pairs of legs, two pairs of antennae, head and thorax joined, and calcareous deposits in the exoskeleton, eg crayfish, crabs, shrimps.

**Cryptic** (coloration or locomotion) protecting through concealment.

**Cusp** a prominence on a cheek-tooth (premolars or molar).

**Cyamids** amphipod CRUSTACEANS of the family Cyamidae that parasitize the skin of the whales; hence the popular name "whale lice."

**Delayed implantation** see IMPLANTATION.

**Den** a shelter, natural or constructed, used for sleeping, for giving birth and raising young, and/or in winter; also the act of retiring to a den to give birth and raise young, or for winter shelter.

**Dental formula** a convention for summarizing the dental arrangement whereby the numbers of each type of tooth in each half of the upper and lower jaw are given; the numbers are always presented in the order: incisor (I), canine (C), premolar (P), molar (M). The final figure is the total number of teeth to be found in the skull. A typical example for Carnivora would be I3/3. C1/1. P4/4. M3/3 – 44.

**Dentition** the arrangement of teeth characteristic of a particular species.

**Digit** a finger or a toe.

**Dimorphism** the existence of two distinct forms (polymorphism = several distinct forms); the term "sexual dimorphism" is applied to cases where the male and female of a species differ consistently in, for example, shape, size, coloration and armament.

**Disjunct** or **discontinuous distribution** geographical distribution of a species that is marked by gaps. Commonly brought about by fragmentation of suitable habitat, especially as a result of human intervention.

**Dispersal** the movements of animals often as they reach maturity, away from their previous home range (equivalent to emigration). Distinct from **dispersion**, that is, the pattern in which things (perhaps animals, food supplies, nest sites) are distributed or scattered.

**Display** any relatively conspicuous pattern of behaviour that conveys specific information to others, usually to members of the same species: can involve visual and/or vocal elements, as in threat, courtship or "greeting" displays.

**Dominant** see HIERARCHY.

**Dorsal** on the upper or top side or surface (eg dorsal stripe).

**Echolocation** for process of perception, often direction finding, based upon reaction to the pattern of reflected sound waves (echoes).

**Ecology** the study of plants and animals in relation to their natural environmental setting. Each species may be said to occupy a distinctive ecological NICHE.

**Ecosystem** a unit of the environment within which living and nonliving elements interact.

**Ecotype** a genetic variety within a single species, adapted for local ecological conditions.

**Elongate** relatively long (eg of canine teeth, longer than those of an ancestor, a related animal, or than adjacent teeth).

**Emigration** departure of animal(s), usually at or about the time of reaching adulthood, from the group or place of birth.

**Enzootic** concerning disease regularly found within an animal population (endemic applies specifically to people) as distinct from EPIZOOTIC.

**Epizootic** a disease outbreak in an animal population at a specific time (but not persistently, as in ENZOOTIC); if an epizootic wave of infection eventually stabilizes in an area, it becomes enzootic.

**Esophagus** the gullet connecting the mouth with the stomach.

**Estrus** the period in the estrous cycle of female mammals at which they are often attractive to males and receptive to mating. The period coincides with the maturation of eggs and ovulation (the release of mature eggs from the ovaries). Animals in estrus are often said to be "on heat" or "in heat." In primates, if the egg is not fertilized the subsequent degeneration of uterine walls (endometrium) leads to menstrual bleeding. In some species ovulation is triggered by copulation and this is called **induced ovulation**, as distinct from spontaneous ovulation.

**Family** a taxonomic division subordinate to an order and superior to a genus (see TAXONOMY).

**Fast ice** sea ice which forms in polar regions along the coast and remains fast, being attached to the shore, to an ice wall, an ice front, or over shoals, generally in the position where it originally formed.

**Feces** excrement from the bowels; colloquially known as droppings or scats.

**Fermentation** the decomposition of organic substances by microorganisms. In some mammals, parts of the digestive tract (eg the cecum) may be inhabited by bacteria that break down cellulose and release nutrients.

**Fin** an organ projecting from the body of aquatic animals and generally used in steering and propulsion.

**Fissipedia** (suborder) name given by some taxonomists to modern terrestrial carnivores to distinguish them from the suborder Pinnipedia which describes the marine carnivores. Here we treat both as full orders: the Carnivora and the Pinnipedia.

**Fitness** a measure of the ability of an animal (with one genotype or genetic make-up) to leave viable offspring in comparison to other individuals (with different genotypes). The process of NATURAL SELECTION, often called survival of the fittest, determines which characteristics have the greatest fitness, that is, are most likely to enable their bearers to survive and rear young which will in turn bear those characteristics. (See INCLUSIVE FITNESS.)

**Flense** to strip blubber from a whale or seal.

**Flipper** a limb adapted for swimming.

**Floe** a sheet of floating ice.

**Fluke** one of the lobes of a whale's tail; the name refers to their broad triangular shape.

**Follicle** a small sac, therefore (a) a mass of ovarian cells that produces an ovum, (b) an indentation in the skin from which hair grows.

**Furbearer** term applied to mammals whose pelts have commercial value and form part of the fur harvest.

**Gadoid** cod-like fish of the suborder Gadoidei.

**Gamete** a male or female reproductive cell (ovum or spermatozoon).

**Gene** the basic unit of heredity; a portion of DNA molecule coding for a given trait and passed, through replication at reproduction, from generation to generation. Genes are expressed as ADAPTATIONS and consequently are the most fundamental units (more so than individuals) on which NATURAL SELECTION acts.

**Generalist** an animal whose life-style does not involve highly specialized stratagems (cf SPECIALIST); for example, feeding on a variety of foods which may require different foraging techniques.

**Genus** (plural genera) a taxonomic division superior to species and subordinate to family (see TAXONOMY).

**Gestation** the period of development within the uterus; the process of **delayed implantation** can result in the period of pregnancy being longer than the period during which the embryo is actually developing. (See also IMPLANTATION.)

**Guard hair** an element of the coat of seals consisting of a longer, stiffer, more bristle-like hair which lies outside and supports the warmer, softer underfur.

**Harem group** a social group consisting of a single adult male, at least two adult females and immature animals; the most common pattern of social organization among mammals.

**Haul-out** behavior of sea mammals pulling themselves ashore.

**Helper** jargon for an individual, generally without young of its own, which contributes to the survival of the offspring of others by behaving parentally toward them (see ALLOPARENT).

**Hemoglobin** an iron-containing protein in the red corpuscles which plays a crucial role in oxygen exchange between blood and tissues in mammals.

**Hierarchy** (social or dominance) the existence of divisions within society, based on the outcome of interactions which show some individuals to be consistently dominant to others. Higher-ranking individuals thus have control of aspects (eg access to food or mates) of the life and behavior of low-ranking ones. Hierarchies may be branching, but simple linear ones are often called peck orders (after the behavior of farmyard chickens).

**Holarctic realm** a region of the world including North America, Greenland, Europe, and Asia, apart from the southwest, southeast and India.

**Home range** the area in which an animal normally lives (generally excluding rare excursions or migrations), irrespective of whether or not the area is defended from other animals (cf TERRITORY).

**Hybrid** the offspring of parents of different species.

**Hydrophone** a waterproof microphone held in position under the sea's surface and used to detect the sounds emitted by sea mammals.

**Hyoid bones** skeletal elements in the throat region, supporting the trachea, larynx and base of the tongue (derived in evolutionary history from the gill arches of ancestral fishes).

**Implantation** the process whereby the free-floating blastocyst (early embryo) becomes attached to the uterine wall in mammals. At the point of implantation a complex network of blood vessels develops to link mother and embryo (the PLACENTA). In **delayed implantation** the blastocyst remains dormant in the uterus for periods varying, between species, from 12 days to 11 months. Delayed implantation may be obligatory or facultative and is known for some members of the Carnivora and Pinnipedia.

**Inclusive fitness** a measure of the animal's FITNESS which is based on the number of genes, rather than the number of its offspring, present in subsequent generations. This is a more complete measure of fitness, since it incorporates the effect of, for example, alloparenthood, wherein individuals may help to rear the offspring of their relatives (see KIN SELECTION: ALLOPARENT)

**Induced ovulation** see ESTRUS.

**Infanticide** the killing of infants. Infanticide has been recorded notably in species in which a bachelor male may take over a HAREM from its resident male(s).

**Jacobson's organ** a structure in a foramen (small opening) in the palate of many vertebrates which appears to be involved in olfactory communication. Molecules of scent may be sampled in these organs.

**Juvenile** no longer possessing the characteristics of an infant, but not yet fully adult.

**Kin selection** a facet of NATURAL SELECTION whereby an animal's fitness is affected by the survival of its relatives or kin. Kin selection may be the process whereby some ALLOPARENTAL behavior evolved: an individual behaving in a way which promotes the survival of its kin increases its

own INCLUSIVE FITNESS, despite the *apparent* selflessness of its behavior.

**Krill** shrimp-like CRUSTACEANS of the genera *Euphausia. Meganyctiphanes* etc, occurring in very great numbers in polar seas, particularly of Antarctica, where they form the principal prey of baleen whales.

**Lactation** (verb: lactate) the secretion of milk from MAMMARY GLANDS.

**Laminar flow** streamline flow in a viscous fluid near a solid boundary; the flow of water over the surface of whales is laminar.

**Lanugo** the birth-coat of mammals which is shed to be replaced by the adult coat.

**Latrine** of a place where FECES are regularly left (often together with other SCENT MARKS); associated with olfactory communication.

**Lead** a channel of open water between ice floes.

**Lob-tailing** a whale beating the water with its tail FLUKES, perhaps to communicate with other whales.

**Mammal** a member of a CLASS of VERTEBRATE animals having MAMMARY GLANDS with which they produce milk with which they nurse their young (properly: Mammalia).

**Mammary glands** glands of female mammals that secrete milk.

**Marine** living in the sea.

**Matriline** a related group of animals linked by descent through females alone.

**Melanism** darkness of color due to presence of the black pigment melanin.

**Metabolic rate** the rate at which the chemical processes of the body occur.

**Migration** movement, usually seasonal, from one region or climate to another for purposes of feeding or breeding.

**Monogamy** a mating system in which individuals have only one mate per breeding season.

**Mutation** a structural change in a gene which can thus give rise to a new heritable characteristic.

**Myoglobin** a protein related to HEMOGLOBIN, found in the muscles of vertebrates; like hemoglobin, it is involved in the oxygen exchange processes of respiration.

**Myopia** short-sightedness.

**Mysticete** a member of the suborder Mysticeti, whales with baleen plates rather than teeth as their feeding apparatus.

**Nasolacrimal duct** a duct or canal between the nostrils and the eye.

**Natal range** the home range into which an individual was born (natal = of or from one's birth).

**Natural selection** the process whereby individuals with the most appropriate ADAPTATIONS are more successful than other individuals, and hence survive to produce more offspring. To the extent that the successful traits are heritable (genetic) they will therefore spread in the population.

**Niche** the role of a species within the community, defined in terms of all aspects of its life-style (eg food, competitors, predators, and other resource requirements).

**Nocturnal** active at nighttime.

**Odontocete** a member of the suborder Odonticeti, the toothed whales.

**Omnivore** an animal eating a varied diet including both animal and plant tissue.

**Opportunist** (of feeding) flexible behavior of exploiting circumstances to take a wide

range of food items: characteristic of many species of Carnivora. See GENERALIST; SPECIALIST.

**Order** a taxonomic division subordinate to class and superior to family (see TAXONOMY).

**Ovulation** (verb: ovulate) the shedding of mature ova (eggs) from the ovaries where they are produced (see ESTRUS).

**Pack ice** large blocks of ice formed on the surface of the sea when an ice field has been broken up by wind and waves, and drifted from its original position.

**Papilla** (plural: papillae) a small nipple-like projection.

**Parturition** the process of giving birth (hence *post partum*—after birth).

**Pelagic** the upper part of the open sea, above the BENTHIC zone.

**Pelvis** a girdle of bones that supports the hindlimbs of vertebrates.

**Phytoplankton** minute plants floating near the surface of aquatic environments (cf ZOOPLANKTON).

**Pinna** (plural: pinnae) the projecting cartilaginous portion of the external ear.

**Pinniped** a member of the order Pinnipedia, aquatic carnivorous mammals with all four limbs modified into flippers; the true seals, eared seals and walrus. Sometimes classified as a suborder of Carnivora.

**Placenta, placental mammals** a structure that connects the fetus and the mother's womb to ensure a supply of nutrients to the fetus and removal of its waste products. Only placental mammals have a well-developed placenta; marsupials have a rudimentary placenta or none, and monotremes lay eggs.

**Pod** a group of individuals, usually applied to whales, with some, at least temporary, cohesive social structure.

**Polyandrous** see POLYGYNOUS.

**Polygamous** a mating system wherein an individual has more than one mate per breeding season.

**Polygynous** a mating system in which a male mates with several females during one breeding season (as opposed to polyandrous, where one female mates with several males).

**Population** a more or less separate (discrete) group of animals of the same species within a given BIOTIC COMMUNITY.

**Predator** an animal which forages for live prey; hence "anti-predator behavior" describes the evasive actions of the prey.

**Process** (anatomical) an outgrowth or protuberance.

**Promiscuous** a mating system wherein an individual mates more or less indiscriminately.

**Puberty** the attainment of sexual maturity. In addition to maturation of the primary sex organs (ovaries, testes), primates may exhibit secondary sexual characteristics at puberty. Among higher primates it is usual to find a growth spurt at the time of puberty in males and females.

**Purse seine** a fishing net, the bottom of which can be closed by cords, operated usually from boats (cf SEINE).

**Race** a taxonomic division subordinate to SUBSPECIES but linking populations with similar distinct characteristics.

**Radiation** see ADAPTIVE RADIATION.

**Radio-tracking** a technique used for monitoring an individual's movements remotely; it involves affixing a radio

transmitter to the animal and thereafter receiving a signal through directional antennae, which enables the subject's position to be plotted. The transmitter is often attached to a collar, hence "radio-collar."

**Receptive** state of a female mammal ready to mate or in ESTRUS.

**Reduced** (anatomical) of relatively small dimension (eg of certain bones, by comparison with those of an ancestor or related animals).

**Reproductive rate** the rate of production of offspring; the net productive rate may be defined as the average number of female offspring produced by each female during her entire lifetime.

**Rhinarium** a naked area of moist skin surrounding the nostrils in many mammals.

**Rookery** a colony of PINNIPEDS.

**Rorqual** one of the six species of baleen whales of the genus *Balaenoptera*.

**Rostrum** a forward-directed process at the front of the skull of some whales and dolphins, forming a beak.

**Scombroid** a bony marine fish of the family Scombridae, with two small dorsal fins, small scales and smooth skin, eg mackerel and tunny.

**Seasonality** (of births) the restriction of births to a particular time of the year.

**Sebaceous gland** secretory tissue producing oily substances, for example lubricating and waterproofing hair, or specialized to produce odorous secretions.

**Seine** a fishing net with floats at the top and weights at the bottom, used for encircling fish.

**Selective pressure** a factor affecting the reproductive success of individuals (whose success will depend on their FITNESS, ie the extent to which they are adapted to thrive under that selective pressure).

**Septum** a partition separating two parts of an organism. The nasal septum consists of a fleshy part separating the nostrils and a vertical, bony plate dividing the nasal cavity.

**Sinus** a cavity in bone or tissue.

**Sirenia** an order of herbivorous aquatic mammals, comprising the manatees and dugong.

**Solitary** living on its own, as opposed to social or group-living in life-style.

**Sonar** sound used in connection with navigation (SOund NAvigation Ranging).

**Specialist** an animal whose life-style involves highly specialized stratagems: (eg feeding with one technique on a particular food).

**Species** a taxonomic division subordinate to genus and superior to SUBSPECIES. In general a species is a group of animals similar in structure and which are able to breed and produce viable offspring. See TAXONOMY.

**Speciation** the process by which new SPECIES arise in evolution. It is widely accepted that it occurs when a single-species population is divided by some geographical barrier.

**Subadult** no longer an infant or juvenile but not yet fully adult physically and/or socially.

**Subfamily** a division of a FAMILY.

**Subfossil** an incompletely fossilized specimen from a recent species.

**Suborder** a subdivision of an ORDER.

**Subordinate** see HIERARCHY.

**Subspecies** a recognizable subpopulation of a single SPECIES, typically with a distinct geographical distribution.

**Surplus killing** a phenomenon where more (sometimes very many more) prey are killed than can immediately be consumed by the killer or its companions.

**Taxonomy** the science of classifying organisms. It is very convenient to group together animals which share common features and are thought to have common descent. Each individual is thus a member of a series of ever-broader categories (individual—species—genus—family—order—class—phylum) and each of these can be further divided where it is convenient (eg subspecies, superfamily or infraorder). The SPECIES is a convenient unit in that it links animals according to an obvious criterion, namely that they interbreed successfully. However, the unit on which NATURAL SELECTION operates is the individual: it is by the differential reproductive success of individuals bearing different characteristics that evolutionary change proceeds.

**Terrestrial** living on land.

**Territory** an area defended from intruders by an individual or group. Originally the term was used where ranges were exclusive and obviously defended at their borders. A more general definition of territoriality allows some overlaps between neighbors by defining territoriality as a system of spacing wherein home ranges do not overlap randomly, that is, the location of one individual's or group's home range influences that of others.

**Testosterone** a male hormone synthesized in the testes and responsible for the expression of many male characteristics (contrast the female hormone estrogen produced in the ovaries).

**Tooth-comb** a dental modification in which the incisor teeth form a comb-like structure.

**Tubercle** a small rounded projection or nodule (eg of bone).

**Underfur** the thick soft undercoat fur lying beneath the longer and coarser hair (GUARD HAIRS).

**Upwelling** an upward movement of ocean currents, resulting from convection, causing an upward movement of nutrients and hence an increase in plankton populations.

**Vector** an individual or species which transmits a disease.

**Ventral** on the lower or bottom side or surface: thus ventral abdominal glands occur on the underside of the abdomen.

**Venule** a small tributary conveying blood from the capillary bed to a vein (cf ARTERIOLE).

**Vertebrate** an animal with a backbone: a division of the phylum Chordata which includes animals with notochords (as distinct from invertebrates).

**Vestigial** a characteristic with little or no contemporary use, but derived from one which was useful and well-developed in an ancestral form.

**Vibrissae** stiff, coarse hairs richly supplied with nerves, and with a sensory (tactile) function, found especially around the snout.

**Zooplankton** minute animals living near the surface of the sea (cf PHYTOPLANKTON).

# INDEX

# Picture Acknowledgments

**Key** *t* top. *b* bottom. *c* centre. *l* left. *r* right.

**Abbreviations** A Ardea. AN Agence Nature. BC Bruce Coleman Ltd. J Jacana. FL Frank Lane Agency

Cover BC, R. J. Tulloch. 1 Anthro-Photo. 2–3 BC. 4–5 NHPA, Philippa Scott. 6–7 Zepha, McCutcheon. 8–9 Zefa, W. H. Muller. 10 J. 11*t* A. R. Martin. 11*b* T. Kasuya. 13 Eric and David Hosking. 14 A. 16, 17*t* BC. 17*b* William Ervin, Natural Imagery. 18 Seaphot. 19 Anthro-Photo, J. Moore. 20*t* Ekdotike Athenon. 20*c* Scala. 20*b* University Museum of National Antiquities, Oslo. 21*t* New Bedford Free Public Library. 22*l* Kingston upon Hull City Museums and Art Galleries. 22*r* National Maritime Museum, San Francisco. 23*t* Faroe Photo, Åsmundur Poulsen. 23*b* P. Morris. 25 A. R. Martin. 28 B. Würsig. 29*t* K. Balcomb. 29*b* W. N. Bonner. 32*t* Biofotos, Heather Angel. 32*b* S. S. Anderson. 33*t* A. 33*b* AN. 34 M. Würsig. 38 A. 38–39 AN. 40, 42, 43 M & B. Würsig. 44*t* D. Gaskin. 44*b* P. Morris. 45 D. Gaskin. 50 F. Bruemmer. 51 BC. 52–53, 56–57 Sea Mammal Research Unit, Cambridge. 56*b* The Mansell Collection Ltd. 57*b* World Wildlife Fund, K. Balcomb. 58 I. Christensen. 63 BC. 65*t* AN. 65*c* BC. 65*t* A. 67*t* M & B Würsig. 67*b* D. A. Sutton. 68 A. 69 William Ervin, Natural Imagery. 70 Anthro-Photo, J. Moore. 71 BC. 74 Institute of Oceanographic Studies, Godalming. 75*t* K. Balcomb. 75*b* W. N. Bonner. 76 B.C. 77 Seaphot. 78 Survival Anglia, D. Bartlett. 79 BC. 80*t* D. Gaskin. 80*b* BC. 82*t* B. Lipton. 82*b* W. N. Bonner. 83 B. Lipton. 84–85 M. & B, Würsig. 85 Survival Anglia, J. & D. Bartlett. 86 A. 90*t* Leonard Lee Rue III. 90*b* William Ervin, Natural Imagery. 91*t* R. A. Luxmore. 91*b* W. N. Bonner. 92 P. Wirtz. 93 U. Schürer. 94 A. Henley. 95*t* B. J. le Boeuf. 95*b* S. S. Anderson. 96–97 S. Stammers. 97 R. M. Laws. 98*t* Museum of the American Indian, New York. 98*b*, 99 W. N. Bonner. 100 R. A. Luxmoore. 101 F. Bruemmer. 102 J. 104, 104–105 A. Henley. 105*c* Natural Science Photos. 105*b* Eric and David Hosking. 108 W. N. Bonner. 109 Prince and Pearson. 110 A. 111 J. 112 L. Shults. 113 K. R. Gordon. 114–115 FL. 116, 117*t* F. Bruemmer. 117*b* B. Lipton. 118 Robert Harding Picture Library. 118*b* J. 119 N. R. Lightfoot. 122*t* A. R. Martin. 122*b* S. S. Anderson. 123 A. R. Martin. 126–127 A. 128*t* W. N. Bonner. 128–129, 129 R. M. Laws. 130 L. Lowry. 131 Luonnonkuva Arkisto. 132 P. Veit. 132–133 Seaphot. 134*t* BC. 134*b* N. R. Lightfoot. 135 J. 137 B. L. Sage. 138*t* Prince and Pearson. 138*b* A. W. Erikson. 139 BC. 142–143*t* J. L. Bengtson. 143*b* AN. 145 A. 146 P. K. Anderson. 148*t* Sirenia Project, DWRC, Florida. 148*b* A. 150 Seaphot. 151 R. Best.

# Artwork

**All artwork** © Priscilla Barrett unless stated below.
**Abbreviations** SC Stephen Cocking. SD Simon Driver. MM Malcolm McGregor

12, 14, 15, 24, 25 SD. 26, 30 MM. 42 SD. 46, 48, 49 MM. 53, 54 SC. 55, 59, 60 MM. 62, 63 SD. 64, 66*t* MM. 66, 71 SD. 72, 73 MM. 77, 79 SD. 80 MM. 84, 88, 89, 91, 93, 94, 99, 102, 119, 130, 142 SD. Maps and scale drawings SD.